THE DANCE BAND ERA

THE "EAGLE"
Coin-Slot Graphophone

TYPE BS GRAPHOPHONE

THE DANCE

BAND ERA

The Dancing Decades from Ragtime to Swing: 1910~1950

Albert McCarthy

Studio Vista

Produced by November Books Limited, 23–9 Emerald Street, London WCIN 3QL.

Published by Studio Vista Publishers, Blue Star House, Highgate Hill, London N19.

Typesetting by Yendall & Company Limited, Riscatype House, 22–5 Red Lion Court, Fleet Street, London EC4.

Printed by Compton Printing Limited, Pembroke Road, Stocklake, Aylesbury, Bucks.

Bound by Webb Son & Company Limited, 303 Chase Road, Southgate, London N14 6JB.

Designed by Tom Carter.
House editor: Tony Russell.
Copy preparation: John Leath.

ISBN 0 289 70218 6

The following illustrations are reproduced by permission of the photographers, copyright holders or owners, as listed: Giuseppe Barazetta 34t; Russ Cassidy 9; Decca Records 22r, 59, 96l, 117bl; Charles Delaunay 133, 138b; EMI 105, 106l, 117tl, 117tr, 147b, 148br, 151t; Bjorn Englund 135, 136t, 136b; Alasdair Fenton 82l, 90t, 96r, 97tl, 97tr, 97b, 110, 114tr, 149tl, 152tl, 169l; Gramophone 51b, 116, obj (outer back jacket) 2nd row r; Pekka Gronow 139b; Max Jones 12, 21, 23, 24–5, 25, 27, 46, 53t, 54, 63t, 66tl, 66tr, 67, 68, 69, 71, 73b, 74t, 103t, 104–5, 107t, 107b, 112t, 114tl, 117br, 123, 124, 126b, 128t, 143b, 156b, 162t; Horst H. Lange 140l, 140tr, 140br; Robert Pernet 134; Philips Records 168; Record Research 10, 11, 14, 15, 16, 28, 33, 74b; Tony Russell obj tl, tr, 3rd row c; Brian Rust 13, 31t, 31b, 32t, 40–1b, 49; Duncan P. Schiedt 26t, 26b, 30, 32b, 62, 65t, 65b, 129, 156t, 157, 158, 159, obj tc, 4th row r; Pete Seago 20, 39t, 42t, 42b, 43b, 53b, 98; Joyce Stone 43t, 82–3, 84t, 84b, 85, 86b, 86tr, 87, 88–9, obj 3rd row l, r; Universal Pix 22l; Leo Vauchant 99l; Edward S. Walker 12, 40bl, 93, 115t, 120t, 120b, 145b, 148bl, 150t, 153tr, obj 2nd row l, 4th row c; Warner Bros. 66b; Tiny Winters 77, 78, 79, 115b, 118b. All other illustrations by courtesy of Ray Coleman, Editor of the Melody Maker.

JACKET PICTURES: *front: Glen Gray and the Casa Loma Orchestra on the boardwalk at Atlantic City. Back: top row: Irene and Vernon Castle demonstrate the foxtrot; Isham Jones leads his 1933 orchestra. Second row: Paul Whiteman and his band in London, 1923; the New Mayfair Dance Band (leader, Ray Noble; vocalist, Al Bowlly) record Goodnight Sweetheart, 193-. Third row: British bandleaders celebrate Henry Hall's 70th birthday on 30 April 1968 (left to right: Harry Roy, Bill Ternent, Joe Loss, Sidney Lipton, Edmundo Ros, Geraldo, Ambrose, Lew Stone: at the piano, Henry Hall). Bottom row, right: Jimmy Dorsey and his band, c. 1944.*

CONTENTS

ACKNOWLEDGEMENTS

As a youth I followed the fortunes of the leading dance bands of the 1930s avidly, pining when a favourite vocalist or instrumentalist left one of the bands I admired for another that did not appeal to me, and rejoicing when the reverse process took place. I could reel off the names of every musician in the top dozen or so bands, and wrote indignant letters to bandleaders when their radio programmes contained an insufficient proportion of hot numbers. Visits to theatres were great occasions when a leading dance band topped the bill, though even here there were dark moments – such as the time Ambrose played two houses without giving trumpeter Teddy Foster, one of my idols, the opportunity to be heard as a soloist or vocalist; I left the theatre vowing that never again would I vote for Ambrose in a popularity poll. I was, I suppose, as fanatical a fan as any who follow the pop groups today, and certainly as pitying as they are of anyone thirty years old or more, whose age, I felt, precluded a true appreciation of the music I enjoyed.

From the dance bands I evolved to an interest in jazz and blues, and have been active in the former field ever since, as a magazine editor and writer. As my involvement with jazz and blues deepened, primarily because of their greater depth and emotional range, I turned away from the dance bands, dismissing them, I regret to say, as 'commercial' – that great critical condemnation of the hard-core jazz fan which assigns an artist to limbo. Well over two decades passed before I again began to take an interest in dance bands; the initial re-awakening was probably due, as much as anything else, to the fact that I had reached the age when one becomes prone to nostalgia.

Some years ago I started to gather material for a lengthy volume on big jazz bands – still only partially completed – and, considering the early developments of arranging, standardisation of instrumentation and many other factors in the growth of bands during the '20s, I became more and more convinced that it was impossible to maintain a clear-cut demarcation line between the early jazz and dance bands. This led me to listen once again, extensively, to recorded dance bands; to read all the available material on the subject – unlike jazz literature, this is scanty – and to renew an interest that had been dormant for many years. This book is the result. Regrettably exigencies of space have led to the omission of several bands and leaders who probably merit mention, but I am not presenting an encyclopaedia of dance bands (though I hope that one day someone will do so) and at least every major figure is, I think, included. While nostalgia must play its part in the consideration of a subject like dance bands, I trust that it has not blinded me, for I have no sympathy with those dance band followers who write as if they stopped living sometime at the end of the '30s.

In the writing of this book I have been greatly helped by many friends and associates. Alasdair Fenton has been of considerable help in constantly checking facts for me and above all in providing me with most of the material on Jack Hylton. Peter Tanner generously gave me permission to draw on his lengthy studies of Ambrose and Fred Elizalde, as did Kenith Trodd in the case of Lew Stone. The various conversations I have had with Mrs Joyce Stone have been immensely helpful in filling out many aspects of the '30s British dance band scene, as have several with Tiny Winters, who was also kind enough to allow me to reproduce several rare photographs in his possession. Dennis Dimmer, Chris Ellis of EMI, and Edward S. Walker have given me the benefit of their knowledge freely and made numerous helpful suggestions. Tony Pollard of *The Gramophone* was good enough to allow me to look through the files of that publication and to give me permission to quote from several articles. For help with information, records and tapes on several European bands I am indebted to Walter Bruyninckx, Björn Englund and Horst H. Lange, and for assistance with the loan of magazines and identification of musicians in photographs I must acknowledge the great help given to me by Charles Fox and Austin Clegg respectively. A special word of thanks is due to Fred Welstead, who spent many hours searching through magazines on my behalf checking vital items of information. Finally, much useful information has been gleaned from such magazines as *Collecta*, *The Golden Years*, *Memory Lane International*, *RSVP*, *Street Singer*, *Vintage Jazz Mart* and, above all, *Record Research*. The latter has been particularly valuable, notably for John McAndrew's columns, which led me to listen to a number of hitherto unfamiliar records.

Although photograph-credits are listed elsewhere, I should like to make special mention of the co-operation and generous help given to me by Ray Coleman, editor of the *Melody Maker*, and Roy Burchell and Max Jones of that publication. The *Melody Maker* itself gives one the opportunity of studying the history of dance music in Britain in considerable depth and is a priceless source of information on the '20s and '30s. By allowing me access to its remarkable photographic files, and granting permission for the reproduction of many rare prints, Ray Coleman has placed me greatly in his debt,

Albert McCarthy

THE
FORMATIVE
YEARS

TREEMONISHA.

No. 27. A REAL SLOW DRAG.

By SCOTT JOPLIN

INTRO. Larghetto. ♩=100

(Treemonisha and Lucy stand on bench in rear of room.)

mf

(Salute partners.)
Treemonisha.

(Slow Drag forward.)

Sa - lute your part - ner, do the drag,   drag,

mf

(All stop.)

(Slow Drag backward.)

drag.................   Stop and move back - ward, do the   drag.

Orchestras whose primary function is to play music to which its listeners can dance have existed for centuries. At first they were confined to courts or the residences of aristocratic patrons; later, they became available to a large public. The development of dance bands, in the limited sense in which the term is used in this book, appears to date from some time about the beginning of the 1910s, a period when syncopated music was gaining wide popular acceptance. Several bandleaders have claimed that they led the first dance group, using what was to become a standard instrumentation of two or more brass instruments, two or more saxophones usually doubling other reed instruments, and a rhythm section that at first usually consisted of a piano, banjo and drums, with sometimes a brass bass or tuba added. What information we have of the period, however, suggests that the violin was a common lead instrument at the time. Before briefly noting one or two of the early leaders who can plausibly claim that they pioneered the modern dance band, it is first necessary to consider the syncopated music that could be heard in the United States at the turn of the century.

Until recent years the gestation period of a new form of popular music seems to have been largely an undercover activity, its creation and formalisation unknown to all but a small group of practitioners and their public. In the case of ragtime, jazz and blues the fact that all these forms were basically the creations of black Americans, an under-privileged and despised racial minority, made it even more certain that their efforts would be ignored or simply overlooked by academic musical circles, which were in any case disinterested in any form of popular music, even contemptuous of it. As a result we know very little of the early development of ragtime, though it is clear that in the latter part of the nineteenth century it surfaced after what might have been a lengthy period of evolution. In all probability the minstrel shows were the chief breeding ground of

Left: a page of Scott Joplin's ragtime opera 'Treemonisha'. Below: Joseph Lamb, one of the pioneer composers of classic ragtime, who lived in musical obscurity until his death in the early '60s. He is shown here outside his home in Brooklyn in June 1958.

early ragtime and certainly the first breakthrough came with the popularity, around 1896 or 1897, of the cakewalk, which used strictly syncopated music and had elements of a march, two-step and polka. It has been claimed that the cakewalk came to the United States via the Caribbean, though its origin may have been African, but for all practical purposes it is one part of the ragtime music that swept the United States, and later Europe, between the 1890s and World War I, though the influence of ragtime extended in attenuated form.

The first true ragtime composition to be published was William H. Krell's *Mississippi Rag*, which appeared early in 1897, in the same year as the first rag by a black American composer was copyrighted – Tom Turpin's *Harlem Rag*. The 'classic' form of ragtime associated with such composers as Turpin, James Scott, Louis Chauvin, Joseph Lamb and, above all, Scott Joplin, originated from the congregation of a group of brilliant writers and performers around Sedalia, Missouri, but in its pure form ragtime had little influence on the early development of dance music. The compositions of Joplin, Scott and other Sedalia figures were too complex to gain wide acceptance, and Joplin's publisher, John Stark, printed his rags more from a belief in their intrinsic worth than from any hope of profit. If the outstanding ragtime composers wrote music that was above the heads of the public, the same cannot be said of the hundreds of lesser talents who popularised and simplified ragtime. They poured out a flood of tunes, in which the words 'rag' and 'ragtime' often signified little more than a jump on to the bandwagon of popular fashion. For two decades American popular music seemed to consist mainly of a type of diluted ragtime, performed by pianists, banjoists, small orchestras and military bands, and the earliest recordings by dance bands are permeated with the influence of this tradition.

The early 1910s showed a very significant development in the sheet music of popular tunes sold by the major publishing companies. Before that, sheet music was essentially sold for performance by pianists or singers. (Another reason why classic ragtime failed to achieve popular success was that the compositions were too difficult for the average amateur pianist to play.) From about 1910 or 1911, however, popular sheet music started to appear with parts for a dance band instrumentation. About that time, and during the next two or three years, the foundations were laid for dance music and dance bands as we now understand them. An important catalyst was the enormous popularity of the basic modern ballroom dance: the foxtrot.

The foxtrot was developed in embryonic form in the United States around 1912, though earlier dances were called the horsetrot and fish walk and the name did not become finalised until 1914. Over the years it has undergone a series of modifications, such as the discarding of the trot part for a less energetic movement called the saunter, which is the basis of the dance as we now know it. Then, in 1924, it was called the slow foxtrot to differentiate it from the quick foxtrot, which subsequently became the quickstep. Several events made the foxtrot an enormously successful innovation, but none more so than the meteoric rise to fame of the dancing team Irene and Vernon Castle. Sponsored by Elizabeth Marbury, a prominent member of the Democratic Party, this pair commenced to exhibit their 'revolutionary' new dance steps in 1914. For one of their engagements, in Philadelphia, they hired an orchestra under the direction of James Reese Europe, whose music in its own way perfectly complemented their dancing. From then on they made Europe their musical director, and he backed the team with an eighteen-piece all-black band during a lengthy road tour and then in a highly successful engagement at 'Castles In The Air' in New York City. The Castles, whose only serious rivals were a dance team of Joan Sawyer and Rudolph [Valentino], sparked off a society dance craze with far-reaching and lasting consequences which they could hardly have foreseen. Though their repertoire included the tango, the one-step and

Victor

$1.25 in U.S.A.   For Dancing

Castle House Rag—One-Step

(Jas. Europe)

Europe's Society Orchestra

Recorded under the personal supervision of
Mr. and Mrs. Vernon Castle

35372-B

VICTOR TALKING MACHINE CO. Camden, N.J.

the maxixe, significantly it was the foxtrot that made the greatest impact, its introduction into Europe following swiftly. In England, it is said to have been pioneered by Stroud Haxton at the 400 Club in Bond Street in July 1914. It received further impetus from its inclusion in popular musical revues of the period, such as 'Tonight's The Night' at the Gaiety and 'Push And Go' at the London Hippodrome. Without this wide public enthusiasm for the foxtrot the history of dance music, and indeed of jazz, would have been profoundly altered.

I have mentioned James Reese Europe, and indeed he seems to be one figure in the history of popular dance music who has received less than his due share of credit in books on the subject, except in Charters, and Kunstadt's *Jazz: A History Of The New York Scene*. Europe was born in Mobile, Alabama, on 22 February 1881, and around 1890 moved with his parents to Washington, D.C., where he commenced his musical training. He made his first trip to New York City in 1904, when he worked as a pianist, following this with spells as musical director with a number of revues. He came to prominence after 1910, when he formed the Clef Club as a centre for black American musicians and entertainers. A disagreement with other members led to his withdrawal, but he set up the rival Tempo Club in collaboration with Ford Dabney and William Tyers, and within a short time found himself at the centre of a booking agency that supplied hundreds of musicians for social functions and dances both in the Manhattan area and as far afield as Chicago. On 11 March 1914 he was responsible for the presentation of a Carnegie Hall concert which featured 125 musicians and singers. The line-up, which reads oddly to modern eyes, included ten pianos, seven cornets, eight trombones and a veritable battery of banjos and mandolins. Another group, billed as the Europe Double Quintet, consisted of three bandolins, a banjophone, two violins, 'cello, string bass, piano and drums. As I have said, the engagement with the Castles gained Europe wide popular recognition, and as a result of this the Victor Record Company recorded his orchestra, some titles bearing the inscription 'Recorded under the personal supervision of Mr. and Mrs. Vernon Castle'.

On the entry of the United States into World War I, Europe was awarded the army rank of lieutenant and given the task of forming a black orchestra to play for the troops overseas. In due course he crossed the Atlantic, leading the 369th Infantry ('Hell Fighters') Band, whose personnel numbered some fifty musicians. A five-week tour of France in February and March

of 1918, during which the band travelled some two thousand miles and performed in over twenty cities, was immensely successful, and one contemporary report commented: 'From the first, the band had a reputation among the troops as the "jazziest, craziest, best tooting outfit in France" and the civilian population in Paris and elsewhere praised it to the skies.'

When the war was over Europe's band returned to the United States in triumph, a million New Yorkers reputedly turning out to acclaim it as it marched from 23rd Street to 145th. All seemed set for Europe's further success, most likely in the developing jazz craze, but on 9 May 1919 an altercation with one of his drummers, Herbert Wright, led to the latter stabbing him and inflicting wounds from which he died a few hours later.

In addition to the 1915–6 Victor recordings, Europe also made titles for the American Pathé company during March and April of 1919. His records have been rather unfairly dismissed by most jazz writers, and it is certainly true that on a strict assessment they have little to offer as jazz. However, the Victor recordings are better viewed as examples of early syncopated dance music with, at times, strong ragtime overtones, and in this light such titles as *Down Home Rag*, *Castle Walk* and *Too Much Mustard* are not without interest, either historically or musically. Both for his association with the Castles and in his own right as an innovator in the field of syncopated music, James Europe merits an honourable place among the pioneers of dance music history.

The society dance craze, which received so much of its impetus from the popularity of the Castles, led to the changing of social patterns that had existed for a very long time. Dance halls, prior to this time, were not considered venues which members of polite society might properly frequent, and in such circles dances and balls were always private functions. The typical line-up of a dance orchestra before about 1912 was violin (the lead instrument), piano, drums and occasionally banjo, and the music was melodically simple. It has been claimed by most writers that the musicians who played in such dance orchestras were not full-time professionals, and that groups were assembled on a casual basis to fulfil engagements as they arose. While undoubtedly true in outline, this view may be a simplification, for it is hard not to believe that some type of permanent group evolved in many instances, when work was freely available; and a few musicians at least must have earned the major part of their income as a result of their ability. With the changing pattern of dance music, full-time professionalism became a necessity for members of a successful orchestra, particularly as society audiences created their own venues in the better class hotels and dance halls, which offered excellent economic opportunities for dance band musicians.

A great deal of speculation has taken place, over the years, about the identity of the first leader who organised a dance band in the accepted sense; several names have been offered as likely contenders. Wilbur Sweatman, a black American clarinettist, who was working with a band around Chicago as early as 1911, has been mentioned frequently, but it seems more likely that what he played was a form of diluted ragtime. In any case, he was basically a vaudeville entertainer, whose forte was the playing of three clarinets at once. Len Kunstadt has discovered an interesting news item, in a February 1923 issue of the *Chicago Defender*, concerning the Black and Tan Orchestra of Los Angeles, a negro group with a line-up of cornet, trombone, two saxophones (of which one doubled violin and clarinet), piano, bass violin and drums. The article claimed that the orchestra had been together since at least early 1914. Probably no single leader was responsible for the creation of dance bands; rather, as a result of the evolutionary trends in syncopated music, a type of standard instrumentation and presentation emerged simultaneously in several areas. It is known that such leaders as Charles Elgar, Charley Straight, Earl Dabney, Paul Specht, Fred Waring, Meyer Davis and Ted Lewis

Dance Records

THE only man who can perform on three clarinets simultaneously, Wilber C. Sweatman, famous as the "rag-time clarinetist," originator of Jazz playing on that popular instrument and the moving spirit of Sweatman's Original Jazz Band, has given Columbia Dance Lists a new shock. Anyone who thinks the limit of Jazz music has been reached will guess again after hearing Sweatman's Band. Earl Fuller contributes still further joy to the Elysian fields of Dancedom and Jockers Brothers play our first selections from "The Rainbow Girl," latest New York success. A "Jazarimba" orchestra furnish a unique novelty in dance music. Prince's Band handles the "populars" in a One-step and Fox-trot and Prince's Orchestra—as only this orchestra can—gives us the waltzes of the month.

W. C. Sweatman
Sweatman's Original Jazz Band

Columbia Grafonola Type G
$110

10-inch Dance Records

REGRETFUL BLUES. Fox-trot. (Hess.) Wilber C. Sweatman's Original Jazz Band.
EV'RYBODY'S CRAZY 'BOUT THE DOGGONE BLUES BUT I'M HAPPY. Fox-trot. (Creamer and Layton.) Wilber C. Sweatman's Original Jazz Band.
} A 2548 10-inch 75c.

Dance Records

Wilbur C. Sweatman's Original Jazz Band

WE saw Sweatman and his jazz experts record their dance coupling of the month. There were times we bet ourselves the drummer would never get his stick back from the ceiling in time for the next "drum"—but he did! Our photograph was taken in the Columbia Recording Laboratory and shows the Sweatman jazz experts "in action" and partially explains the "action" to be found, in their Columbia dance recordings! The Sweatman crowd are surely saturated with syncopation. While playing they swing and beat time with their entire anatomy. It is their thorough feeling of the music which enables them to play such rag riots of jazz pyrotechnics as "Good-bye Alexander" and "Darktown Strutters' Ball."

GOOD-BYE ALEXANDER. (Creamer and Layton.) Medley One-step. Introducing "Oh Frenchy." (Conrad.) Wilber C. Sweatman's Original Jazz Band.
THE DARKTOWN STRUTTERS' BALL. (Shelton Brooks.) Medley Fox-trot. Introducing "I'm Sorry I Made You Cry." (Clesi.) Wilber C. Sweatman's Original Jazz Band.
} A 2596 10-inch 85c.

Wilbur Sweatman was a popular vaudevillian in the early 1920s, noted for his ability to play three clarinets at once. The top picture shows him on stage with his band during 1923.

started their careers early in the 1910s, but, while we are unable to say for certain who was the first man to lead a dance band, it is not unreasonable to mention the important pioneer activities of Art Hickman and Isham Jones.

Hickman is the man whom some historians favour as the first real dance band leader and, though this cannot be substantiated, there is no doubt of his singular importance as an

innovator in the field. His first band, assembled in 1913, arose almost accidentally when his wish to hang round the holiday camp of a well-known baseball team led him to suggest to the team's manager that he organise a group to provide dance music in the evenings. Many newspapermen were at the camp, and their enthusiastic reports of the band led to it being booked for a season at San Francisco's St Francis Hotel, with an instrumentation of cornet, trombone, piano, two banjos and drums, to which in a short while a violin and string bass were added. In the next few years Hickman's reputation grew, and he was resident at the St Francis and other hotels in the San

Francisco area, having by now increased his personnel to ten by the addition of two saxes. He received a further boost in popularity when his tune *Rose Room* became a nation-wide hit. (He later had another success with *Tears*.) In 1919 Florenz Ziegfeld heard him in San Francisco and took the band to New York, where it was an immediate success; after a brief return to San Francisco, it gained a feature spot in the 1920 edition of 'Ziegfeld Follies'. In 1921 Hickman's band was chosen to open the Coconut Grove at the Ambassador Hotel in Los Angeles, but, though once more a great popular success, Hickman became weary of the dance band business and retired from music. The band continued under the leadership of Frank Ellis or Earl Burtnett. Hickman died in San Francisco in 1930, but his historical importance cannot be challenged, and it is worth noting that his line-up of ten musicians was unusually large for the period before the early '20s. An innovation which was not to be widely copied for over a decade was the use of a string bass instead of the more usual tuba or brass bass, and Hickman's retention of this instrument throughout his band-leading career suggests that he wished to achieve as much rhythmic flexibility as was possible at the time. In 1920 a small group known as Art Hickman's New York London Five played in the Criterion Roof Garden in London and recorded a number of titles for the HMV label, but those I have heard are undistinguished.

Isham Jones led bands throughout most of the '20s and '30s, one '30s group being of exceptional musical interest. His career and output will be discussed in the chapter on the American '30s bands, but a brief consideration of his early years is relevant here. He became a proficient musician, beginning on the string bass, in the early years of the century and initially led a small ensemble in his home town of Coaltown, Ohio. By the time he was twenty he was leading a dance orchestra in Saginaw and Bay City, now playing piano and saxophone, and in 1915 he moved to Chicago to continue his studies on the latter instrument. He worked in Chicago at first as a member of a trio consisting of saxophone, piano and drums; then, after a variety of casual jobs, he organised his first full dance band of any consequence for location work at the Green Mill. As his popularity grew Jones moved to the Rainbow Gardens and the College Inn, and then went out on a tour that finally led him to New York, though for the rest of his musical life Chicago always remained his home base. In his early years in Chicago, Jones, himself a highly proficient musician, paralleled the efforts of Hickman in San Francisco in shaping some of the basic characteristics of the new dance music, particularly instrumentation, voicings, and the balance of rhythmic and melodic qualities that became a hallmark of the better bands. According to James T. Maher, a perspicacious student of American popular music:

During the years that dance orchestras were groping their way towards some musical rationale, some grammar of harmony, rhythms and instrumental colourations, the role of the arranger was undefined. [Isham] Jones wrote his own arrangements. 'They were good, and they were tough to play', according to *Metronome* magazine. Arriving on the heels of the first white 'jazz bands' with their often frenzied sounds and tempos, the Jones orchestra moved towards a more relaxed, smoother kind of dance music.

Later Maher remarked of the Jones band that 'they seemed to have learned very early a lesson that white bands had to re-learn in the '30s from the relaxed swing of Bill Basie: take it easy'. It is certainly notable that even Jones's earliest records have a more flowing rhythmic and melodic quality than those of contemporary recording bands, and the overall influence that he had on the development of dance music remains incalculable.

Another bandleader who claims a pioneering role in the development of dance band music is the Californian Eddie

Left: the Seven Spades toured the British music halls in 1917, billed as 'The Greatest Combination of Ragtime'. They were in fact Ciro's Club Coon Orchestra with the addition of Louis Mitchell. Above: the Original Dixieland Jazz Band, who took Britain by storm in 1919. Left to right: Tony Sbarbaro, Eddie Edwards, Nick La Rocca, Larry Shields and Henry Ragas. Local pianist Billy Jones replaced Ragas for most of their British engagements.

Elkins. While leading small bands at the Alexandra and Ambassador Hotels in Los Angeles around 1918, Elkins was spotted by Al Jolson, who brought him to New York. There Elkins played at the Pavilion Hotel and Knickerbocker Grill with a ten-piece band, earning (he was to claim) $2000 a week. During 1923–5 the band was a big-selling Columbia attraction. After working in major hotels throughout the United States, Elkins became MD for two film studios between 1928 and 1930. In the late '30s he was still active in hotel and radio work. He has himself said that he was one of the creators of modern dance music.

The upsurge in the new syncopated forms of music that swept the United States during the years with which we are dealing did not take long to find a reflection in Europe, for a characteristic of the present century is that Europe has failed to provide any development in indigenous forms of popular music. This aspect has received surprisingly little attention from scholars, though incidental information concerning it can be gleaned from a number of works that have documented the development of jazz and dance music in various European countries. As yet, however, the list of countries dealt with unfortunately excludes several that are important if an overall study of American domination in the field is to be attempted.

One of the few writers to touch upon this subject has been the Finnish musicologist Pekka Gronow, who has made some provisional observations on the diffusion of American jazz and dance music in Europe during the early decades of the century. He points out that at the turn of the century there was a crisis in European popular music, caused mainly by rapid urbanisation, that resulted in many forms of rural folk music becoming obsolete. The strong influence of American syncopated music began with ragtime at the end of the 19th century; records, sheet music and visiting American brass bands and minstrel shows acted as transmitters of the new music. From roughly 1905 to World War I, ragtime numbers, albeit often mediocre, were commonplace items in the lists of tunes written by European composers.

When jazz and dance music began to dominate American popular music, it was inevitable that those countries which had strong contacts with the United States would be the first to be influenced by it, notably Britain, France, Belgium and Germany. However, Gronow points out that the frequency of contacts was only a secondary factor; it was of even greater importance that jazz and dance music were first accepted in urbanised industrial areas. Czechoslovakia is a case in point. The Czech record company Supraphon has issued a two-LP set covering part of the history of Czechoslovakian jazz – though much of it would be considered, quite rightly, as dance music by most jazz followers – and it is instructive to find that all the musicians featured came from the industrialised Czech part of the country. Gronow also mentions that his own country, Finland, lagged far behind Sweden in industrial

development, and that jazz attained popularity in Finland much later than it did in the rest of Scandinavia. He concludes that there seems definite evidence that the popularity of jazz in Europe has correlated positively with urbanisation.

The most obvious characteristics of early European jazz and dance music are the adoption of a standard instrumentation as in the United States (though inevitably there were minor variations) and a syncopated 4/4 foxtrot rhythm, with slight improvisation apart from occasional melodic or rhythmic embellishments. In Western Europe this phase relates to the early '20s, in Finland to the early '30s, and in the USSR to the '40s.

Britain, by virtue of its close contacts with the United States, its industrialisation and, above all, the lack of any language barrier, was, not unexpectedly, the first country to be strongly influenced by American popular music in all its forms. By the turn of the century there were innumerable records by British artists in the ragtime manner, though orchestral, as distinct from solo, performances were rather uncommon. During World War I a number of small orchestras played a form of syncopated music that was strongly ragtime-influenced, but, while their records are of historical interest, their relationship to the better British jazz and dance groups of the '20s is at the most peripheral. Edward S. Walker, the foremost historian of early British jazz and syncopated music, has pointed to the interesting fact – one that I have already observed in most of the very early dance records I have heard – that in Britain the replacement of the violin as a lead instrument came years later than in the United States. The time-lag between the USA and Britain in adapting standard dance band instrumentation was, in all probability, due to Britain's involvement in World War I some years before the United States. An inevitable result was that new directions in syncopated music and dancing were no longer followed as speedily in Britain as they used to be. It is a virtually impossible task to identify the first modern British dance band, and again it is probable that a number of leaders worked simultaneously towards the same end. British dance bands really evolved during the early years of the '20s, the

The Original Dixieland Jazz Band at Hammersmith, London 1919 – left to right: Billy Jones, Larry Shields, Nick LaRocca, Emile Christian, Tony Spargo. Other reproductions on this and facing page are advertisements for early 'talking machines'.

OAK

$35.

MAHOGANY

$40.

THE STANDARD.—The Standard Cabinet as made for a clockwork motor Graphophone, has two rows of drawers, with pegs to hold 200 records or cylinders, besides space for other attachments. The cabinet has a roll-top cover. The Standard intended for a Graphophone with an electric motor differs from that described and illustrated above in having a closet on one side for holding the battery. The drawers in this cabinet will accommodate 100 cylinders.

Standard Cabinet in oak finish, . . . **$35 00**
" " in mahogany finish, . . **40 00**

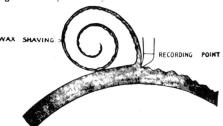

---

dance craze getting fully under way after the armistice. Some well-known leaders commenced their activities around 1919, but for all practical purposes we must look to the following decade for significant developments in the music.

With radio still in its research stage during the 1910s, the new music was diffused by sheet music and above all by records. These were still crude by modern standards but their popularity was widespread, and by 1912 double-sided discs were normal. A good deal of ragtime, though mainly in its most commercialised variety, appeared on American records, performed by pianists, banjoists and military bands. As for nationally-known dance bands, their first boom years on record were in the early '20s, but there were numerous releases before this. European countries were quick to cash in on the interest in the new syncopated forms, both by releasing items from American-made masters and by offering records in the idiom by locally known artists. An Edison advertisement of 1907 assured prospective customers that, whether they wanted to hear grand opera or ragtime, the company had the requisite selections available. Clearly, ragtime was well known in Britain by this time. British companies were quite happy to make money out

of American music, but this did not prevent at least one of them from indulging in scurrilous anti-American propaganda. A 1906 advertisement assured prospective purchasers that 'our records are made in Britain by British workmen with British capital. We keep employed thousands of craftsmen at a good living wage.' The good living wage was in fact thirty shillings a week.

Advertisements for records and record-players in the years up to the close of World War I are frequently fascinating and sometimes bizarre, and I cannot conclude without quoting a few of the more outlandish examples. The Ko-Hi-Ola, for instance, combined Grandfather's clock, phonograph, secret chamber and record compartment. The advertisement claimed: 'The Ko-Hi-Ola is more useful than the ordinary phonograph, more ornamental than the usual style of Grandfather's clock and has exclusive features not found in other machines.' An ingenious aid for the lazy phonograph owner was the 'Metrola', which, it was said, 'could wind any phonograph by electricity, insuring perfect time and tone'. The advertisement went on to mention that it was easily attached in place of the handle, upkeep was negligible, and it couldn't get out of order. There were other

Columbia New Process Disc Records

7-in. Disc Record, 50c each; $5 per doz.

10-in. Disc Record, $1 each; $10 per doz.

Grand Opera Disc Records, (10-inch diameter) **$2 Each**
14-inch Disc Records, - **$2 Each**

All of the above records may be used on any Disc Graphophone. The larger records have greater volume, and are characterized by a delightful roundness and fulness of tone.

List of selections furnished upon application.

Record Cabinet No. 5

This cabinet is for **disc records,** and will accommodate one hundred of them.

Price, $20.00

This Cabinet is made of dark oak highly polished and is ornamental in design. It has **two** shelves or racks which hold the records upright. It is a handsome piece of furniture.

Type AH Graphophone
Uses all flat records

Specifications

Double-spring Motor.
Very Elaborate Cabinet—piano finish (new design).
Analyzing Reproducer.
22-inch Horn, black, with polished brass bell, with metal elbow.
Ornamental, Detachable, Horn Supporting Arms.
100 Needles.
Two-part Needle Box.

PRICE, complete, as above, **$30**

PRICE, equipped with 30-inch brass horn, with 16½ inch bell, otherwise as above, **$40**

PRICE, equipped with 36-inch aluminum horn, otherwise as above, **$45**

Type AU Graphophone

Uses all flat records

Specifications

Spring Motor.
Japanned Bed Plate.
Analyzing Reproducer.
16-inch Japanned Horn, with metal elbow.
Horn Supporting Arms.
100 Needles.
Two-part Needle Box.

PRICE, complete as above, **$12**

PRICE, equipped with 16-inch Horn with polished brass bell, otherwise as above, **$13.50**

Analyzing Reproducer for Disc Graphophones

Reproducer bar pivoted on delicate points, practically eliminating friction.
Reveals tones hitherto indistinguishable.

Greatly increases volume and enriches quality
Price, $5

Send $3 and any disc reproducer and we will give you in exchange this newest improvement in talking machines.

The Analyzing Reproducer
is actually one of the greatest improvements in talking machines. It must be heard to be appreciated.

COLUMBIA ANALYZING REPRODUCER

Record Cabinet No. 4
Same as No. 5, but made of solid mahogany.
Price, $25.00

---

marvels offered to adventurous buyers, such as the 'Clayola' – a phonograph that was fitted into a piano – or the 'Marveola' talking machine, whose manufacturer assured possible purchasers that its name derived from its having been deemed marvellous by acoustic experts, and that it 'seemed to operate with human intelligence'. Probably few of these devices achieved any great commercial success, but perhaps, somewhere, working models may be preserved in a museum.

As the 1910s closed, dance music and dance bands gained in

Amongst the oddities included in the early gramophone advertisements above are (top left) rare 14-inch diameter records.

sophistication and became an international form of entertainment, aided by technological advances in radio and recording. The frequently crude strivings of the pioneer bands and musicians soon began to sound dated or even absurd, but to them goes the credit for making possible the halcyon decades that followed.

UNITED STATES – THE TWENTIES

Dance music, in common with most forms of popular entertainment, received its greatest fillip during the '20s from the growth of radio. During World War I radio had been in its research stage, but subsequently it experienced a phenomenal rise in popularity; from being the hobby of a wealthy minority, it became an immensely potent force in the lives of the majority of Americans. Technological developments enabled the producers of radio sets to market them at a price within the reach of most sections of the community, and sales figures soared from the $60 million of 1922 to over $800 million seven years later. A federal census of 1930 stated that over twelve million families owned radio sets; not unexpectedly, the smallest percentage of ownership was found in the Southern states, where low-income groups were prevalent.

Initially many of the early radio stations were low-powered, their function that of serving a local community, but before long powerful ones arose which were capable of reaching audiences over a wide area. It was a further logical step to create major networks with facilities for transmitting programmes coast-to-coast. The more far-sighted dance band leaders were quick to realise that these developments offered them a ready-made opportunity to establish national reputations. The early growth of radio was not without its seamy side, and federal codes for broadcasters were drawn up to combat the activities of unscrupulous operators. By the late '20s the United States Government found itself battling against pirate radio stations, operating with enormous 100,000 or even 150,000 wattages from just inside the Mexican border. These stations were capable of being heard throughout most of the country, but their programmes were increasingly beamed at rural audiences. The Government fulminated, but there was little it could do about it without the willing co-operation of the Mexican authorities. This was not readily forthcoming, for Mexican feelings had been offended by the action of the American and Canadian governments in appropriating the whole of the long waveband to themselves.

During the early '20s a number of dance bands first acquired localised reputations by association with specific radio stations, and then went on to national fame through exposure over major networks. The great ambition of any band that obtained broadcasting opportunities was to create enough enthusiastic response from its listeners to gain a sponsor. (Until quite recently all American radio survived as a result of commercial advertising.) It was not long before sponsors realised that the growing popularity of the dance bands made them an attractive proposition, as a means of gaining large listening figures. Non-sponsored programmes gave little-known talent the opportunity to establish sufficient popularity to draw the attention of advertisers in search of new names to be featured on their programmes. Almost inevitably, however, the quest for the largest possible listening audiences led sponsors to favour names or formulas of proven success. The great black bands of the day were seldom, if ever, featured regularly on sponsored programmes, while leaders with a yen for experimentation were discouraged from following their inclinations if it was felt that their music would be too advanced for widespread acceptance. Despite this, most of the leading white bands of the '20s experienced little difficulty in attracting sponsors, and their programmes, transmitted at regular times on regular days, attracted huge audiences, who became eager to see their favourites in the flesh.

The '20s also saw the growth of dance halls in any town with a sizeable population. Some of these halls were remarkably ornate in style, and a number became nationally famous from broadcasts. As well as providing a great deal of work for local musicians, they also performed a role of considerable importance in creating centres where touring bands could play, either for a period or for one night. Equally important, an increasing number of hotels realised that a good dance band could enhance their reputation, so they provided ballrooms for their patrons, some of which rivalled the major dance halls in their ostentation and glitter. Regular broadcasts from hotels became commonplace; the bands eagerly seized the opportunity of attracting a mass audience which could support them on profitable tours, while the hotel managements were only too willing to exploit the publicity – the names of their hotels were constantly mentioned in the course of these radio shows.

For a while the record industry suffered from the popularity of radio. Though records were an important source of revenue and publicity to bandleaders, several at least regarded them as less valuable than regular broadcasting opportunities. By 1924 the boom years that immediately followed World War I were but a fading memory to the record manufacturers; many, indeed, viewed radio as heralding the death of their industry. However, behind the scenes the record companies had been experimenting with electric recording, and it was through this revolutionary technical advance that they fought back and attained a new prosperity that was to last until the depression caused another catastrophic recession. Most outstanding technical developments are loudly heralded from their initial application, but American Columbia and RCA Victor, who shared the patent with Western-Electric, did not announce the new system for a year after they commenced to use it. The reason was that they were fearful that the improved sound made possible by the electric process would at one stroke render their whole catalogue obsolete. Both companies began to re-record the major part of their best-selling repertoire by the new method; the only visible sign on the records was an encircled W (on Columbia's) or the letters VE (on RCA Victor's). Then, having satisfactorily completed the programme, they broke the news. The fury of their rivals was intense, but, faced with such a *fait accompli*, they had no option but to pay up and use the new techniques, or to continue with the acoustic method and, probably, ultimately face bankruptcy. A few did attempt to ignore the development, but none successfully. Record buyers were now faced with a major problem; though the new technique gave far greater clarity and overall presence to their records, the playing machines then current were inadequate to cope with it. Within a short time, however, manufacturers were marketing improved gramophones capable of playing the electric recordings to the best advantage. It was the familiar pattern of one technical advance begetting another.

It is outside the scope of this book to dwell in any detail on the activities of the record companies during the '20s, other than those which have a direct bearing on the dance band field, but the appearance of the first long-playing record is worthy of note. In 1932 RCA Victor issued several long-playing items, a number of which had been specially recorded rather than made up from 78 rpm masters, and numerous mini-long-players have been released over the years before the microgroove era. Lack of adequate players led to the swift demise of the RCA Victor series; other examples, usually made by narrowing the grooves, proved to be unsatisfactory because the surfaces rapidly deteriorated. These latter records were normally achieving playing times of five to six minutes a side. One such experiment involved cardboard-based records, but buyers unhappily discovered that, however careful they might be in playing them, there seemed no way of preventing the grooves detaching themselves from the base as the turntable revolved! The real pioneer of the long-playing record was the Edison company, who, in an effort to combat declining sales in 1926, introduced records with a playing time of 24 minutes. They achieved this by retaining a record speed of 80 rpm but narrowing the grooves to 400 per inch, the finest groove ever issued by a commercial company. These records required a special adaptor and needle for use with the Edison player, but, as a result of their delicate grooving and low volume, they were not a success with the public, and after a short life had to be withdrawn. Ray Wile, the foremost authority on Edison records, has printed a list of these releases, but, though there are some dance band records they are of slight musical significance.

The outstanding regularly-constituted dance bands – using the term 'dance bands' in a broad sense – in the United States during the '20s were probably the Coon-Sanders Nighthawks, Jean Goldkette's, Ben Pollack's, Isham Jones's and Paul Whiteman's. Because Isham Jones led his greatest band in the following decade, he will be covered in the chapter dealing with the pre-swing bands of the '30s. As for the great black bands, such as McKinney's Cotton Pickers, Fletcher Henderson's, Luis Russell's, Bennie Moten's and Duke Ellington's, they were essentially large jazz units, and are thus outside the scope of this book. It is true that bands like McKinney's and Russell's were normally playing for dancers in the late '20s, and also that at this period a strict distinction between jazz and dance bands can justifiably be criticised, but – to generalise – the groups above were basically jazz units and should be analysed as such. The overall musical achievements of the large black bands were in the main greater and of more lasting significance than those of the dance and show units, but developments in arranging techniques were not the exclusive prerogative of either, but crossed stylistic barriers. In selecting the five bands I have named as the outstanding ones of the '20s, I can foresee objections from admirers of George Olsen, Ben Bernie, Abe Lyman and numerous other leaders, but, while any of these bands, and indeed others, might occasionally produce records equalling or even surpassing some of those by the chosen five, I do not believe that they matched them in influence or potential. In a period when the future pattern of dance music was being moulded on a trial-and-error basis, it is clear, in retrospect, that even the outstanding bands were amazingly inconsistent; in the case of Jean Goldkette, for example, one has to search hard to

A scene from Republic's musical Atlantic City *with the Paul Whiteman Orchestra and Constance Moore.*

discover his band's worth from records. It is also revealing that a number of little-known bands showed remarkable talent on individual records – several of the more interesting will be briefly mentioned in later stages of this chapter – but here it is difficult to judge accurately on a limited number of releases. Judging bands on their recorded output alone can no doubt lead to distorted evaluations, but the problem is that four decades later no practical alternative method is available to us. There were, I am certain, outstanding bands which never recorded, particularly those based a considerable distance from major recording centres, and no doubt some were inhibited by studio conditions from performing at their best. Many years of listening to bands, however, both in person and on record, has convinced me that in the majority of cases records do give an accurate picture of a group's capabilities and basic style. In-person judgements, on the other hand, are far from error-free, because of the intrusion and unconscious influence of extra-musical factors.

To the public at large the 'King Of Jazz' during the '20s was Paul Whiteman. The son of a director of musical education for the city's public schools, he was born in Denver, Colorado, on 28 March 1890, though a profile on one of a set of cigarette cards issued in Britain chauvinistically claimed his birthplace as Lancashire! His musical studies commenced at the age of seven and a decade later he was a member of the Denver Symphony Orchestra. In 1911 he moved to San Francisco and worked with classical and dance groups. It was then that he first heard jazz, as he recalled in an autobiography, titled, unsurprisingly, *Jazz*.

We first met – jazz and I – at a dance hall dive on the Barbary Coast. It screeched and bellowed at me from a trick platform in the middle of a smoke-hazed, beer-fumed room. And it hit me hard. Raucous? Yes. Crude – undoubtedly. Unmusical – sure as you live. But rhythmic, catching as the small-pox and spirit-lifting.

It would be interesting to know which group Whiteman heard; we can be reasonably sure that it was not an authentic jazz unit. The experience was to alter his career drastically, for he decided his future lay with the new music, and was determined to capture the improvised sounds he heard within an orchestrated framework and to create a new art form – 'symphonic jazz'.

When the United States entered World War I, Whiteman secured a post as musical director with the navy, organising a forty-piece band that was the precursor of his later civilian groups. After his discharge he returned to leading more conventional dance bands, making a hit at the Alexandria in Los Angeles where he became a favourite of the movie colony. It was while working at this hotel that he was heard by S. W. Straus, who persuaded him to head east and open the new Ambassador Hotel in Atlantic City. It was a fortunate choice of location, for, soon after he commenced the engagement, the Victor Talking Machine Company had its annual convention in Atlantic City, and one of its executives was so impressed with Whiteman's music that he immediately signed the band to a recording contract. Whiteman stated more than once that he was so scared of recording that he put off the first session on no fewer than four occasions, but he overcame his nervousness and went on to make a version of *Whispering* that sold a phenomenal 1,800,000 copies.

In 1920 Whiteman decided that the time had come to move to New York, and on 1 October he commenced what was to become a lengthy and historic engagement at the Palais Royal on Broadway. The social climate that prevailed in the higher ranks of the dance band world at that time is made clear by Whiteman in his book: 'we could look out and see the Vanderbilts, Drexel Biddles, Goulds and the rest dancing to our music. Lord and Lady Mountbatten, cousins of the Prince of Wales, were among the distinguished guests one night.' One success followed another, and in 1921 the Whiteman band made a triumphant debut at the Palace Theatre, following this a year later with an initial Broadway appearance in 'George White's Scandals Of 1922' at the Globe Theater. In March 1923 the band sailed for England, appearing in the revue 'Brighter London' at the

Hippodrome and also playing at the Grafton Galleries before a society clientèle. On their return they were greeted by rapturous crowds and musicians playing from planes, rafts and piers. The entertainment world lay at Whiteman's feet, and, no longer satisfied with leading a conventional dance group, he decided that the time was ripe to fulfil his earlier dreams of 'symphonic jazz', conceiving the then revolutionary idea of leading a large group in a jazz concert at a symphony hall.

Whiteman's concert at the Aeolian Hall, New York City, on 12 February 1924, was historic. He led a 23-piece orchestra in a programme titled 'An Experiment In Modern Music', playing standard Whiteman pieces like *Whispering*, some with contrasted 'legitimate' and 'jazz' scoring; *Kitten On The Keys*, featuring composer Zez Confrey at the piano; various semi-symphonic arrangements of Irving Berlin numbers; and a suite of serenades by Victor Herbert. The evening closed with George Gershwin at the piano, performing his new composition *Rhapsody In Blue* with the orchestra in an arrangement by Ferde Grofe. The concert was an immense success, with both Whiteman fans and the critics, and the audience included Jascha Heifetz and Igor Stravinsky. It was repeated later at Carnegie Hall, where Whiteman had initially hoped to introduce it. From then on Whiteman could do no wrong with the American public, receiving the then astronomical fee of five thousand dollars for a single broadcast, and undertaking theatre tours, with ever larger orchestras, that were invariably sell-outs wherever he played. The souvenir programme of his 1925-6 tour explains that Whiteman 'confined his repertoire to pieces which were scored and forbade his players to depart from the script', a strange admission from a man who was billed as the 'King of Jazz'. Most of his concerts now included not only semi-symphonic arrangements of popular songs but performances of light classical items such as Rimsky-Korsakov's *Song of India*, sometimes arranged in a medley form with titles like *Tchaikowskiana*. Early in 1926 Whiteman once more visited London, this time appearing at the Albert Hall, and subsequently presented concerts in Paris, Berlin and Vienna before returning to the United States. It is a little-known fact that the Albert Hall concert, which included Gershwin's *Rhapsody In Blue*, was recorded, but presumably recording techniques of the day were not equal to the task, for the results were never released.

Late in 1927 Whiteman reversed his previous policy and actually introduced some genuine jazz musicians into his band, most of them from the recently disbanded Jean Goldkette orchestra. Foremost among them was the legendary cornetist 'Bix' Beiderbecke, an archetypal figure of the 'jazz age' whose short but brilliant career has been highly romanticised in Dorothy Baker's novel *Young Man with A Horn* and the film which the book inspired. Others included the Dorsey brothers, Frank Trumbauer and Eddie Lang. As long as he led a band thereafter Whiteman employed a number of jazz instrumentalists, two of the most famous in the '30s being trombonist Jack Teagarden and trumpeter Bunny Berigan. For the jazz musicians the Whiteman band meant economic security, for by the mid-'20s the leader was paying his men what had up to then been unheard-of salaries, but few of them could have been entirely happy with the music they were called upon to play. (Beiderbecke has the additional problem that he was a poor reader, and found the complex arrangements very hard to master.) At about the same time Whiteman heard two young vocalists performing at the Metropolitan Theater in Los Angeles and was so impressed with them that he offered them a contract. Their names were Bing Crosby and Al Rinker. With Harry Barris they were to form Whiteman's famous 'Rhythm Boys' vocal trio.

Left: Paul Whiteman and his band, 1923. Below: Zez Confrey, whose novelty pieces like Kitten On The Keys *were popular in the '20s.*

In 1930 Whiteman again achieved a notable triumph, in what was, for him, a new medium, when his entire band and entertainers were given the feature role in the film *The King Of Jazz*, the first in the lengthy list of 'band' films. Shortly after its completion, Bing Crosby left to start his career as the most famous popular vocalist of his day, but it is worth recalling one Whiteman story about him. The Whiteman band was undertaking a lengthy engagement at the Paramount Theater in New York, at a reputed fee of $12,500 a week; the only stipulation the management of the theatre made was that Crosby should not be allowed to sing solo! Soon after Crosby started his solo career, Whiteman pioneered another development when he engaged Mildred Bailey as a vocalist, the first time a female singer was booked as a regular attraction with a band.

During the early '30s the Whiteman band continued to be immensely popular, and present the type of programme with which it was associated, but under the impact of the swing bands its style began to sound dated, and in 1938 Whiteman attempted to modernise his group by commissioning arrangements from Tutti Camarata and others. The attempt was not successful, possibly because the group included too many musicians whose roots were in the pre-swing era, and Whiteman finally broke it up and set about organising a swing-oriented band. His first effort was a failure, but late in 1940 he reorganised once again, this time with excellent musical results. In 1942 his band recorded for Capitol, one of the titles, *Travellin' Light*, having a vocal by the great jazz singer Billie Holiday; three years later he re-created some of his early successes for the same company. The loss of musicians called up for war service caused Whiteman to break up this unit, and, though afterwards he occasionally organised bands for short tours, he never again led a group on a regular basis. During the '40s he worked for a TV network as musical director, and as late as 1955 conducted a regular series, but his activity at this period was prompted more by a desire to remain in music than by economic need, for Whiteman was a wealthy man. In 1956 the American record company Command made an LP titled 'Paul Whiteman – 50th Anniversary' on which former Whiteman employees such as Jack Teagarden, Jimmy and Tommy Dorsey, Hoagy Carmichael, Joe Venuti and Johnny Mercer were featured in a tribute to their leader. Whiteman retained an interest in the music business until his death, on 29 December 1967. At his funeral service four days later a large group of musicians, many of them former sidemen, played his favourite tune *When Day Is Done*.

When one considers Whiteman's vast recorded output it is clear that the passing of time has shown up his more ambitious performances as the least satisfactory. At their best they are melodic trifles grossly inflated, at their worst ridiculous. A particularly blatant example of over-arranging is the 1928 recording of *Sweet Sue*, a slight but agreeable popular tune which has become a standard over the years, presented here in a pretentious concert version that at times runs close to burlesque. For half its length it meanders along without purpose or direction, the burlesque character heightened by a wispy falsetto vocal from Jack Fulton; then the brass breaks into double tempo, leading in a beautiful solo by Bix Beiderbecke which highlights the absurdity of all that has gone before – only to give way to a ponderous ensemble close. In this instance there is the important saving grace of a Beiderbecke solo, but nothing worthwhile enlivens the 'concert' versions of such pieces as *Metropolis*, *La Golondrina* and *Liebestraum*. Yet there are occasional exceptions among the concert performances; *When Day Is Done*, despite an excess of tempo changes and a rather fussy score, is impressive for the quality of the actual playing, as indeed is *Song Of India*. In general the best that can be said about Whiteman's self-styled concert recordings is that the quality of musicianship is normally a great deal higher than the level of taste.

Whiteman's first recording was *Wang Wang Blues*, made in September 1920 and originally intended as a test. This is performed in a style that has overtones of the Original Dixieland Jazz Band, though it may be that there was no direct influence but rather the employment of a then conventional method. His next session produced the famous *Whispering* and *Japanese Sandman*, both rhythmically indebted to ragtime and completely devoid of any ODJB influence. *My Man*, recorded a year later, is similar in character but is more formally arranged and shows an advance in technical resource, as indeed does the Henry Busse hit *Hot Lips* which, mediocre in itself, does incorporate section patterns which are used more fully in the slightly later *Any Time, Any Place*, where the brass riffs against the reeds' melody line. It would be easy to deride these efforts, but they are no worse and in some instances a great deal better than similar performances by contemporary bands. At this period many musicians were developing arranging techniques, and experiments with new instruments and the blending of different sounds were taking place on a hit-or-miss principle. It was to be a year or two before the problems were satisfactorily solved by arrangers such as Don Redman, but the latter's score of *Whiteman Stomp*, recorded by the Whiteman band in late 1927, proves beyond any doubt the superlative skill of the musicians in handling what was a tricky chart.

In the closing years of the '20s Whiteman led his most impressive band. Not only did it include a number of gifted

Above: a film still of the Paul Whiteman band in the late '20s. The guitarist (far left) is the late Eddie Lang, the saxophonist second from the right the late Frankie Trumbauer. Right: as late as 1939 Whiteman was still being billed as 'The King of Jazz' in British record supplements. Far right: another Whiteman extravaganza film of the late '20s or early '30s. The guitarist is Eddie Lang; behind him is violinist Joe Venuti.

soloists – Beiderbecke, Eddie Lang, the Dorsey brothers and others – but it possessed in Bill Challis a talented and skilled arranger who worked to extend the melodic and harmonic horizons of the music. Whiteman's most prominent arranger was Ferde Grofe, said to be the first man to score written parts for a dance band, but Grofe's real inclination lay towards light music, of which he was a prolific composer, perhaps his best known work in this idiom being *Grand Canyon Suite*. Challis, and to a slightly lesser extent his fellow arranger Lennie Hayton, was little concerned with this aspect of Whiteman's music, and his scores of such numbers as *Changes, Lonely Melody, Love Nest, Dardanella* and *San* have many felicitous touches, hallmarks of a fine craftsman. These performances involved personnels that varied from ten to twenty or more, and all had brilliant, lyrical, solos by Beiderbecke. Even though the Whiteman band never swung in a convincing manner, there are passages where Challis manages to inject an unusual rhythmic surge into ensemble statements. This is particularly so in *Dardanella*, where the ensemble playing is of a high order and Beiderbecke's solo is helped by some incisive bass support from

Steve Brown. These recordings show that, while the Whiteman band was, as a group, incapable of turning out an authentic jazz performance, it could at least provide a setting for a jazz soloist that was not totally inept. The commercial success Whiteman enjoyed at this time was in part due to the vocals by Bing Crosby and the Rhythm Boys, but even his most ephemeral performances reflect his insistence on the highest musical standards and his ability to hire the best instrumentalists available.

During the early '30s Whiteman's public success was unbroken, but recordings like *Announcer's Blues, It's Only A Paper Moon* and *Ain't Misbehavin'*, though featuring excellent solos by Bunny Berigan, Frank Trumbauer and Charlie and Jack Teagarden, show that his attempts to come to terms with the new developments that were to culminate in the swing era lacked conviction. By the mid-'30s his music began to sound anachronistic.

During his heyday Paul Whiteman played the role of the successful entertainer in the classic showbiz manner. A big man in every sense of the term – he weighed over 280 lb – he exuded an air of joviality and love of high living. He let it be known that his musicians were the highest paid in the business, that his fees were astronomical by the standards of the day, that he lived in a luxurious manner, and that he and his entourage travelled in the height of comfort, frequently in Cadillacs equipped with cocktail cabinets and other trimmings of the good life. His success may have been due in part to his exploitation of two important characteristics of popular taste: basic conservatism, and a love of novelty. In addition he gave an air of respectability to popular music, appealing to his public's latent snobbery with light classics and Gershwin's *Rhapsody In Blue*. Jazz writers have never forgiven Whiteman for his 'King of Jazz' tag and seem reluctant to this day to credit him with any worthwhile achievements, but, while much of his recorded output may rightly be condemned as pretentious, even absurd, blanket condemnations of his total output are grossly unjust. It is probably true that Whiteman succeeded best when his own inclinations towards 'symphonic jazz' were least in evidence, but

22

by his insistence on a high quality of performance, and his willingness to pay well to obtain the leading instrumentalists, there is little doubt that he did help to raise the level of popular music, though his influence may have been more oblique rather than direct. Ironically, though he was credited with directly furthering dance music and jazz, after 1924 and the success of the Aeolian Hall concert Whiteman never led a dance band as such, but fronted a showband. Perhaps Herman D. Kenin, president of the American Federation of Musicians, most aptly summed up Whiteman's role when, in an address delivered at his funeral service, he described him as 'King of the Jazz Age' In the flamboyance of his personality and the spectacular nature of his public successes Whiteman was well equipped to live that role. Today there is a Whiteman museum where all the original band arrangements are stored, with records, broadcast transcriptions and memorabilia. The Whiteman legend may be hard to sustain on a musical level, but to his former public it remains undimmed.

It is logical to follow the Whiteman story with that of Jean Goldkette, for the influx of jazz musicians into Whiteman's band late in 1927 followed directly upon the break-up of the Goldkette band. Goldkette was born in Valenciennes, France, on 18 March 1899, lived his boyhood years in Greece, studied briefly in Russia, and went to the United States in 1911. Although initially intending to follow a career as a concert pianist, he worked in popular music, playing for a time with a small group at Lamb's Café in Chicago. About the end of World War I he moved to Detroit forming his first dance band

in 1921 and commencing to record for Victor in 1924. He then acquired the foremost ballroom in Detroit, the Greystone, and went into management, operating numerous Jean Goldkette orchestras. He also controlled the group that subsequently became the Casa Loma Orchestra, and the famous McKinney's Cotton Pickers.

Goldkette's original ideas seem to parallel Whiteman's; indeed, at one time his major group was billed as 'The Paul Whiteman Of The West'. Late in 1926, however, he decided to have a nucleus of jazz musicians within his band and to feature them extensively. In fact he had already, at various times, employed Joe Venuti, Eddie Lang, Bill Rank and Fud Livingston, but, on records at least, they were allocated little solo space. As a result of his business interests Goldkette appears to have been casual about the direction of his primary band, but when Frank Trumbauer and Bix Beiderbecke joined, to be followed a few months later by the Dorsey brothers, he realised that he had an exceptional unit and took a great pride in its musical achievements. For about a year, from late 1926, Goldkette led a potentially great band, which he took to New York to play at the Roseland Ballroom, where it created something of a sensation. The high salaries paid to the sidemen, however, and the *prima donna* behaviour of many of its stars, caused it to break up, and it made its farewell appearance at the Roseland late in 1927. Goldkette formed a new band that continued to record until 1929 and, though in his later years he was chiefly occupied with his booking and management agency, he led groups sporadically until the mid-'40s. In the '50s he returned to working as a

The Jean Goldkette Orchestra, 1926–7. Left to right: Bill Challis, Spiegan Wilcox, Andy Riskin, Bix Beiderbecke, Don Murray, Howdy Quicksell, Doc Ryker, Chauncey Morehouse, Fred Farrar, Ray Lodwig, Bill Rank, Frankie Trumbauer, Steve Brown. Right: Ben Pollack in the late '20s.

concert pianist, but in 1959 lent his name to a Camden LP that re-created some of his hits of the '20s. Though he had a long career in the music business, his great days ended with that farewell engagement at the Roseland.

Goldkette's Victor recordings of 1924-5 are unexceptional, those of early 1926 no less so. The year in which Beiderbecke, Trumbauer and others were included in the personnel produced some twenty-four recorded titles, but unfortunately Goldkette gave in to pressure from recording directors and did not use his more advanced arrangements, mainly written by Don Challis and Don Murray. Instead he produced almost entirely commercial titles, such as the eminently forgettable *In My Merry*

Oldsmobile (in waltz and foxtrot versions), *Hush-A-Bye* (another waltz) and *Sunny Disposish*. The last had the distinction of being mentioned in John O'Hara's famous novel *Appointment In Samarra*, but there is little in the performance to indicate why O'Hara singled it out. Irritatingly, two of the recordings most likely to reveal the band at its best, *Stampede* and *Play It, Red*, remain unissued, and we are left with only a few items whose musical content sustains the reputation that the band enjoyed at its peak. *Clementine*, arranged by Bill Challis, is one example, for apart from the fine Beiderbecke solo there are good passages by Eddie Lang and Joe Venuti, excellent ensemble playing, and, throughout, an impressive rhythmic lift. For the rest, parts of *I Didn't Know*, *My Pretty Girl* and *Slow River* reveal neat arranging touches and spirited ensemble playing, but we are left with the inescapable conclusion that the music with which Goldkette scored his great success at the Roseland Ballroom never got on to record. What it was like only a surviving member of the band – like Bill Rank, trombonist in the peak

years, who not long ago assured enquirers that the greatness of the band was no myth – or someone who heard it at the Roseland could tell us.

Ben Pollack could reasonably claim to have led the first white band in the United States that stressed hot performances and gave jazz soloists a high degree of freedom. It has been said with some truth that his was the first large white jazz band. Pollack, an excellent drummer who recorded with the Friars Society Orchestra (later New Orleans Rhythm Kings) as early as 1922, was born in Chicago on 22 June 1903, and after a thorough and varied training formed his own band for a Californian engagement in 1925. It was here, in August of that year, that he hired a 16-year-old clarinettist named Benny Goodman. Early in 1926 the band returned to Chicago, working in clubs like the Rendezvous and the Blackhawk until the summer of 1927, when it again made tracks for California. A few months later Pollack took his band, including Jimmy McPartland, Glenn Miller, Benny Goodman and Gil Rodin, to New York, where it became

established at the Park Central Hotel for a number of years. After good reports of its Californian engagement Victor had signed the band in 1926 and it recorded for this company until the close of 1929. Members of the band also made dozens of titles under numerous pseudonyms for other companies, not always with Pollack's blessing – hence, perhaps, one of the pseudonyms they used: 'Ben's Bad Boys'. In the mid-'30s Pollack re-formed with an entirely new personnel that in late 1934 became the nucleus of the Bob Crosby band. Two years later he was back again with a new group, which included Harry James, Shorty Sherock, Irving Fazola and Freddy Slack. For the rest of the '30s Pollack led other bands that included famous musicians, usually acting as a front man and seldom playing drums. In the '40s he assembled bands for others, for a while had his own record company (Jewel), owned a restaurant in Hollywood, and until his death on 8 June 1971 sometimes led Dixieland groups. Over the years he discovered an astonishing number of musicians who subsequently became famous, though

after the 1926-9 period he seemed unable to maintain stable personnels for very long. Several of his '30s recordings are worthwhile, particularly for the solo talent displayed, but his greatest impact on the dance band world was certainly in the '20s.

The trouble with Pollack, during his peak years as leader between 1926 and 1929, was that he realised he led an outstanding band, strong in jazz soloists, but longed too for commercial success. As a result he constantly compromised with his music, introducing novelty effects and showing a desire to be known as a showbiz personality. Thus, in 1928, he forsook the drums, because he felt that he might not be recognised as the leader in that role. (His replacement, Ray Bauduc, was in fact a better drummer.) He also took to singing on records, which did not add to their worth. Though his soloists were on the whole featured quite extensively, most of his '20s records repeat the Goldkette story in a less dramatic form.

Most of Pollack's arrangements are by unknown hands, but some of the recorded titles were arranged by Glenn Miller, and Benny Goodman has singled out these scores as particularly praiseworthy. It is probable that 'Deed I Do, recorded in December 1926, is a Miller arrangement; the writing is extremely professional for the period, and solo passages are well integrated with the ensemble. Benny Goodman is heard to advantage, and Miller's 8-bar contribution, interestingly enough, is much influenced, stylistically, by Miff Mole. Regrettably, Pollack's singing is influenced by no one but himself. That the band kept

abreast of arranging developments is shown by the 1929 *My Kinda Love* which, apart from the excellent solos by Goodman and Jack Teagarden, displays ensemble integration of a high order. For the rest, Pollack's records are a strange mixture of good and utterly mediocre scores, worthwhile solos frequently offset by dismal vocals, and a forward-looking approach uneasily co-existing with commercial banality. The band's many pseudonymous records were occasionally good jazz performances, but unfortunately a high proportion were, at the insistence of A & R men, in a deliberately burlesque vein.

If asked to name the dance band of the '20s that produced the most consistently interesting recordings, I should be tempted to settle for the Coon-Sanders Nighthawks. Their peak years of popularity were between 1926 and 1932, when drummer Carleton Coon died, but the band had been in existence for some years beforehand. It grew from a chance meeting of the two leaders at a Kansas City music store in December 1918, when both were home on leave from the army. They struck up a friendship, and after their army discharge started working together in small, casually assembled bands, usually of seven or eight musicians, which played at clubs and private functions. Coon was born on 5 February 1894 at Rochester, Minnesota. His parents shortly afterwards moved to Lexington, Missouri, where, it has been said, Coon became friendly with black dock workers, who influenced his musical outlook. A few years later the family moved to Kansas City. Sanders was slightly younger – he was born at Thayer, Kansas, on 15 October 1896 – and his initial musical activity was as a boy soprano, followed in turn by work as a concert pianist and as a singer in the Kansas City Opera Company. He also enjoyed a considerable reputation as a baseball player – hence his nickname as 'The Old Left-Hander' – but by the early '20s had decided to make dance music his career, a profession which he followed for most of his life.

From 1919 to 1921, when it made a recording for Columbia,

Top left: Jean Goldkette (inset) with his orchestra during 1924; bottom left: later in the '20s. Below: Ben Pollack and his Central Park Hotel Orchestra, early 1929; left to right: back row – Eddie Bergman, Larry Binyon, Jack Teagarden, Al Beller; front row – Al Harris, Harry Goodman, Jimmy McPartland, Benny Goodman, Dick Morgan, Vic Breidis, Gil Rodin. Ben Pollack is seated.

The Coon-Sanders Original Nighthawks: left to right – Nick Musolina, Pop Estep, Joe Richolson, Carleton Coon, Tom Beckham, Joe Sanders, John Thiell, Orville Knapp(later a bandleader in his own right) and Harold Thiell. Inset are photographs of the co-leaders Carleton Coon and Joe Sanders. This picture was taken in the closing months of 1923.

the personnel of the band – which billed itself as a 'Novelty Orchestra' – varied little. Its popularity was boosted by a series of pioneering broadcasts from the Muehlebach Hotel, which went out over WDAF ('Kansas City Star'), a moderately powerful station. Shortly after the broadcasts commenced the leaders set up the 'Nighthawks Club' (the transmissions took place in the early hours), encouraging listeners to send in requests for tunes by letter, telegram or telephone. The success of the move led to Western Union installing a ticker tape between Sanders's piano and Coon's drums, so that telegrams could be acknowledged during transmissions. As the broadcasts gained the Nighthawks a wider audience they planned their first trip away from Kansas City, and in May 1924 opened a three-month engagement at a Chicago roadhouse. Next they did a short tour for MCA, then returned to take up residence at the Congress Hotel in October. In the following two years there were a number of personnel changes, and the band that moved into the Blackhawk Hotel in October 1926 consisted of Joe Richolson, Bob Pope (trumpets), Rex Downing (trombone), Harold Thiell, John Thiell, Floyd Estep (saxophones), Joe Sanders (piano), Russ Stout (banjo, guitar), 'Pop' Estep (tuba) and Carleton Coon (drums). This engagement represented a triumph for the Chicago office of the Music Corporation of America (MCA). Previously the hotel had featured no entertainment, and it took a great deal of lengthy negotiation by MCA representatives to persuade the management to change their policy. Several members of the band, too, were sceptical about the value of the job, thinking that the hotel – having no tradition of live music – might find it difficult to attract audiences. In fact the engagement led to the greatest years of commercial success that the band was to enjoy.

In the years that followed, the Nighthawks were resident every winter at the Blackhawk, and had a nightly broadcast over the powerful WGN (owned by the *Chicago Tribune*) and a weekly half-hour on an NBC coast-to-coast programme. When the winter job terminated the band undertook highly successful road tours; its reputation had spread virtually nation-wide, as a result of the regular broadcasts and fast-selling Victor records.

(But it was not always featured to the best advantage in New York, where radio executives imposed limitations on the co-leader's announcing and reading out requests.) Flaunting the outer trimmings of success, all the band-members possessed identical cars, each in a different colour, with the names of the band and the individual owners embossed on the rear. The arrival of the band in this fleet must have impressed inhabitants of the towns in which they played one-nighters.

During the spring of 1932 the Nighthawks returned to Chicago to take up residence in the College Inn of the Hotel Sherman. The band's popularity showed no sign of abating, the personnel had been stable for years, and the contract with MCA had another fifteen years to run, but suddenly disaster struck; Coon contracted a jaw infection and died on 4 May, aged thirty-eight. Although profoundly shocked, Sanders continued to lead the band, taking on the additional responsibility of caring for Coon's family, who discovered that Coon's happy-go-lucky attitude on the stand unfortunately mirrored his personal mode of living. Within a few months, however, he was forced to give up, partly because the public was unwilling to accept the band without Coon. In 1935 he formed a new band and returned to the Blackhawk, working there regularly for the remainder of the decade and also less frequently in the '40s, when he combined the roles of occasional bandleader and Hollywood studio musician. With the decline of the big band business Sanders returned to an earlier career and throughout the '50s was a regular member of the Kansas City Opera Company, but in the latter years of his life he suffered from failing eyesight and other health problems, and a stroke in 1964 led to his death early the next year. Throughout his career he had maintained voluminous scrap books and other memorabilia, which his widow presented to the Kansas City Public Library, who now keep it readily available to researchers. In the post-Nighthawks period Sanders was a prolific composer of popular music, some of which was fairly widely performed, but his name and those of other members of the Coon-Sanders band are kept alive today through the flourishing Coon-Sanders Nighthawk Club.

In considering the Nighthawks' recordings one must remember that some of the formulas which made the band so successful as a broadcasting unit cannot be utilised in a different medium. The broadcasts obviously owed much to the personalities of the leaders, expressed through their announcements, acknowledgements of requests, and vocal duets. These last could of course be reproduced quite satisfactorily on record, as titles like *Wabash Blues*, *After You've Gone* and *Alone In The Rain* confirm. These, like Sanders's individual vocals on *Alone At Last* and *Here Comes My Ball and Chain*, now have a distinctly period flavour. Today, the qualities that make listening to the Coon-Sanders recordings an enjoyable experience are technical expertise and a relaxed rhythm that was by no means commonplace among white bands of the period. Coon, on recorded evidence, was a proficient drummer, but no doubt his value to the band lay as much in his personality as in his musical skill; in bookers' terminology, he was an ideal front man. But it was unquestionably Sanders who guided and shaped the band's music. He wrote most of its arrangements, his skill being particularly evident in the scores of the hotter numbers it recorded. He is said to have worked hard to develop flexibility in his writing for the saxophone section, and if some numbers – *Tennessee Lazy*, for example – reveal the unfortunate influence of Guy Lombardo, *Keepin' Out Of Mischief Now* and others testify to his success in meeting this challenge. In the more jazz-inclined performances, like *High Fever*, *S.L.U.E. Foot* and *Rhythm King*, the excellence of the whole is due not only to the musicians' technical brilliance but also to Sanders's awareness of their individual strengths and limitations. By limitations I mean, for example, that the band had no major jazz stylist capable of sustaining lengthy solos. Sanders compensates for this by restricting solo space, leaving room instead for frequent breaks, which are always performed with *élan* and unfaltering technical expertise. It may even be that some of the breaks are fully scored, though they normally give the impression of spontaneity. Sanders's arrangements sustain a neat balance between short solos and ensemble passages, and show his ability to use conventional scoring techniques of the period in a fresh manner. Above all, they are as strong rhythmically as they are melodically. Though not a creative innovator, Sanders was a thorough professional, and this ensured a steady flow of scores that highlighted the band to the best advantage. If we make the necessary allowances for period characteristics, they remain to this day an impressive tribute to his intelligent musicianship and versatility.

In concentrating on the bands that produced the most rewarding records of their day, there is the inevitable danger that many other excellent groups will receive less than justice. It is worth making it clear that the conciseness of the accounts that follow is dictated by exigencies of space.

Certain leaders were active for many years who, unable to maintain stable personnels, or lacking long spells of economically rewarding work, produced their outstanding records in the brief periods when circumstances favoured them. One such was Bert Lown, who was born at White Plains, N.Y., on 6 June 1903. After working as a sales executive and public promotions officer, he opened a theatrical booking agency in 1926, which increasingly led him to place bands for clubs, house parties and private functions. From 1928 he was a leader in his own right, and remained so, though continuing his activities as a booker, until 1941, latterly working as musical director for prominent hotels in Argentina, Brazil and Uruguay. After leaving the band business he became a leading executive in various war relief organisations, and since 1946 has been associated with the Muzak Corporation. He is also a long-standing member of ASCAP, on the strength of compositions such as *Bye Bye Blues*, *Tired*, *By My Side* and *My Heart And I*. Though a leader for over a decade, Lown had his most musically rewarding period in one specific engagement at New York's Biltmore Hotel, between 3 December 1929 and June 1932, during which he recorded for Columbia, Perfect, Victor and Hit-Of-The-Week. Just prior to his opening at the Biltmore Lown had recorded three excellent titles for Columbia with a studio group that contained Miff Mole, Jimmy Dorsey, Adrian Rollini and Carl Kress, and his regular band at the hotel included, at various times, Frank Cush, Glenn Miller, Adrian Rollini, Al Philburn and Spencer Clark – in itself a guarantee that he had set his sights on maintaining worthwhile musical standards.

Too many Lown records are rendered painful by vocalists who, even when one allows for period conventions, can only be dismissed as appalling; readers with a taste for the bizarre in vocalising are recommended to hear *Tomorrow's Violets* and *Redskin*. Certain Lown records, however, are advanced for their time, notably *Here Comes My Ball And Chain*, *Jazz Me Blues*, *Big City Blues*, *Loving You The Way I Do* and *Blues In My Heart*. With a nucleus of talented soloists in the band, it is not surprising that individual contributions frequently catch one's attention, but the modern-sounding brass passages and well varied score of *Blues In My Heart*, or the crisp section work and skilful arrangement of *Loving You The Way I Do*, prove that the band, at its best, could offer serious competition to most contemporary dance orchestras. They also suggest that most of its records are not representative of its potential.

There were several bands whose music reflected one aspect of the '20s, and their bright, brash and carefree performances retain a certain nostalgic charm for the present-day listener. One such band was led by George Olsen. Born in Portland, Oregon, in 1890, Olsen organised his first band at college, deciding to make music his career in 1915. His big break came in the '20s, when, at the urging of singer Fanny Brice, the impresario Florenz Ziegfeld brought him east to appear in Eddie Cantor's show 'Kid Boots'. Subsequently his band was featured in the original Broadway productions of many famous American musical comedies. He commenced recording for Victor in the pre-electrical era, achieving his first big hit with a late-1925 version of *Who* which sold over a million copies. His earliest recordings were in the peppy, restless style that then seemed to many the epitome of jazz, but by the end of the '20s he had added strings to his line-up and achieved a smoother sound, and was known as much for the featured vocals by Fran Frey and various trios as for any individuality of instrumental approach. In 1930 Olsen moved back to the West Coast and became popular in Hollywood, continuing to lead a band in the ensuing years, though its style increasingly lacked distinction. He retired in 1951 and began a restaurant business in Paramus, New Jersey, providing his patrons with background music from tapes of his old records. He died there on 18 March 1971.

A reissue LP of Olsen's most famous recordings gives a fair cross section of the band's repertoire, including novelty numbers like *Horses* and *Sax-O-Phun*, show tunes of the calibre of *Who*, *Sunny* and *The Girl Friend*, and collegiate favourites like *Doin' The Raccoon* and *All American Girl* (into which Fran Frey's two vocal choruses cram the names of no fewer than twenty-six colleges). One title, *A New Kind Of Man, With A New Kind Of Love*, is, somewhat surprisingly, an attempt at a straightforward jazz performance and features a solo by a temporary member of the personnel, Red Nichols. In general the appeal of these performances lies in their musical evocation of an era that has long passed. While playing standards were by no means negligible, the material and scores neither called for nor produced very much individual or collective creativity.

Two further bands whose music faithfully reflects the frenetic 'jazz age' of the '20s are the California Ramblers and,

far less predictably, Fred Waring's Pennsylvanians. Waring, who celebrated fifty years in the music business in 1966, is best known today for his stylised 'Glee Club' presentations, and since the mid-'30s his instrumentalists have been subsidiary to vocalists and choirs. During the '20s, however, he led an immensely popular dance band. Born in Tyrone, Pennsylvania, on 9 June 1900, he studied violin at high school and was, appropriately, a member of its glee club. In conjunction with his brother Tom and a neighbour, Poley McClintock, he formed a youthful band, which, on leaving college, he called Waring's Banjo Orchestra and led with some success, adding steadily to the original personnel. After enduring the vicissitudes that are part of most bandleaders' early careers, Waring commenced a series of broadcasts over WWJ in Detroit. They were highly successful in bringing his music to the notice of a wider public, and, dropping the banjo to become full-time leader, he renamed the group Waring's Pennsylvanians. The band soon became a great favourite on the collegiate circuit, and after a notable engagement at the Metropolitan Theater in Hollywood was signed to an RCA Victor contract, its first release, *Sleep*, becoming a tremendous hit. In the succeeding years Waring rivalled Paul Whiteman – his major influence – as a show attraction. Highlights of his career included periods as the headliner in the Broadway show 'Help Yourself', starring in the very popular film *Syncopation* (1929), and a lucrative overseas engagement at the Ambassadeurs Club in Paris. Though not, by all accounts, a man who inspired much affection in his musicians, he kept key members of his band for lengthy periods; Fred Culley joined as assistant conductor in 1925 and remained in that role until his death in 1966, while Stuart Churchill, who joined him in 1929, was a featured vocalist for over twenty-five years.

Waring has the reputation of being a perfectionist in everything he does. This care was illustrated by his thorough preparation upon accepting an offer in 1930 to make regular broadcasts. He hired a sound studio and in seven days the band produced something like two hundred transcriptions for him to study balance, blending of sounds, and many other aspects of radio transmission. In the same year he also organised his own musical comedy, which later opened in New York as 'The New Yorkers' with a score by Cole Porter. By 1933 Waring was reputedly the highest paid bandleader in radio and theatre, which may have influenced his decision to cease making records, a policy to which he steadfastly adhered for a decade. His subsequent concentration on his glee club stemmed from his high school interest and from hearing the famous Hall Johnson Choir, but his accomplishments in this field are irrelevant to the central theme of this book.

Above: Fred Waring's band, early '30s. Right: the Ipana Troubadours, led by Sam Lanin (seated at piano). Sponsored by Ipana Toothpaste, they could be heard over many radio stations by early 1928. Evidently they were also good customers of the theatrical costumiers.

A small selection of Waring's '20s recordings has been reissued, and such titles as *Collegiate, Any Ice Today Lady?* and *Wob-a-ly Walk* contain the peppy rhythms, novelty effects and vo-do-de-o vocals beloved of TV and film producers in search of period atmosphere. By the '30s Waring's music had become more sophisticated, with a smoother balance and tauter section work, though there is still little that rates higher on musical than on nostalgic appeal. In several respects Waring was a pioneer in dance band recording – *Collegiate* was the first recording by a dance band to feature a vocal chorus; *Nashville Nightingale* the first recording of a George Gershwin tune; *Oh, Donna Clara* the first recording of a rhumba. Regretfully, though, one concludes that throughout his career Waring's perfectionist criteria were applied to what was essentially trivial material.

The California Ramblers, by contrast, while producing their fair measure of '20s ephemera, were basically a very musicianly group, whose better records possess qualities still apparent forty years or more after they were made. The band was misnamed, for most of the personnel came from Ohio. Its upward career was initiated when two of its members called on Ed Kirkeby (who became very prominent in the following decade as Fats Waller's manager) and asked if he could help to get them work in New York City. At first, under the leadership of banjoist Ray Kitchenman, the band worked in New York as accompanists to a singer called Eva Shirley, but before long it broke up as a result of internal dissension. Kitchenman persuaded Kirkeby to let him re-form it, using as his basis a small orchestra, led by violinist Arthur Hand, which included Adrian Rollini, Jimmy and Tommy Dorsey, and Loring 'Red' Nichols. After a trial run at Shanley's Dance Hall on Broadway, the California Ramblers took up location at the Post Lodge, Pelham Bay Park, Westchester County, calling their base the California Ramblers Inn. They were immediately successful and for just over a decade enjoyed a lucrative career, recording prolifically under their own name for Columbia and under numerous pseudonyms for other labels. (Kirkeby has said that the band waived all royalties for their Columbia recordings on condition that they were free to record under *noms-de-plume* for other companies.) Their style was firmly rooted in the '20s, and it is surprising that they lasted beyond the decade. One of

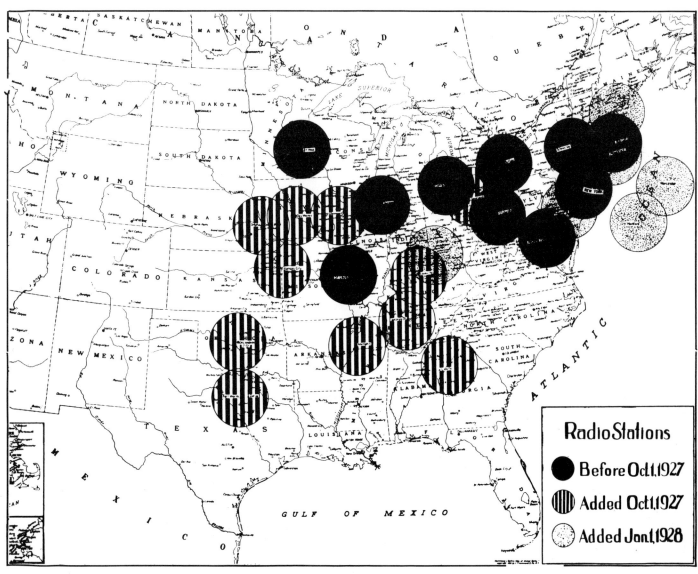

Radio Stations

● Before Oct.1,1927

▥ Added Oct.1,1927

○ Added Jan.1,1928

the regular personnel in the mid-'20s was trumpeter Bill Moore, a light-skinned black who 'passed'; the Ramblers were thus one of the first racially mixed groups, but whether Moore would have remained if the audiences had realised the fact is open to doubt. An unusual pioneering effort by the Ramblers took place on Easter Sunday of 1923, when they were featured, on WMCA, New York, in the first programme of sacred music to be broadcast, performed by a jazz dance band group. The reactions were far from favourable, many listeners considering the whole idea blasphemous.

The personnel of the California Ramblers underwent many changes over the years but always included a nucleus of jazz musicians; hence the band has been well represented on re-issue LPs. The Ramblers must share with Pollack the distinction of being one of the earliest white bands regularly to present dance music that was strongly jazz-influenced. Even such unlikely looking titles as *Vo-Do-De-O Blues* and *Dustin' The Donkey* include a number of reasonable solos, and when the band turned to less ephemeral material and dispensed with vocal choruses it produced such excellent performances as *Static Strut*, *Arkansas Blues* and *Stockholm Stomp*. The last-named was in all probability the finest record that the Ramblers made, combining fresh solos from Abe Lincoln, Bobby Davis, Chelsea Quealey and Adrian Rollini, with crisp, well-scored ensemble playing. The early arrangements that the Ramblers used were at least as good as, and sometimes better than, those heard on contemporary records by such bands as Fletcher Henderson's and Paul Whiteman's; an unexpected by-product of their success was the influence they exerted on Fred Elizalde's band at the Savoy Hotel in London, during the time when he had ex-Ramblers musicians within his ranks. It is fifty years since the Ramblers were formed, forty years since they disbanded, but their records conclusively show that they were one of the earliest dance bands to combine functional appeal with a concern for musical values well beyond that of mere professionalism.

An early band which has been completely ignored by re-issue compilers, but produced records that were in many ways very forward-looking for their day, was the Benson Orchestra of Chicago. It worked at the Marigold Gardens – a venue notorious for its association with gangsters – and though carrying the name of its manager, Edgar A. Benson, was under the musical direction of pianist Roy Bargy. The band went to Camden, New Jersey, to record for the first time in September 1920, but it made its first really interesting records at a session seven months later, including the first recording of *San*. Of particular note is a version of *No-Ja*, which features possibly the earliest use of stop-time on record, clarinettist Matt Amaturo soloing against fill-ins by the full band. This and other titles suggest that the band was ahead of its time in its deployment of section arranging and solo instrumentalists playing against a section in harmony. A September 1921 recording of *Wabash Blues* proved to be the band's most popular seller, sales exceeding 750,000 copies.

Late in 1921 Bargy had a disagreement with Benson and formed his own band, including many members of the Benson Orchestra. His replacement as leader was another pianist, Don Bestor, and a new member of the personnel was saxophonist Frankie Trumbauer, who stayed until April 1924, when he left to join Ray Miller's band in New York. Trumbauer is heard in a solo chorus on *Think Of Me* and also on *I Never Miss The Sunshine*, a finely scored and played performance at slow tempo that includes a piano duet from Bestor and Charley Straight. *Somebody's Wrong* is another attractive title, worth hearing for a very good muted trumpet soloist, probably Herb Carlin. Best

Top left: Art Landry and his Commodore Band. Bottom left: Don Voorhees and his band; the first trumpeter on the left is Red Nichols. This was the band which Voorhees formed for the Columbia Recording System in 1928. Right: Cass Hagan.

of all is a really spirited version of *Copenhagen* with first-rate solos by, amongst others, the Chicago clarinettist Volly de Faut.

In 1925 a trumpeter named, not inappropriately, Fred Hamm, took over the leadership of the band, and Bestor followed Bargy's example in forming his own group, which recorded spasmodically well into the '30s. From this point Hamm, and some other leaders, recorded under their own names with the subtitle 'A Benson Organization', but their output, though not without interest, is not comparable to the early Benson releases. In its use of well-written and imaginative scores, its standard of execution, and its willingness to chart new territories, the Benson Orchestra's only rival in its earliest years was Paul Whiteman, though unlike Whiteman it is now remembered only by record collectors and, presumably, a few elderly people who heard it in person. Edgar Benson, whose 'cello playing was not exactly revered by other musicians, is still alive and active at the time of writing, though now in his eighty-first year.

Other popular leaders of the '20s sometimes recorded above-average performances. Cass Hagan (born 1904) led several bands that have been highly rated by musicians, his personnel at different times including such stars as Red Nichols, Pee Wee Russell, Al Philburn, Lennie Hayton, Tommy Dorsey and Bix Beiderbecke. Unfortunately few of his records reflect the reputation his bands enjoyed, but *Variety Stomp* and *Melancholy Charlie*, apart from good solos by trumpeter Bob Ashford and baritone saxophonist Jack Towne, offer powerful ensemble playing. Hagan retired from music in 1937 but is remembered with affection by musicians for his interest in jazz and for the

unusual freedom he afforded jazz soloists who were members of his band. Paul Specht led a successful band for many years and was a prolific recorder, though little of his output was particularly striking, but jazz fans owe him a debt for featuring The Georgians, probably the first 'band within a band' in the tradition of Bob Crosby's Bob Cats or Tommy Dorsey's Clambake Seven, and one that subsequently led an independent existence under its leader Frank Guarente.

There were numerous other proficient and musicianly bands recording dance music by the end of the '20s, all of whom could produce the occasional outstanding performance, even if none could lay claim to any high degree of individuality. Those led by Hale Byers, Tom Gerunovich, Henry Halstead, Vincent Lopez, Benny Meroff, Vic Meyers, Jesse Stafford and Herb Wiedoeft were among the most noteworthy. Two veteran leaders deserving of mention are Ben Bernie – 'The Ole

Above: the Georgians, a small group from Paul Specht's orchestra, probably the first 'band within a band'; left to right – Arthur Schutt, Johnny O'Donnell, Frank Guarente, Chauncey Morehouse, Ray Stillwell. Below left: Abe Lyman and his band, from a '30s musical film. Opposite, top: banjoist/guitarist Harry Reser, who recorded hundreds of titles for many companies; here he is with his regular 'Syncopators' of the late '20s. Opposite, left: Abe Lyman celebrates 20 years in show business, 1938, with Paul Ash (seated), Freddie Rich (piano), Clyde McCoy (trumpet), Russ Morgan (trombone), Jimmy Dorsey (clarinet) and Will Osborne (far right). Lyman himself plays drums.

Maestro' – who was born at Bayonne, New Jersey, in 1894 and died at Beverly Hills, California, in October 1942, and Abe Lyman, who was born in Chicago in 1897 and died in retirement in 1957. Both led bands for over two decades and recorded extensively, Bernie's output of 1926–8 including such good titles as *Jig Walk*, *Rhythm King* and the deterringly named *When Polly Walks Through The Hollyhocks*, all of which combine strong rhythmic attack by the ensemble and creditable solos from trumpeter Bill Moore and saxophonist Jack Pettis, amongst others. Lyman, whose brother Mike was the owner of the Trent Café in Los Angeles, at which Bing Crosby secured his first professional job, started as a show drummer but soon switched to the role of personality leader. Over the years he managed to combine popular appeal with reasonable musical standards, his '20s recordings of *Too Bad*, *Shake That Thing*, *Everybody Stomp* and *Bugle Call Rag* highlighting fierce ensemble passages and good solos by such musicians as trumpeter Ray Lopez and clarinettist Zip Keyes. Later performances in a more overtly commercial manner, of which *Breezin' Along With The Breeze*, *Tenderly* and *Wistful And Blue* are

typical, feature skilful arrangements and a high level of technical expertise. An early leader about whom no biographical information is available was Ray Miller, who, during the mid-'20s, led a band that made some particularly spirited records with solos by such jazz stars as Muggsy Spanier and Frankie Trumbauer. Titles like *Weary Blues*, *That's A Plenty*, *Angry* and *Stomp Your Stuff* merit reissue, and no doubt there are other recordings by Miller that are equally interesting.

Particularly intriguing to record-collectors are those bands that took part in only one or two recording sessions, made a couple of outstanding titles, and never went into a studio again. Are these recordings typical of their creators? If so, several obscure bands must be assumed to have been superior to many that became nationally famous. Or is one hearing an average band spurred, by the hope of gaining wide recognition from recordings, into playing well above itself? As an illu-

stration of the problem the bands of Phil Baxter and the Harris brothers will serve admirably. The Harris Brothers' Texans recorded six titles at three Dallas sessions in November 1928, October 1929 and January 1931. If one heard only *Gut Bucket Shuffle*, with its fierce attack, clean section work and excellent solos, one could be forgiven for thinking that here was a remarkable band indeed. Alas, the original coupling of *Louisiana, That's My Home* not only has an incredibly poor vocal but is otherwise utterly mediocre, and the two 1931 performances are if anything worse. *Somebody Stole My Gal* and *The Pay-off* from 1928 look promising but I have not been able to hear them. One is left with the feeling that any band that could make *Gut Bucket Shuffle* must have been potentially outstanding. The position with Baxter is less clear-cut. He was born in Navarro County, Texas, on 5 September 1896, and led a band from the early '20s through at least part of the '30s, though

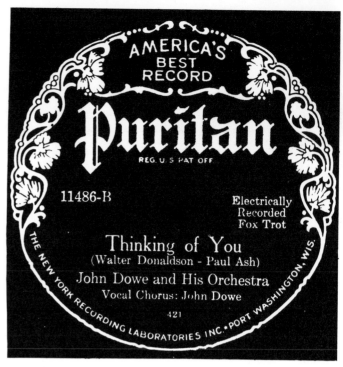

Lower left: the late Russ Columbo, Bing Crosby's greatest crooning rival. He accidentally shot himself with one of his collection of revolvers. Lower right: Rudy Vallee, the first popular singing idol of the '20s.

from 1932 he had to curtail his activities as a result of arthritis. Since 1940 Baxter has been inactive in music, but as a member of ASCAP he has continued to draw royalties on such early hits as *Piccolo Pete, Going, Going, Gone* and *I'm A Ding Dong Daddy*. The session that has interested collectors for some years took place in Dallas on 20 October 1929, resulting in four titles that were released on Victor. *I Ain't Got No Gal Now* features fine solos from trumpeter Roy Nooner and an unidentified clarinettist, and, apart from an indifferent vocal is a performance on all counts superior to the norm of the day. Just how typical this is of Baxter's normal output is something we are unlikely to resolve at this date. Baxter did make one other set of recordings in St Louis in October 1925, but, good as they are, the group was a small six-piece, so direct comparison with the Victor recordings is impossible. There were of

course many other bands like Baxter's and the Harris brothers' throughout the United States, a fact that in itself points to the constantly rising standards of dance music during the late '20s. As the decade came to its end, with the country in the depth of a catastrophic depression, the future of dance music and dance bands must have seemed to most people of little consequence. Probably nobody would have believed that six years later the greatest band boom in American history would be firmly under way.

BRITAIN—
THE
TWENTIES

While this book is concerned in the main with dance bands rather than with out-and-out jazz groups, it is worth recalling that during the '20s, and to a slightly lesser extent the '30s, the division between dance music and jazz was much less clearly defined than it subsequently became, and that the majority of the public saw little distinction between them. For this reason the visit of the Original Dixieland Jazz Band to Britain in April 1919 was not without its importance for the future of dance music in this country.

The ODJB opened at the London Hippodrome as part of the musical revue 'Joy Bells' on 7 April and, since the audience included a strong contingent of American soldiers, received a tumultuous reception. The star of the show, the famous comedian George Robey, possibly sensing a threat to his position, reacted less than ecstatically, and presented producer Albert de Courville with an ultimatum: either he or the ODJB would have to go. The ODJB went, but their setback was only temporary, for after a tour of variety theatres they secured an engagement at the Hammersmith Palais de Danse, commencing on 28 November 1919 and running, in all, for nine months. Their pianist J. Russell Robinson was forced to return home shortly after the band arrived in England; his replacement was the English ragtime stylist Billy Jones, and this is the earliest example of a European musician playing regularly with an American jazz group. When the band finally left Britain in July 1920 they had achieved a great popular triumph and inevitably their influence was to be felt in the years ahead, though often in an oblique rather than direct form.

It is not possible to detail the developments in dance music during the '20s in a strict chronological sequence, for historical processes in popular music, as in other fields, tend to be diffuse. But highlights can be pinpointed accurately enough, when one considers the subject in retrospect. Though the '20s were to some extent a period when the foundation was being laid for the '30s, during which British dance music reached its peak, it would be unfair to innumerable fine musicians and bands to discuss their '20s output solely as a stage on the way to something better. If no band during the '20s was able to produce a consistent body of recorded work to equal that of Roy Fox, Ray Noble and Lew Stone in the following decade, one has to remember that many of the techniques that made the latter possible were being forged by a process of trial and error. Moreover, a number of records were being released that today, over four decades later, still stand up well enough on a strictly musical level.

The opening chapter suggested that the popularity of the foxtrot with the dancing public was perhaps the major factor in the development of dance bands as we now know them. The years between the two world wars in Britain were notable for the popularity of dancing as an entertainment and relaxation at all levels of society. As the dancing craze grew, and hotels, both famous and obscure, engaged dance bands for their patrons to dance to, and dance halls arose in most towns with a population sufficient to support them, the stage was set for an enormous increase in the number of jobs available to musicians. It was not until the '30s that dance bands made their greatest impact in the variety theatres, though here again the precedence had been firmly established in the preceding decade. However, as in the United States, the development of radio as a popular source of entertainment did most to establish dance bands as national institutions.

Older readers who cast their minds back to the early days of broadcasting and the emergence of dance bands to the forefront of popular entertainment will almost inevitably recall the Savoy Orpheans. This was not, however, the first dance band to broadcast; the honour in fact belongs to Marius B. Winter, whose group was first heard on the radio on 26 March 1923, broadcasting from the attic of Marconi House in London. A year later Winter became the first dance band leader to be used in commercial radio (on Radio Paris). He also claims that he

was the first to use a signature tune and to play linking music between numbers. However, his impact was slight, whereas the Savoy Orpheans became nationally famous.

There had been live music at the Savoy Hotel since at least 1916, when a group known as the Savoy Quartette took up a residence for an engagement that was to last until 1920. The music of this unit was strongly ragtime-oriented, and though their records are not without interest they fall outside the scope of this chapter. What happened at the Savoy between 1920 and the arrival of the Savoy Havana Band is obscure, though it is hard to believe that no live music of any description was featured during this period.

In 1919 the American saxophonist Bert Ralton left Art Hickman's band in New York, reputedly going to Havana, where he formed his own group. During either 1920 or 1921 (the latter year seems more likely) he arrived in England, opening with his New York Havana Band at the Coliseum in

Below: the late Bert L. Ralton at an early recording session, with his New York Havana Band. Right, top: the Savoy Orpheans in 1923. Bottom: a few years later at the Lucerna Palace, Prague; left to right – Frank Herbin, band porter (behind piano), Frank Guarente, Max Goldberg, unknown German bassist, Tony Thorpe, Tony Morello, Les Huntington, Teddy Sinclair (leader), Cyril Hellier, Jeff Golicheff, unknown Russian pianist, Charles Remue, Eddie Bave, Billy Barton.

March 1922. Some months later – the exact date is uncertain – he opened at the Savoy Hotel, changing the name of his group to the Savoy Havana Band. The band made its initial broadcast, from a BBC studio, in April 1923, and five months later it became the first dance band to have regular weekly broadcasts, by now relayed from the Savoy Hotel. At the end of the year Ralton left to go to Australia and the leadership of the band passed to violinist Reg Batten. Its personnel now included the American saxophonist Rudy Vallee, who was destined in a few years time to become one of the United States' first singing idols, and Billy Mayerl, pianist and composer of popular novelty pieces. The position from 1924 onwards is somewhat hard to unravel, for it appears that Reg Batten was at some time in the next two years deputy leader of the Savoy Orpheans, while Cyril Newton directed the Havana Band. However, by late 1926 Batten was back as leader – probably he had held this position for some time before – and the personnel included two future stalwarts of the Ambrose band in trumpeter Max Goldberg and trombonist Tony Thorpe. In the autumn of 1927 another violinist, Teddy Sinclair, had assumed the

leader's role, but by the end of the year the Savoy engagement had been terminated. During 1928 the band, with many members of the Savoy personnel, was re-formed by Reg Batten and Cyril Newton, but, though it made some records, it does not appear to have enjoyed more than a very brief existence under its new name of the Original Havana Band. In January 1927 the Havana band's creator, Bert Ralton, died in South Africa as the result of an accident while on safari.

While the Savoy Havana Band enjoyed considerable popularity, it somehow never gained the public esteem accorded to the better-remembered Savoy Orpheans. This band was formed in 1923 under the leadership of Debroy Somers, who had been at the Savoy as a musical director in the preceding years. (This supports the view that some form of live music was presented there between the departure of the Savoy Quartette and the arrival of the Havana Band.) Though the initial personnel is known with some certainty, a great deal of confusion surrounds later changes, but it is probable that Carroll Gibbons was present at some point during 1923 or 1924, at about the same time as Rudy Vallee. Billy Thorburn, who became well known for his 'The Organ, The Dance Band And Me' programmes during the '30s, was the pianist from 1924 to 1926, and between these years other distinguished names within the band included Arthur Lally, Sidney Kyte and Reg Batten. Debroy Somers left in 1926, which was probably when Cyril Newton assumed leadership for a limited duration; by January 1927 Carroll Gibbons was definitely the musical director. He joined at about the same time as the American trumpeter Frank Guarente, who had, since September 1924, been leading his 'New Georgians' in various European countries.

At the end of 1927 William de Mornys, the manager of the Orpheans and the Havana Band, withdrew both – the result of a long-standing grievance over the management's refusal to allow them to fulfil outside engagements. De Mornys, who divides his years of retirement between London and the Isle of Wight, held the musicians' contracts, including those of their recording activities for EMI. The contracts with the Savoy were in fact due to expire on the last day of December and it seemed likely that some at least of the musicians would agree to new contracts offered them by the Savoy management. The result of this was that in January 1928 Reg Batten became leader of the 'New Savoy Orpheans' which included within its ranks the Americans Sylvester Ahola and Irving Brodsky, while Carroll Gibbons and Teddy Sinclair became co-leaders of the 'Original Savoy Orpheans' with trumpeters Frank Guarente and Max Goldberg amongst the personnel. The latter orchestra set off on a tour of Germany almost immediately and recorded in Berlin two months later, but upon its return to Britain disbanded. The New Savoy Orpheans fared only fractionally better, for their engagement at the Savoy terminated on 30 September 1928 and they also broke up. However, Reg Batten reorganised the band a month later under the Original Savoy Orpheans name and it played in the pit of the Gaiety Theatre for the show 'Topsy and Eva', finally disbanding when the production was taken off. This was not quite the end of the story, for in 1929 Ben Evers formed a stage band, using the name 'Savoy Orpheans', which led to a legal wrangle and the break-up of that group. Then the name was revived in 1930 and 1931 for bands led by Ben Loban and Jack Hart respectively. In 1932 the Savoy Hotel won an action for the exclusive right to the use of the name 'Savoy Orpheans', but already, a year previously, the Savoy Hotel Orpheans under the direction of Carroll Gibbons had taken up residence. This latter band

The Savoy Orpheans. Left: at a 1922 recording session, with Billy Mayerl (piano), Bert Ralton (saxophone), Ramon Newton (seated in front of Ralton) and George Eskdale (trumpet, on right). Far left: in 1923; above: c. 1924.

The Boston Orchestra.

J. Brannelly   A. Ure   H. Jacobs   C. Gibbons   Reg. Pursglove

Left: the Savoy Orpheans, c. 1923. This page: the London Lyrics Band (Lew Stone in the centre) and (below) the Boston Orchestra; left to right – Joe Brannelly, Alec Ure, Howard Jacobs, Carroll Gibbons, Reg Pursglove.

had little in common with the earlier groups except the shared name.

Although the Savoy Hotel management did not look with any favour on their bands making many outside appearances, they made an exception early in 1925. In the United States Paul Whiteman had started his concert career with a programme of 'Symphonic Syncopation' and it was decided to present a similar concert at the Queen's Hall, London. For the occasion, on 3 January 1925, the Savoy Orpheans performed in conjunction with the Savoy Havana Band and the Boston Orchestra, and so successful was the concert that two others were given shortly afterwards. The selections played read strangely to modern eyes, for such jazz standards as *Eccentric* and *Beale Street Blues* are to be found alongside pretentious-sounding titles like *Chaliapinata* and *Wagneria*. It was much too early for such concerts to be recorded but studio re-creations by the Savoy Orpheans, augmented by the Savoy Havana Band and the Selma Four, give an idea of how some of the numbers must have sounded. These records, *Fantasie Of Syncopated Favourites* and *Savoy English Medley* being typical, now retain only a quaint period interest, though the standard of musicianship is quite creditable.

The Savoy Orpheans and Havana Band were the highest-paid dance bands contracted to EMI during the '20s, and they made over three hundred records between 1922 and 1927. (The Sylvians, who were the house band at the Berkeley – the Savoy's companion hotel – but played at the Savoy for a few months in 1927, added a few dozen more.) In assessing these records it must be remembered that the bands' main function was to provide melodic dance music for the Savoy patrons, including a fair number of waltzes, show medleys and straight renditions of popular songs of the day, many of which represented far from challenging material. Many of the records are thus without interest on musical grounds, and a collector who was unlucky enough to find only the more mediocre items might well assume that these were very dull bands indeed. However, a very small proportion of this considerable output is worthwhile, mainly the performances in a 'hot' vein. That the Savoy Orpheans were not uninterested in jazz is shown by the fact that on 4 May 1927 four titles were recorded for the HMV label – *Sax Appeal*, *Snag It*, *Tampeekoe* and *Windy City Blues* – which were due to be issued as by the 'Savoy Hot Heads', but unfortunately all were rejected. On titles such as *Stomp Off, Let's Go* and *Copenhagen*, for example, or the earlier *Eccentric*, the Orpheans play with an unexpected drive and rhythmic mobility, while in the two takes of *Oh! Eva*, recorded in September 1924, the differences in the solos prove that the musicians did sometimes improvise even at this early date. The best titles by the Savoy Havana Band that I have heard are *Farewell Blues* and *Henpecked Blues*, recorded in November 1923, which feature excellent lead trumpet work, possibly by Jimmy Wornell, and fine soprano saxophone playing by Ralton. However, there are probably many other good performances to be discovered, no doubt masked on occasion by unlikely-looking titles. The Savoy bands introduced many to dance music, and in a transitional phase their historical importance was considerable.

A common factor in many of the better British dance bands of the '20s was the presence of American musicians. Union policy regarding the use of Americans in British bands was surprisingly liberal at the time, and numerous well-known jazz stylists can be found in their personnels. Such stalwarts as Frank Guarente, Sylvester Ahola, the Starita brothers and Rudy Vallee played at different times with the Savoy bands, and in due course Fred Elizalde's band at the Savoy would include Chelsea Quealey, Bobby Davis, Adrian Rollini and Fud Livingston. Nor was this co-operative outlook extended only to individual American musicians, for from 1923 through to the early '30s various American bands played club and theatre dates quite frequently. Paul Whiteman was in England during 1923 and again in 1926; Paul Specht was in residence at Lyons Corner House in 1923 and at the Kit-Cat Club in 1925, the club bringing in Ted Lewis too in the latter year. Lewis also led his band in a show at the London Hippodrome, a doubling of venues repeated in the same year by the Vincent Lopez orchestra. Paul Specht's Canadian Orchestra, directed by

Orville Johnson, was at the Kit-Cat Club in 1926, and three years later Abe Lyman and his band were resident there in addition to appearing at the London Palladium. Gus Arnheim was at the Savoy Hotel in 1929 and a year later Hal Kemp, with the late Bunny Berigan as a member of the personnel, could be heard at the Café de Paris and the Coliseum. The full list of musicians who played in Britain during the '20s might still produce some surprises; the Princeton Triangle Band played at the New Princes Restaurant of the Piccadilly Hotel in the summer of 1924 and also at an unspecified location for the regatta week at Cowes, while Will Vodery's Orchestra, resident at the Plantation Club in New York, appeared at an English private party and 'proved once more that black faces, like Oriental china, blend admirably with eighteenth-century decoration'. It appears that there were a great many American visitors to British shores during the '20s who played as individuals or as members of touring bands, and the subject would repay further research.

By the middle '20s dance music and dance bands had become enormously popular and it is worth glancing at a few of the comments that appeared on the subject in Britain's leading record magazine, the *Gramophone*. The first issue of the *Gramophone* appeared in April 1923 and contained 'A Note On Some Dance Records' by James Caskett, a pseudonym for Christopher Stone, who was to become one of the first broadcasters to attain fame as a disc jockey (though the term would have been distasteful to both him and the BBC at the time). He wrote:

Every month new and more exciting dance tunes are produced which, as they weary us, we discard for newer and still more exciting ones. For it is notorious that jazz tunes, admirable as they are, do soon become a burden. Where are *Beets And Turnips*, *After You Get What You Want*, *Swanee*, and the rest? The gramophone is most convenient; no need to be careful of the life of the records, you can wear them out and get the latest.

Later in his note Stone went on to recommend records by Paul Whiteman and the Bar Harbor Orchestra. In June 1923 an unknown reviewer praised the technical excellence of many dance band musicians, adding:

To the gramophone dance record we owe one social improvement. The 'Wallflower' in the dance room is disappearing. Young folk have the opportunity to practice at home to music supplied, via the gramophone, by first-class bands. Up to date and up to tempo, these records have killed the shyness that used to overtake the infrequent dancer on entering a ballroom. This country is following the Continental lead, where everybody dances.

Ambrose, then resident at the Embassy Club, was commended for his violin-playing; it 'has a special soothing quality, which makes one almost forget that the saxophone and the drum are the really essential instruments for modern dance music.' Two months later the correspondence column had a letter from one C. W. L. Lamotte of Cambridge, replying to a writer in the previous number who described foxtrots and dance music as 'contemptible and unoriginal fripperies' and 'an enormous rubbish heap'. Mr. Lamotte asks: 'Can anyone claim that *Kitten On The Keys* (by one of our greatest living masters) is unoriginal? Further, it is a melody that, under the baton of Richard Strauss, recently calmed a panic-stricken Viennese audience.' *Kitten On The Keys* was a popular novelty piano piece of the day, written by the American performer Zez Confrey, and certainly not normally the type of number that one would associate with concerts conducted by the late Richard Strauss.

Dance records continued to be noticed with regularity in the

Al Starita.

columns of the *Gramophone* during the '20s, though it was, and remains, primarily a magazine for classical music followers. In February 1929 the first article on any aspect of jazz or dance music appeared within its pages, some quotations from which will appear in a later paragraph, but meanwhile other magazines had commenced publication which were devoted solely to dance music and dancing.

Returning to the subject of American musicians who played their part in the development of dance music in this country, we should mention Al, Ray and Rudy Starita. These brothers were of Italian extraction, Rudy having actually been born in Naples two years before his family emigrated to the United States. In 1921 they formed their own band which in due course gained itself a following as the 'Paul Whiteman of New England',

but two years later Ray and Al decided to go to England and were for a time members of the Savoy Orpheans, though it is not easy to pinpoint the exact period. In 1925 Al Starita became leader of a Jack Hylton-sponsored band that played at the newly opened Kit-Cat Club in London and recorded as Jack Hylton's Kit-Cat Band or Hylton's Hyltonians. His brother Ray, who had returned to the United States for a holiday after leaving the Savoy Orpheans, arrived back in Britain with Rudy Starita, who had been working with the Mal Hallet band. Within a short while Ray had obtained the job of leading the Piccadilly Revels Band at the Piccadilly Hotel, including Rudy in the personnel, and for the next year or two the Staritas were very active in British dance music circles. Early in 1928 a switch occurred when Al became the leader of the band at the Piccadilly, Ray moving to the Ambassadors Club, and the former remained in residence until October 1930, when pianist Sid Bright took over the band. The brothers continued to be active during the '30s, though Ray returned to the United States in 1932, but their major contributions to British dance music occurred in the preceding decade. Two 1927 recordings by the Piccadilly Revels Band have been reissued on the LP 'Jazz In Britain – The 20's' and *Go, Joe, Go* in particular is interesting for its complex arrangement, high standard of musicianship, and good trumpet solos by Freddy Pitt and/or Andy Richardson.

In the later '30s Rudy Starita owned a photographic store in

Left: Rudy Starita (seated) with his band, late '20s. Below: Manuel 'Liz' and Fred Elizalde.

London and was little involved in music, but he did emerge to play as featured vibraphone soloist with Joe Loss, in a 1938 broadcast. By 1942 he had returned to music, leading his Starlites, but how long he remained in this role, and what he did afterwards, is not known.

Without doubt Fred Elizalde's band at the Savoy Hotel was the most advanced group playing in this country during the '20s, so much so that it is astonishing that Elizalde ever secured the engagement in the first instance. He was born in Manila in 1907 and together with his elder brother Manuel spent his youth in the United States. The Elizalde family was a wealthy one and Fred's parents frowned upon his interest in jazz and dance music. Their decision to send Manuel to Cambridge was in part undertaken in the hope that it would make contact with musicians less likely. When Fred and Manuel arrived at Cambridge in the Autumn of 1926 the former had already led a dance band in the United States and made some now rare recordings, and it was only a matter of months before he recruited students to form the Quinquaginta Club Ramblers. (One of them was Maurice Allom, later well known as a prominent cricketer.) The band had not been in existence long before it recorded for Brunswick and HMV, Elizalde also making solo piano items of his own compositions. *Stomp Your Feet* has been reissued on the 'Jazz In Britain – The 20's' LP and is a very promising performance despite the inadequacies of the rhythm section.

When Manuel left Cambridge Fred had gained a considerable reputation in dance band circles and was asked to write technical articles for the *Melody Maker*, in addition to which

he continued his recording career. His compositions included an ambitious symphonic jazz suite titled, unbelievably, *Heart Of A Nigger*; such was the prevailing ignorance about racial matters at the time that Elizalde apparently considered the name in no way insulting to black people. When it was performed by Ambrose and his Orchestra at the London Palladium in May 1927 the title was changed to *Heart Of A Coon*, in what was presumably meant to be a conciliatory gesture, but in any case it proved to be too advanced for the Palladium audiences and it was to be five years before Elizalde was able to record it.

During 1927 Elizalde recorded a number of titles for Brunswick, using mainly members of Ambrose's Orchestra. *Stomp Your Feet* and *Clarinet Marmalade* prove his proficiency as an arranger, the scores for both titles showing a skill in the use of dynamics and instrumental textures that was by no means commonplace at the time. Late in the year it was announced that Elizalde had been asked to form a band to play at the Savoy Hotel, then one of the prestige jobs of the dance band business. Manuel – known as 'Lizz' throughout his musical career – went to the United States to recruit some American musicians for the band and returned with Chelsea Quealey, Adrian Rollini and Bobby Davis from the California Ramblers. Trumpeter Quealey was considered at the time the equal of Bix Beiderbecke and Red Nichols – an evaluation that in the former instance now seems extremely eccentric – while Davis was a highly proficient reed player whose professionalism was an asset to any group. The star, though, was Rollini, the only outstanding soloist in jazz history to use the unwieldy bass saxophone as his major instrument, though he also liked to play instruments of his own devising such as the goofus and hot fountain pen. The former sounded similar to a harmonica though it looked like a saxophone, while the latter was a miniature clarinet with a range of an octave.

The band opened at the Savoy, playing opposite Reginald Batten's Savoy Orpheans, late in December 1927 and on New Year's Eve broadcast for the first time. The *Melody Maker* printed an ecstatic review but the Savoy's patrons were a great deal less enthusiastic, dancers complaining to the management that they were unable to recognise the tune and had to hang around on the dance floor while the band played long out-of-tempo introductions. Above all they were enraged by Elizalde's refusal to accede to their requests for waltzes. The BBC was also bombarded with irate letters concerning the lack of melody in the Elizalde performances, though to some extent these were offset by others from more musically sophisticated listeners. Within a few months the management of the Savoy, no doubt regretting that they had ever booked the band, insisted that it should play more simple arrangements, and that violins be added to the personnel. For a while a compromise was reached, whereby Elizalde also featured a small group from within the band in hot performances. Despite everything the band held the job at the Savoy until July 1929, various personnel changes taking place meanwhile. Some of the well-known musicians who were in its ranks at different times include the talented American arranger and reed player Fud Livingston, pianist Billy Mason, and violinist Benjamin Frankel, who in later years was to become widely known as a straight composer. In 1928, owing to the efforts of banjoist/guitarist Len Fillis, Elizalde was persuaded to offer Al Bowlly a job as singer with the band. Bowlly came to London from Germany and was heard on a number of Elizalde's recordings, though he was still a few years distant from his enormous popular success of the ensuing decade.

During July 1928 the Elizalde band played a six-week engagement at the Restaurant des Ambassadeurs in Paris; having returned to the Savoy, it commenced a series of regular broadcasts on 1 October. Despite the disenchantment of more conservative dancers Elizalde must have succeeded in winning over some of the Savoy's clientele, for in the autumn of 1928 Reginald Batten's contract was not renewed, and Elizalde was asked to divide his band into two units, with the full orchestra

only being used for peak dancing periods and broadcasts. In November the band topped the *Melody Maker* readers' poll, the next four places being held by Ambrose and his Mayfair Hotel Orchestra, the Savoy Orpheans directed by Reginald Batten, Jack Payne and the BBC Dance Orchestra, and Ray Starita's Ambassadors Club Orchestra respectively. Around this time it also appeared in a short film titled *Christmas Fantasy*. Opposition from radio listeners continued unabated and the BBC cut the band from its list of broadcasting units, subsequently restoring it for a while before again, in the spring of 1929, denying it air time. This was a bitter blow to Elizalde, for radio broadcasts were essential to commercial success; moreover, he had no recording contract at this period. There was a record date in 1929 for Parlophone, but two of the four titles made were never released, though one of the two issued performances – *Nobody's Sweetheart* – is by a section of the full band and must be rated as one of Elizalde's most impressive recordings, by virtue of the excellent solos from Quealey, clarinettist Max Farley, Davis, Livingston and Rollini, framed by cohesively scored and executed ensemble passages.

Late in April 1929 the Elizalde orchestra opened at the London Palladium for a three-week engagement with a personnel of twenty-three and two dancers. Al Bowlly was featured as vocalist but earned rebukes in some reviews for what was described as poor enunciation and lack of pitch in the upper register. On 23 June the band took part in a concert organised by the *Melody Maker* and held at the Shepherds Bush Pavilion; both the full orchestra and a smaller group, which concentrated on hot performances, were heavily featured. Just before the concert Chelsea Quealey and Fud Livingston had left the band, but their deputies Norman Payne and Arthur Rollini proved to be more than adequate substitutes, particularly on the more rhythmic pieces. The full band played pop numbers of the day like *Lover Come Back To Me*, *Let's Do It* and *A Precious Little Thing Called Love*, many with vocals by Al Bowlly, while the small group was given its head on such titles as *Nobody's Sweetheart* and *Savoy Stomp*, the latter a new Elizalde composition. The concluding work was a somewhat pretentious composition by Elizalde titled *Bataclan*, described in programme notes as 'a fantasy on life in three movements', but the audience was probably happier when the encores proved to be hot versions of *Tiger Rag* and *Sweet Sue*. The band personnel had put in many hours of extra rehearsal time in preparation for the concert and must have felt well rewarded by the warmth of the reception they were accorded; but the end of the Savoy engagement was at hand. In July the management of the hotel terminated Elizalde's contract, replacing him with Al Collins and his Orchestra, a proficient but entirely uninspired group from Claridge's. Collins was followed by Gus Arnheim's Coconut Grove Orchestra from Los Angeles, and then by a variety of bands prior to the return of Carroll Gibbons, in 1931, as resident co-leader, with Howard Jacobs, of the Savoy Hotel Orpheans.

By all accounts Elizalde was not by nature a business man, nor, it would seem, a very far-sighted individual, for after leaving the Savoy he led the band on a tour of northern and Scottish music halls which, predictably, proved to be disastrous. The modern arrangements were met with incomprehension or downright hostility by the audiences; the greatest humiliation was incurred at Edinburgh, where the band was forced to give way to the resident pit orchestra. One report – probably apocryphal – claims that part of their trouble in Scotland stemmed from their inability to play reels! By the end of the year Elizalde, understandably discouraged, was forced to disband, and though in the following spring he led the pit orchestra at the Duchess Theatre in London, using his own music for the show 'The Intimate Review', his involvement in dance music and jazz was drawing to a close. During 1932 and 1933 he made his last recordings, for Decca, but most of these were quite commercial. In the autumn of 1933 Elizalde left for Spain, where he studied with Falla, subsequently becoming recognised as a composer and conductor in the classical field. Today it is believed that he is the director of a broadcasting network in the Philippines.

A rather interesting insight into the clientele of such hotels as the Savoy at this period, and into the social conditions of which they were a part, is given by Stanley Jackson.

No expense was spared to present his [Elizalde's] orchestra as a symbol of super-sophisticated entertainment. The musicians used to sit on a platform turret like a medieval castle and painted in red, gold and silver. Elizalde himself was soon the darling of London society and brought huge nightly bookings to the restaurant. For his opening appearance, Mrs Louis Oppenheimer gave a dinner party for 120 guests and presented him with laurel wreaths, but Elizalde began to grow weary of the glitter and ultimately returned to his first love.

It might be that Elizalde's social background was one reason for his having been booked by the Savoy management in the first instance, for, in terms of his music at the time, it was rather as if the present musical directors of the Mecca ballrooms were to engage an avant-garde jazz group to supply the music for their dancing public. Some years later, in the course of an interview with Stanley Nelson, Benjamin Frankel summarised the position: 'Potentially we had one of the finest combinations ever, but somehow, in spite of fine orchestrations for the time, and the

Fred Elizalde (at piano) with his Savoy Hotel Band. Adrian Rollini is third from the left.

quality of the players, we never quite played the music that we had latent in us.'

Just what direction Elizalde's music might have taken if he had been given a free hand can be partially surmised from an article that appeared under his name in 1929, entitled 'Jazz – What Of The Future'. Some of his ideas have a prophetic ring, but many years were to elapse before they became accepted at all widely. For one thing he foresaw a development in new rhythms, with the performance of a single number using a variety of rhythmic signatures, getting away from the set system of verse and chorus. 'I am not definitely opposed to melody', he said, 'but to me it is an entirely secondary consideration as far as dance music is concerned.' Avant-garde thoughts indeed for 1929! The following month produced a reply, signed by Bert Ambrose and headed 'Come, Come Mr Elizalde'. The predictions, said Ambrose, were absurd, and he added rather tartly, 'Being laid up with influenza during the past week or so, I took the opportunity of listening to the music broadcast from the Savoy, and there can be no doubt that Mr Elizalde is carrying out his "no melody" threat.' He saw no future in the use of rhythmic variations within a number, commenting that 'if I tried it out at the Mayfair Hotel I feel certain that the floor would be empty in a minute'. The month after, 'Needlepoint' of the *Melody Maker* (the late Edgar Jackson) wrote of his reactions to the two articles, coming down heavily on the side of Elizalde. His concluding sentence is interesting: 'Dance records are listened to far more often than they are played for dancing.'

When one listens to Elizalde's records the restraining hands

An early photograph of Jack Jackson.

of recording directors are everywhere obvious, but now and then the potential of the band is partially realised. His initial dates were undertaken in May and June of 1927, for Brunswick and Parlophone respectively, and represent a promising debut despite occasional uncertainties in execution and a stodgy rhythm section. *Stomp Your Feet* has already been mentioned, but its original coupling, *Clarinet Marmalade*, like *Hurricane* from the Brunswick session, is well played and has an interesting alto solo from Lizz Elizalde; both numbers show a strong Red Nichols influence. One of the earliest recorded piano solos, *Siam Blues*, is only partially successful, though a number of individual touches are evident, but a band date in August resulted in new recordings of *Stomp Your Feet* and *Clarinet Marmalade*, superior to the Parlophone versions by virtue of their being played by professional musicians. On these titles Jack Jackson – the same Jack Jackson who is now a well-known disc jockey – takes pleasant Red Nichols-inspired trumpet solos, and Elizalde himself is heard in an advanced solo for the period on the former number.

January 1928 saw the first recordings by Elizalde in an uncompromising jazz style that included the American contingent of Adrian Rollini, Bobby Davis and Chelsea Quealey. The themes used were *Dixie* and *Tiger Rag*, and while all three American stars play well it is Rollini who steals the honours with an outstanding solo on *Dixie*. A session of two months later produced one of Elizalde's best recordings in *Sugar Step*, notable for the cohesion and relaxation of the ensemble passages, but this title and its session-mate *Arkansas Blues* are marred by mediocre sound quality. Most of the remaining 1928 recordings are extremely commercial and though well played, with occasional worthwhile solos and felicities of scoring, are of slight interest. An exception is *Somebody Stole My Gal*, which has spirited solos from three Americans and Elizalde himself. The piano solo *Grown Up Baby* is unusually introspective in mood and highlights Elizalde's advanced harmonic conception. The session supervisor for Parlophone may have been a little more

liberal than his Brunswick equivalent, for an April 1929 Parlophone date resulted in two of the band's best titles, *Singapore Sorrows* and *Nobody's Sweetheart*. The former, by the full group, benefited from an arrangement by Fud Livingston and impeccable ensemble playing, the latter, by a hot contingent, maintained a high solo level with contributions by Quealey, Max Farley, Davis, Livingston, Elizalde and Rollini. Livingston was an imaginative arranger and composer and it is unfortunate that his association with Elizalde was of such short duration.

Elizalde's post-Savoy recordings for Decca are mainly disappointing, one of the few bright spots being his solo of *Vamp Till Ready*, a personal composition with more than a hint of the better known popular song *Hallelujah*, which suggests that he was steadily gaining in rhythmic flexibility.

It is unfortunate that pressure from the Savoy management, recording officials and BBC producers forced Elizalde constantly to compromise with his music; if he had been given a free hand his achievements might have been considerable, though it is possible that he might have dissipated his talents in the production of arid pseudo-symphonic works. Even so his actual successes were by no means insignificant, and his influence certainly brought about rhythmic improvements in the dance music performed by most leading British bands in the last years of the '20s.

The space devoted to the various bands that played at the Savoy Hotel might give the impression that this establishment enjoyed a monopoly in the field, but this was certainly not the case. Historically the Savoy Orpheans and Savoy Havana Band were important because of their pioneering role in dance band broadcasting. (It has been claimed that certain technical factors influenced the BBC in preferring the Savoy for early outside broadcasts.) What may have been an historical accident in the case of Elizalde's residency further strengthens the links between the Savoy and the expansion of dance music during the '20s. However, other hotels featured excellent bands, the nightclubs were taking an increasing interest in the quality of the music they offered their patrons, and inevitably radio was the means of establishing a whole new group of leaders and bands. The first outside broadcast by a dance band took place on 24 May 1923, the group being Ben Davis's Carlton Hotel Dance Band; in the following year Henry Hall (whose story will be told in the chapter devoted to the '30s) began broadcasting with his Gleneagles Hotel Orchestra. In 1925 Jack Payne was heard regularly with his Hotel Cecil Orchestra, and on 16 February 1926 the first BBC house band made its initial broadcast. This was the London Radio Dance Band, under the direction of violinist Sidney Firman, a group that was resident for a season or two at the Cavour Restaurant in London. In 1928 the BBC decided that the time had come to form its own resident dance band and Jack Payne was appointed as musical director, the billing changing in the space of four years from 'The BBC Dance Orchestra directed by Jack Payne' to 'Jack Payne and his Orchestra'. During this period the band broadcast on every weekday afternoon – no dance music was broadcast at all on Sundays – in addition to numerous evening shows, and it is hardly surprising that Payne became a household name. His career and musical output will be discussed later.

As soon as dance bands became popular the BBC found itself face to face with the problem of song plugging, a subject with which it appeared to become neurotically obsessed from then on. The BBC executives struggled incessantly and comically to try to prevent song plugging; in 1929 they went so far as to prevent leaders announcing the songs they were playing, and to ban all vocal choruses because they would make the titles obvious. After a few months the protests of listeners forced them to

Right, top: Ray Noble (in front of bass) and a session band, with Max Goldberg (far left), Bill Harty (drums) and Al Bowlly (seated on floor at front). Noble often conducted from a sound-proof box.

remove the restrictions. The only leader who escaped the ban was Jack Payne who, not unnaturally, was tightly controlled by the BBC in any case. To the music industry song plugging seemed quite a natural development, for the sale of sheet music was the economic base of the music-publishing firms, and clearly sales could be boosted considerably if songs were regularly broadcast by top bands. It is a moot point whether there were any bandleaders totally guiltless of co-operation with song pluggers; the fact that their remuneration for broadcasts was not particularly high, and that they often paid for special arrangements out of their own pockets, must have induced in many a willingness to accept payment on the side for plugging certain numbers. In the case of the really prominent bands it has been reported that the music-publishing houses were even willing to provide full arrangements, specially tailored to each band's style, of the numbers they were particularly keen to have played over the air. So one can only be amazed that the BBC went to such lengths in fighting a battle it was bound to lose.

Many famous bandleaders who came to prominence in the '30s – Roy Fox, Ray Noble, Harry Roy, Lew Stone – were active in varying degrees during the preceding decade, but as their major achievements are firmly related to the '30s it seems logical to write of them in the appropriate chapter, taking a backward glance at their earlier careers where it is relevant. In the case of Jack Hylton and Bert Ambrose, however, there are reasons for making an exception, in one case on stylistic grounds and in the other because later developments were only extensions of an approach already established by the late '20s.

Jack Hylton was born at Great Lever, near Bolton in Lancashire, on 2 July 1892, and his interest in music was aroused in the early 1900s when his father became the licensee of a public house and in his spare time ran the local Socialist club, a venue where singing acts were a nightly event. His first professional engagement was as a boy soprano and assistant pianist with a pierrot troupe, at the Welsh resort of Rhyl; then in 1909 he secured a job as conductor of an orchestra with a touring pantomime. Four years later he went to London for the first time and worked as a cinema organist and assistant pianist in a night-club. He spent the war years in an entertainment division of the army. Upon his discharge he resumed his career in music, in the summer of 1919 composing popular songs and selling them to holidaymakers on the promenade at Blackpool. Returning to London during the autumn, he found that the era of jazz and dance music was under way and that dance halls were springing up on all sides. He joined a group that was playing at the Queen's Hall Roof in Langham Place in the capacity of relief pianist, and this proved to be the first step of a career in dance music that spanned the next two decades.

Since he was the only musician in the band who could read music, Hylton soon became a permanent member and arranger, and in May 1921 the group journeyed to Hayes in Middlesex, to record for the first time. The session fee was £5 a man; Hylton claimed that he should receive extra for his arrangements but the other musicians objected, finally agreeing that the words 'directed by Jack Hylton' should appear on their HMV recordings, though the same group's Zonophone discs were issued as by Jack Hylton's Jazz Band. During the next year or two Hylton enlarged the band and accepted residencies at such locations as the Grafton Galleries and the Piccadilly Hotel; an important addition to the line-up was trombonist Lew Davis. By the mid-'20s Hylton had decided to concentrate on stage engagements and tours, building up a band that was essentially the British equivalent of Paul Whiteman's in America. The basic approach of his show band, which made its initial broadcast in 1926, altered little through the years and his post-1926 career will be related in the '30s chapter.

Throughout an extensive recording career Hylton only occasionally featured performances in a hot or jazz-inclined vein, though he did from time to time include jazz soloists within his personnel. The fact that his early Zonophone releases are given a 'Jazz Band' labelling is misleading; most of them bear no relation to authentic jazz. Hot items are as likely to be found on HMV, where the band name carried no such connotation. During the early '20s Hylton recorded prolifically, but the bulk of his output is only of slight musical interest. *Bullfrog Patrol*, from a November 1921 date, is unusually well scored for the period and the rhythm is less jerky than usual, while *Seven Or Eleven Blues* and *Louisville Lou*, recorded at different sessions two years later, are mildly interesting. An untypical performance from 1927 is *Grieving For You*, which is deliberately scored and played in the style of Red Nichols, with neat and well-executed solos by Eric Pogson, Jack Jackson and Lew Davis, the latter two adopting the mannerisms of Nichols and Miff Mole respectively. The title was originally issued as by Jack Hylton's Rhythmagicians and whether Hylton himself had any active part in its production is a matter for conjecture. Jack Hylton's Kit-Cat Band recorded 51 titles during 1925–6; when the Kit-Cat engagement terminated it produced a further 41 by May 1927, now billed as Hylton's Hyltonians. The leader and musical director of this band was in fact Al Starita, and during the Kit-Cat period a few interesting titles were made, including *Riverboat Shuffle* and *Milenberg Joys*, the latter having creditable solos from trumpeter Tom Smith and trombonist Ted Heath. The Hyltonians made brisk, well-played versions of *Brown Sugar* and *Number Ten*, and in general the Hylton-sponsored band made slightly more meritorious records than those directly controlled by Hylton himself.

Bert Ambrose is one of the most famous names in British dance music history and by the close of the '20s he had already been active in the field for over a decade. Born in London in 1897, Ambrose emigrated to the United States when a youth, and after violin studies secured his first professional engagement as a member of a cinema orchestra in New York. In 1917 he was appointed musical director of the Club de Vingt at the Palais Royal, New York, and remained in this position until 1920, when he was heard by Luigi, owner of the Embassy Club in London, and persuaded to return to England to lead the band at this high society venue. In 1922 he went back to the United States and for a while was musical director at the Clover Gardens, New York, but once more Luigi enticed him back and that winter Ambrose and his Embassy Club Orchestra were in residence at the Bond Street club. They began to record for Columbia the following May, but these early sides are of little interest and, as Luigi did not allow broadcasting from his club, Ambrose's reputation was confined to a very limited circle. During 1926 there was an important addition to the personnel with the arrival of the saxophonist Joe Crossman, a musician destined to become a key member of several important bands in the years ahead.

Early in 1927 Ambrose was offered the post of musical director at the Mayfair Hotel at the then astonishing salary of £10,000 a year. He accepted, though in fairness to his former employer he took only Joe Crossman from the Embassy band with him to his new location. (The pianist of the Embassy group, Max Raiderman, became its leader.) He travelled to the United States to recruit five musicians, the best known of whom was Henry 'Hot Lips' Levine, who made a name for himself in the '30s with a popular broadcasting and recording group known as the Chamber Music Society of Lower Basin Street. The British members of the personnel, apart from Crossman, included violinist Sidney Lipton – later a popular bandleader himself and today director of music at the Grosvenor Hotel, London – reed man Jack Miranda and trumpeter Dennis Radcliffe. The band opened at the Mayfair Hotel on 27 March 1927 and was an immediate success, soon afterwards being offered a recording contract by Brunswick. In June it made its initial stage appearance at the London Palladium.

Ambrose's first Brunswick records – at least two of which were arranged by Fred Elizalde and possibly conducted by him – were well played but have little of the character of his

Above: Jack Hylton's first show band of the late '20s. Below: a c. 1922 line-up – left to right, Bernard Tipping, Basil Wiltshire, Bert Heath, unknown, Hylton, Jack Raine, Chappie d'Amato, Dick de Pauw and Bert Bassett.

better-known releases, a number being marred by indifferent vocals. By early 1928 there had been changes in the personnel, the work permits of the original American contingent having expired, and Joe Brannelly, an American banjoist/guitarist who had recently joined the band, was sent home to recruit Perley Breed (saxophones), Sylvester Ahola (trumpet), and Leo Kahn (piano). The late Max Bacon, a long-term Ambrose stalwart,

was now present on drums, with Ted Heath replacing Sam Acres on trombone. Broadcasts from the Mayfair Hotel commenced on 20 March 1928 and continued at fortnightly intervals. Just before this the band made its first recordings for the Gramophone Company (now EMI), the titles being issued on the HMV label. At this time, and through the '30s, HMV (His Master's Voice) was the prestige label of the Gramophone Company, and record dealers who obtained the right to stock its releases considered it a success symbol. Ambrose's association with the Gramophone Company, however, was not an altogether happy one, for Jack Hylton was the big name on HMV, and such top American bands as Paul Whiteman, Jean

Billy Mayerl (standing) wrote many popular novelty pieces for piano in the '20s and later led a flourishing 'School of Syncopation'.

Goldkette, George Olsen, Fred Waring and Nat Shilkret were released on the label too. An unfortunate result, for Ambrose, was that he was restricted as to the material he could use. One outstanding title did come from these sessions, for the 1928 recording of *Singapore Sorrows* not only contains excellent solos by Crossman, Radcliffe and Heath but is also notable for a superb score by Lew Stone, who had joined the band as an arranger.

Dissatisfied with his treatment by the HMV recording directors, Ambrose switched in 1929 to the new Decca company, which assured him that he could not only choose top numbers to record but would also be allowed to include some of his less commercial items. Changes in personnel brought in the American clarinettist Danny Polo, who joined direct from the famous Jean Goldkette Orchestra; arranger and pianist Bert Read (replacing Leo Kahn); and vocalist Sam Browne, who was to remain with Ambrose until 1945. The 1929 Decca recordings were on the whole rather disappointing, in part because of poor sound quality, but two titles worthy of reissues are *Body And Soul* and *Sugar Is Back*, the former the first recording of the famous Johnny Green number. Ambrose had heard Gertrude Lawrence singing this on a broadcast and, as Green was in London at the time, secured his permission to record it. *Sugar Is Back* features an advanced arrangement and includes an excellent trumpet solo by Ahola. The Decca supplement of August 1929 surmised: 'There will be an enormous demand for these (referring to *Precious Little Thing Called Love/Sugar Is Back*), not only for dancing, but for those who appreciate and enjoy hearing dance music played by an orchestra of which each individual member is a master artist.'

There was a temporary termination of Ambrose's broadcasts from the Mayfair Hotel during 1929, when the management resisted the BBC's ban on announcements and vocal choruses, but by the autumn they were resumed and the band had the key spot from 10.30 pm to midnight on Saturday. These broadcasts, and the success of his records, made Ambrose a national figure, and as a new decade arrived his reputation as the leader of a dance band with uniquely high standards of musicianship and sophistication spread to Europe and ultimately to the United States.

Readers will have noticed that the evaluation of records in this chapter has been influenced by jazz criteria. The basic problem here is that very few recordings of ballads, or popular numbers

of the day presented straight, now stand up very well on musical grounds, and it is in general the hot or jazz-inclined performances that show the bands of this period at their best, though in the following decade this was no longer so. During the '20s the dividing line between dance music and jazz was recognised only by a very small minority of record-collectors and radio listeners. Moreover, most of the British musicians with jazz aspirations sought to emulate the technical expertise and polished sound of such white American stylists as Red Nichols, Miff Mole, Jimmy Dorsey and Frankie Trumbauer, as the hot recordings of the period clearly testify. The sophisticated music of the white New Yorkers was considered the epitome of jazz, and when the classic Louis Armstrong Hot Five and Seven recordings first appeared in Britain they were dismissed as crude, while blues in their purest form were virtually unknown and would have been met with incomprehension if they had been issued. Some years were to pass before the first glimmering of genuine appreciation of jazz with a strong Afro-American flavour: it took even longer for it to have any influence on British musicians.

It has been said that radio made the dance bands and television destroyed them. This simplification ignores several economic and social factors, but the first part of the statement contains more than a grain of truth. Records were important in spreading the popularity of the dance bands, but quite frequently it was success gained from broadcasts that led to bands being sought after and built up by the record companies. One suspects, however, that the attitude of the BBC to the success of the dance bands was somewhat ambivalent, for the Calvinistic Sir John Reith, Director-General during the peak years of the dance band era, could hardly have considered them of much value in furthering his fervently held belief that radio should be primarily a medium for the spread of cultural and moral enlightenment. However, popular art has its own momentum, and by the close of the '20s dance music had emerged from its early phase of technical and instrumental experimentation, with its inevitable crudities, and in the hands of its leading exponents was combining popular appeal with high musical standards. Every development in a genre such as dance music, or jazz, is based on what has gone before, and for that reason the band-leaders and musicians of the '20s, both famous and obscure, deserve credit for making possible the halcyon years to come.

UNITED STATES— THE THIRTIES

The early depression years following the Wall Street crash of 1929 found every department of the entertainment industry concerned, like society at large, with survival rather than expansion. A number of prominent bands folded and there was a temporary decline in the emergence of new ones, yet in retrospect it is surprising that so many bands and individual musicians managed to achieve a sort of economic security at a time when the major part of their public was living in conditions of extreme poverty. One reason for this is that in periods of disaster there is a demand for entertainment as a means of escape from the harsh realities that are a part of everyday life. In such circumstances the purchase of a record or a ticket for a concert seems less an extravagance than an act that will help sustain morale and remind one that more normal times may be just around the corner.

Record companies were badly hit in the depression years, and several went out of business. Unfortunately record firms have never been very willing to disclose sales figures on individual items, except when they happen to have a million-seller on their hands, but documents from the once powerful Gennett concern, one of the depression's victims, reveal that in its final years it was pressing quantities as low as 25 and 50 of certain releases. The few artists who continued to record regularly during this period were those lucky ones whose releases were assured reasonable sales, though a hit record then was one that sold around ten thousand. The worst year for record sales was 1932, when the total number sold throughout the United States was about 6 million; whereas in 1927 sales had reached 104 million (some sources have claimed 130 million). After the depression there was a revival and from 1938 figures soared once more to the 140 million mark in 1942.

An important new company to emerge during the mid-'30s was Decca, which, after a year or two of uncertainty, established itself as a major concern through its policy of selling records by major artists like Bing Crosby, Guy Lombardo and Isham Jones for 35 cents. This company also worked hard on its hillbilly (later Country & Western) and race (blues and gospel) catalogues, for it found that the rural buyers of these items remained faithful to their favourites even in time of economic disaster. In addition Decca signed many of the prominent bands of the day, a move that enabled them in later years to realise handsomely on their modest initial investments, when reissues of such items became a profitable part of the LP era.

A crucial aid to the record companies as the '30s progressed was the technical development of jukeboxes. As these machines became a part of the American way of life and penetrated into even the smallest rural communities, they opened up new avenues of sales and paved the way for the creation of the hit parade. They were also important in a fashion that the record companies could not have foreseen, for rural Southern areas demanded their own music and thus boosted the sales of hillbilly and blues records – an event that in a decade or two was to transform American popular entertainment. The emergence of a mass market for hillbilly and blues records, and its far-reaching consequences, will be discussed in a later chapter.

Turning to the pre-swing dance bands of the '30s, we can fairly say that most of the leaders who had built their reputations during the preceding decade were more concerned with refining and developing techniques of arranging and presentation than with seeking new directions. By the middle '30s a schism had developed between the revolutionaries – the swing bands – and those leaders who followed a more conservative path. The trade papers and fan magazines of the day enthusiastically supported the swing bands and tended to condemn the others, but such a blanket dismissal of the 'straight' dance bands is manifestly unfair. Admittedly there were numerous bands that enjoyed great popular success but certainly contributed nothing of musical value. Against these must be counterpoised bands such as that led by Isham Jones, which reached its highest musical level in the '30s and can claim to have been amongst the greatest

Glen Gray and his Casa Loma Orchestra. Gray is seventh from the right.

dance units in the history of the music. In the middle there were many others which could be labelled 'commercial' – the great critical swear-word of the '30s – but which tempered a popular approach with respectable musical criteria.

Categorising bands became a commonplace of critical writing in the '30s, and it sometimes led to gross oversimplification. On the other hand, there were leaders who chose to follow a particular path; one of the most economically rewarding was to organise a society band to perform in the plusher hotels and night-clubs. The music played by such groups seemed to be designed to make no demands on the attention of its listeners, however illiterate their musical tastes might be. It helped to have a personality leader, such as a pianist who could perform in a flashy style that gave an illusion of musical depth. Bands led by pianists of this type flourished; Carmen Cavallaro and Eddie Duchin were perhaps the most successful. George Simon quotes a former Eddie Duchin sideman as wryly remarking: 'I'll say this for the man, he was the only musician I've ever known who could play a thirty-two bar solo with thirty-two mistakes and get an ovation for it afterwards.' The recorded evidence left by

GLEN GRAY and His Famous
CASA LOMA
Orchestra

the bands of Cavallaro, Duchin and Wayne King (The 'Waltz King') may offer nothing of genuine musical interest, but in their time they gave a great deal of pleasure to thousands of listeners and it is doubtful if they themselves would have claimed any ambition to scale musical heights.

It does become clear, when one listens to the recordings of the non-swing dance bands popular with American audiences during the '30s, that few were the equal of their leading British contemporaries. Despite the United States' predominance in jazz and dance music, no American dance band of the period, except Isham Jones's, appears to me to have left such a worthwhile body of recorded work as did, say, Ambrose and Lew Stone in England. However, although on the whole the '30s in the United States belong to the swing bands, it is worth turning now to some others who played an important role in the development of dance music at the time, among the most interesting of which is the Casa Loma Orchestra.

This band has been somewhat unfairly treated in most critical books, in particular getting short shrift from jazz writers. The band was founded in the late '20s, first recording in 1929, and several of the original members, including Glenn Gray Knoblauch and Pee Wee Hunt, had played with a Jean Goldkette group. At the close of a Toronto engagement Knoblauch

dropped his surname and with Hunt and others reorganised the band on a co-operative basis in New York City, subsequently being billed as the leader. From then on the Casa Loma Orchestra was part of the dance band scene well into the '40s, but its most important period was undoubtedly during the early '30s. The band operated on two levels, on the one hand presenting popular numbers of the day in a more or less straightforward fashion with vocals by Kenny Sargent, and on the other offering a series of instrumental pieces, written and arranged by the band's banjoist/guitarist Gene Gifford, that were entirely distinctive in their field. Some of the most famous of Gifford's numbers were *White Jazz*, *Black Jazz*, *Maniac's Ball*, *Blue Jazz* and *Casa Loma Stomp* – the latter apparently borrowed in part from the tune *Oh Susannah* – all of which were widely copied by other bands in both the United States and Europe, not least by Lew Stone, whose recordings of several of these titles closely follow the originals. These scores have been spoken of slightingly by most jazz critics but their influence on other bands was extensive, indeed at times overwhelming. It is not without significance that Benny Goodman, for example, was utilising the Casa Loma style only a few months prior to the commencement of his trend-setting 1935 Victor recordings, as his late 1934 version of *Cokey* demonstrates. The influence of the Casa Loma

Orchestra was not confined to white bands, for Fletcher Henderson, Earl Hines, Jimmie Lunceford and the Mills Blue Rhythm Band all recorded numbers reflecting the impact of Gifford's scores. The full scope of the Casa Loma influence is worthy of a chapter in itself.

It is interesting to learn that Gifford at one time worked as a draftsman, for his scores have about them the precision of an engineering blueprint, and their execution calls for a high degree of technical facility on the part of their interpreters. Technical skill was certainly not lacking in the Casa Loma Orchestra, though many hours of tedious rehearsal must have been necessary before the numbers were mastered sufficiently for public presentation. It is the mechanical quality of the Casa Loma recordings that has attracted most criticism, and certainly at times the swing of the band sounds somewhat laboured, but the inescapable fact is that for the early '30s these were remarkably advanced scores, and were played with an ensemble precision that was at the time virtually unique. A more valid criticism of Gifford's writing is that he frequently – but not always – failed to use riffs satisfactorily at the close, so that after a technically arresting opening and middle section there followed a succession of repetitive phrases that represented an anti-climax to what had gone before. If Gifford had been able or willing to pay more attention to the overall form of his numbers, and had not tediously prolonged his final riffs, their impact would have been musically more satisfying, but whatever his failings he was a genuinely original arranger who deserves sympathetic consideration in any historical account. Many critics have claimed that the Casa Loma performances of the Gifford scores were unswinging, but contemporary audiences had no such reservations and enthusiastically hailed the band as the hottest then in business, while Kenny Sargent's singing of the better ballads pleased those who demanded a less frenetic type of music. It has been said also that the band lacked major soloists, but its records show that several were at least highly competent, and clarinettist Clarence Hutchenrider was occasionally outstanding.

The first Gifford score to make an impact was that of Joe

'Wingy' Manone's *San Sue Strut*, recorded in February 1930. It is a performance of impressive precision, which builds up tension steadily, bar by bar, as it progresses; the climax is logical because for once Gifford avoids monotony in the final riffs. Nine months later the band recorded their first version of *Casa Loma Stomp*, followed in 1931 by *Black Jazz* and *Maniac's Ball*, two archetypal performances. *Black Jazz*, unexpectedly slow in tempo, features superb ensemble playing and two good solos, from Hutchenrider on clarinet and an unidentified trumpeter, while *Maniac's Ball* is in the more familiar up-tempo vein and includes brilliant unison passages, excellent solos by Hutchenrider and tenor saxophonist Pat Davis. It ends, however, in total anti-climax, with a series of clichés played with an élan they hardly merit. There is one particularly impressive passage, after twelve bars from the reeds, where a brass fanfare is played, each instrument falling into line unerringly. *White Jazz* and *Blue Jazz* are perhaps better-known titles – as much through the cover versions as the originals, outside the United States – but the latter reveals a diminution of Gifford's arranging skills and has not withstood the test of time very securely. There were, of course, numerous other recordings of the Gifford/Casa Loma combination, and his arrangements of numbers not written by himself, such as the perennial *Royal Garden Blues* and *Alexander's Ragtime Band*, both recorded at a session in December 1930, are instantly recognisable as his work. The relaxed ensemble playing on the latter, and the first-rate trumpet solo in plunger style, make some of the standard criticisms of the band hard to sustain. In December 1933 Gifford stopped playing in the band and turned his attention to full-time arranging, a great deal of it free-lance work. He returned to the band in 1948 for a further year but subsequently devoted most of his time to

working as a radio engineer, arranging for various groups on a part-time basis until his death early in 1971.

When Gifford left the band in 1935 the style had been clearly defined and it was to remain substantially unaltered for several years. The orchestra made a number of popular instrumental recordings in its latter years, including *Study In Brown*

– with ingenious use of low-register clarinets – *Stompin' Around, Malady In F* and *Jungle Jitters*. Its final hit in this vein was the two-part version of *No Name Jive* recorded in 1940. Gifford's replacement was Larry Clinton, an arranger who achieved considerable popularity during the swing era, for he was able to produce at will riff themes that were usually

Above: the Casa Loma Orchestra, 1932. Left: the rhythm section of the 1937 Casa Loma: Stanley Dennis (bass), Jack Blanchette (guitar), Joe Hall (piano), Tony Briglia (drums), with Glen Gray.

built out of stock clichés. As important as the loss of Gifford was the departure over the years of several of the original members of the band; this led to a steady decline in musical accomplishments in the period before the disbandment of the group in early 1950. Six years later Glen Gray was the nominal leader on numerous Capitol LPs, including two that re-created Casa Loma successes of the past, but from then until his death on 23 August 1963 he was virtually inactive as a musician.

Other Casa Loma stalwarts have continued their musical careers. Pee Wee Hunt achieved considerable commercial success in the '40s with burlesque Dixieland recordings in the style of his famous *Twelfth Street Rag*; this has enabled him to lead a small group until today. Trumpeter Sonny Dunham, who became well known for his features with the Casa Loma Orchestra (the most popular being *Memories Of You*), branched out as a leader early in 1940 and to this day heads a band that works in Florida, though he now plays trombone. Clarence Hutchenrider, the most distinguished of the band's soloists, left it in 1944 as a result of failing health, but after some years away from music returned to working around the New York City area, where today he leads a highly successful trio. The remaining Casa Loma musicians of the peak years appear to have drifted into non-musical occupations.

In retrospect the Casa Loma Orchestra can reasonably be said to have been the most influential white band in the United States during the early '30s. It was perhaps a transitional band, providing a link between the dance orchestras who could turn out creditable hot performances and the swing groups of the Goodman and Dorsey variety. Whatever its failings – and the lack of a really good rhythm section was a perennial one – it deserves credit for its pioneering spirit and for the technical expertise of its personnel. If imitation is indeed the highest form of flattery the Casa Loma Orchestra was certainly flattered to a remarkable degree in the early years of its existence.

It was remarked earlier that musicians admire technical skill without giving much consideration to questions of stylistic merit, and the career of Jimmy Dorsey amply demonstrates this fact. Throughout his life Dorsey was revered by all other alto saxophone players for his consummate ease of execution and masterly technique; the list of those who paid tribute to him includes Johnny Hodges, Charlie Parker and Ornette

Coleman. Critics might refer disdainfully to Dorsey's solos as a collection of technical doodles, but musicians who played alto knew just how difficult those 'doodles' were to execute. When the Dorsey Brothers Orchestra was formed in 1934, Jimmy and his trombonist brother Tommy were already veterans of the big band and recording-studio scene, and had had records issued under their names, made with pick-up groups. Their prowess was recognised and envied by fellow musicians, and it augured well when other first-class soloists and section-men became members of the band, but somehow the results – at least judging by its records – were curiously disappointing, and a great deal more was promised than was actually achieved. This may have been in part due to the temperamental differences that divided the Dorseys, a subject which for years occupied the same role in American musical journalism, at times when news was difficult to come by, as the weather does in British conversation. The music of their band undeniably reflected an uncertainty of direction, embracing a high proportion of big band Dixieland scores alternated with straightforward ballad interpretations and, occasionally, more adventurous items that looked forward to the swing era. The ballads were usually sung by Bob Crosby in a style heavily influenced by his famous brother. An example is *Basin Street Blues*, where his vocal contrasts oddly with George Thow's plunger solo; but on the whole his singing was as unexceptional as the scores. It is only on a small percentage of the instrumental numbers that the full potential of the band is even partially realised.

The line-up of the Dorsey Brothers Orchestra had one unusual feature, for apart from the conventional rhythm and saxophone sections the brass consisted of only one trumpet (George Thow) and three trombones; the latter included not only Tommy Dorsey but, for part of the band's life, Glenn Miller. It was he who provided many of the arrangements, also writing special numbers such as the march-type *Dese Dem Dose*. As in his arrangements for Ray Noble's American band, which will be discussed later, there is a fussiness and over-elaboration about his work that was not conducive to cohesive performances. Some of the Dixieland-styled recordings were reasonable, the best being *Dippermouth Blues* and *That Eccentric Rag*; the former contained an assured clarinet solo by Jimmy Dorsey and a creditable attempt at the traditional trumpet solo by Thow, while the latter had accurate section playing, a fleet clarinet solo by Jimmy Dorsey, and competent tenor saxophone work from Skeets Herfurt, who on other records mars his solos by the use of square, on-the-beat phrasing. The less stylised instrumentals *Stop, Look And Listen* and *By Heck*, however, showcase the talents of the band more effectively. Glenn Miller was responsible for the arrangement of *Stop, Look And Listen* and it is one of his best for the band, looking ahead to the swing era in its employment of call-and-response patterns for the sections; both the Dorseys and Thow take worthwhile solos. *By Heck* is the most satisfying title that the band recorded and offers ensemble work of a high quality, excellent solos by the Dorseys and Thow, crisp playing from a rhythm section sparked by drummer Ray McKinley, and a cohesiveness of solos and ensemble that is missing in most of the band's recorded output. If the orchestra had stayed together and had concentrated on this type of material it might well have made a far greater impact. As it was, the conflicts between the co-leaders became more acute, and finally Tommy walked off the stand during a performance, leaving Jimmy to retain most of the personnel as the basis of the first regular band billed under his leadership. Tommy Dorsey was, by all accounts, a singularly determined man with a great will to succeed in his field, and the frustrations he experienced as co-leader of the Dorsey Brothers Orchestra probably only steeled his ambitions in the succeeding years, when he went on to lead one of the most professional and versatile bands of the swing era.

When Ray Noble arrived in the United States in 1934 he had built up a tremendous reputation with his British recordings, which sold well on the American market. His initial band was organised for him by Glenn Miller, who had just left the Dorsey Brothers Orchestra, and included in its ranks such outstanding musicians as Bud Freeman, Claude Thornhill, Johnny Mince and Will Bradley. Everything pointed to an emulation of Noble's British success, yet, despite a number of interesting recordings over the next few years, his American output cannot be compared in its consistency of musical accomplishment with what he had done in Britain. Miller had expressed his admiration for Noble's arranging before their association, and it has been claimed that it was while working for Noble that he discovered the famous reed voicing of clarinet over four saxophones that subsequently became his trademark. His arrangements, however, reveal the failings that were apparent in his scores for the Dorsey Brothers Orchestra, particularly in the more jazz-inclined items such as *Bugle Call Rag*, *Way Down Yonder In New Orleans*, *Chinatown, My Chinatown* and *Dinah*. These numbers have been singled out because over the years they have sometimes received a disproportionate amount of praise, the reason for which is puzzling. *Bugle Call Rag* is an extraordinarily gimmicky arrangement, introducing snippets from Ravel's *Bolero* and various other numbers during the course of a performance that has only the saving grace of an attractive tenor solo from Bud Freeman. *Way Down Yonder In New Orleans* is another cluttered score that allows the soloists little freedom. *Chinatown, My Chinatown* and *Dinah* are certainly better, the latter employing riffs capably and allowing the soloists enough room to build coherent solos, but overall they are little more than professionally competent. In a few months most of the jazz soloists had drifted away, their talents neglected by the arrangements they

Above: the Dorsey Brothers Orchestra, 1935. Kay Weber is in the centre, flanked by Tommy (left) and Jimmy Dorsey (right). Right, top: Jack Crawford – a rival to Paul Whiteman in the girth stakes. Bottom: Jan Garber and his band follow the popular '30s tradition of being photographed on the waterfront.

were called upon to perform.

Though he had made numerous British records that were successful in a jazz-influenced vein, Noble's real strength lay in his sensitive approach to the better type of popular song, where his voicings were often startlingly fresh. He was fortunate to have Al Bowlly with him during the first year or two of his American band-leading career, and Bowlly's vocals frequently provide the highspot of his American recordings. Titles such as *Down By The River*, *The Touch Of Your Lips*, *Soon* and *With All My Heart* have excellent Bowlly vocals, and the arrangements, though seldom as distinctive as those on Noble's British recordings, are at least highly professional. Overall, Noble's American output, despite numerous individual contributions of merit, lacks any great impact and the best of it is that on which Bowlly is featured. Bowlly returned to England in 1939 and Noble moved to Los Angeles, where he combined the roles of bandleader and radio personality successfully for many years, subsequently retiring from music and settling in Jersey, where he lives still.

Interestingly enough, Noble has claimed that he preferred the band he led in Los Angeles to the more star-studded New York outfit, in all probability because these lesser-known musicians were more willing to adjust their approach to Noble's requirements. The basic reason for the partial failure of Noble's American records is that he was unable to get musicians with strongly individual styles to adapt their tone and phrasing to the extent necessary for his arrangements to be

JACK CRAWFORD
"THE CLOWN PRINCE OF JAZZ"
AND HIS ORCHESTRA
Exclusive Management
MUSIC CORPORATION of AMERICA
NEW YORK · CHICAGO

JAN GARBER
And His Greater
COLUMBIA RECORDING
ORCHESTRA
Exclusive Management
MUSIC CORPORATION
of AMERICA
NEW YORK
CHICAGO

performed successfully; whereas in England he had worked for long periods with a core of leading London musicians, who, from frequent association, became the ideal interpreters of his scores. For the dance band and jazz arranger or composer, lengthy association with sympathetic musicians is essential, if his work is to be performed as he would wish.

Jazz musicians often dismay their followers by revealing distinctly unhip likings for bands or performers dismissed by purist critics as beneath notice. Louis Armstrong's attachment to the sound of the Guy Lombardo saxophone section has been well known for years; it even inspired gruesome attempts at emulation on some of his own records in the early '30s. In an interview with Orrin Keepnews he enlarged on this.

When we were at the Savoy in Chicago, in 1928, every Sunday night we'd catch the Owl Club, with Guy Lombardo, and as long as he played we'd sit right there. Zutty [Singleton], Carroll Dickerson and all the band. We didn't go nowhere until Lombardo signed off. That went on for months. Music for me, music that's good, you just want to hear it again!

It is difficult to write with any objectivity on the Guy Lombardo band, for it has become an institution and somehow criticism seems almost an irrelevance. Gaetario 'Guy' Lombardo was born in London, Ontario, on 19 June 1902, and after family promptings organised a quartet that included his brothers Carmen and Lebert on flute and drums respectively. It made its debut, perhaps appropriately, at the local Mothers' Club. By the early '20s Guy was leading a band on a semi-professional basis, making his American debut at the Clare-mont Hotel, Cleveland, in 1924. Three years later the band moved to Chicago where, despite poor business at their resident job, they managed to get a 15-minute broadcast over a local station. The response was astounding and they were called upon to play for a further 45 minutes – broadcasting schedules in those early days must have had a flexibility unknown in later years – and by the following week they had found a sponsor. In 1929 Lombardo first played in New York at the Grill Room of the Hotel Roosevelt; he subsequently set up an astonishing record by playing a season there every year until 1962, with only one year's absence. Although the Lombardo band clinched its unique reputation during the '30s, and is therefore discussed in this chapter, its popularity has never waned during the following decades, and it is still, in 1971, as active as ever. Up to the swing era Lombardo occasionally played hot numbers; an early (1928) recording of *Sweethearts On Parade*, for example, reveals a proficiency in this department that would astound those familiar only with the band's later output. When the swing bands got under way, however, Lombardo decided, wisely, to stick to 'The Sweetest Music This Side of Heaven' – to use the most familiar description of his style. To the chagrin of many jazz fans Lombardo unexpectedly holds the record of drawing the largest crowd in a single evening to Harlem's famed Savoy Ballroom, regarded as

Right, top: Guy Lombardo in the early '40s. Bottom: the 1934 Lawrence Welk band. Below: Lombardo directs his famous saxophone section. For decades Lombardo has successfully presented the 'Sweetest Music This Side of Heaven', and Welk is still an immensely popular TV bandleader.

a bulwark of the large jazz bands. He once commented that as long as he did not attempt to play jazz he found considerable acceptance among black audiences.

The style of the Lombardo band has been set by the saxophone section, led by Carmen, which employs an exaggerated vibrato. Brass instruments – never employed in any considerable number – usually phrase in a clipped, staccato manner, while the rhythm section is frequently more felt than heard. These factors have given the band an instantly recognisable style, one that is unlikely to call for any degree of concentration from the most casual of listeners; but in commercial terms it has paid off handsomely. Lombardo has been clever enough to select his numbers with his audiences very much in mind, concentrating on the better-known standards. Critics may ridicule the Lombardo style, and those seeking creativity within the field would swiftly turn away from it, but however many and however valid the criticisms may be, the average fan of the band knows for sure that he is going to be able to recognise the melody from the opening bars. This, I believe, is the reason for the Lombardo band's longevity, which is rivalled only by Duke Ellington's.

Since 1935 Lombardo has recorded for Decca – initially he was with Columbia – and it is claimed that over 25 million records by the band have been sold, a figure that seems more than likely. Amongst the many hits created by Lombardo can be numbered *You're Driving Me Crazy, Little White Lies, It Seems Like Old Times, Heartaches, Boo Hoo, A Sailboat In The Moonlight* and *Little Girl*; Carmen has also been responsible for writing big-selling numbers of the calibre of *Coquette* and *Sweethearts On Parade*. To most critics musical conservatism is to be deplored; to Guy Lombardo and his musicians, seven of whom have been with the band for periods of well over forty years, it has been a means of unprecedented survival in an industry noted for its high mortality rate.

Another bandleader who gained full public acceptance during the '30s and has survived to the present day is Lawrence Welk, but the records that I have heard by the band make Lombardo sound almost progressive by comparison. Other

Top left: Freddy Martin in the film The Big Beat. *Though not himself a jazz musician, his saxophone-playing was greatly admired by many famous jazzmen. Right: Gus Arnheim, who for many years held sway as leader at the Coconut Grove in Los Angeles. Lower right: Arnheim and his orchestra in an early '30s film.*

prominent dance bands of the '30s, such as those led by Sammy Kaye, Kay Kyser and Shep Fields, were as much variety acts as musical aggregations. A society band that was always well rehearsed and musicianly was that led by tenor saxophonist Freddy Martin, whose playing attracted the admiration of such leading jazz soloists as the late Leon 'Chu' Berry (until his death in a car accident the star of the Cab Calloway band), the late Johnny Hodges, and Eddie Miller of the Bob Crosby band. Martin was born in Cleveland in 1908 and was raised in an orphanage after the death of both parents. He first studied the drums and later the C-melody saxophone, and as a young man played with local bands, in the process becoming friendly with Guy Lombardo, who was resident at a club called 'The Music Box'. Branching out as a leader, he met

Ted Lewis, whose 'is everybody happy?' became known to millions. His band for many years included Muggsy Spanier and George Brunies.

little initial success. He worked as a sideman for several years after his first band broke up, and finally came to national prominence during the mid-'30s, when he was resident at the Bossert Hotel in Brooklyn, and secured a recording contract with Brunswick. Many of his early records had vocals by Elmer Feldkamp, but the basis of his style was the employment of three tenor saxophones against two trumpets and trombone, with strings. In the later '40s Martin commenced recording for RCA Victor and still does so, having contrived in some fashion to survive the great changes in the field of popular entertainment. In 1969 he was resident at the famous Coconut Grove restaurant of the Hotel Ambassador in Los Angeles, where he first played in 1938. Martin's records tend to blandness but the standard of musicianship displayed is invariably of a high order.

For many years the Coconut Grove was the home of Gus Arnheim's band, which first became resident there in the late

'20s. Arnheim himself was born in Chicago and first worked in a group called the Syncopated Five, in which Abe Lyman played drums. Subsequently he took theatre jobs, then played for a year or two as Sophie Tucker's accompanist, then worked again with Abe Lyman. He formed his first band in 1927 and it became immensely successful at the Coconut Grove, a favourite haunt of Hollywood film stars. He took leave of absence in 1929 to play at London's Savoy Hotel and the Ambassadeurs Club in Paris. In 1930 he engaged the Rhythm Boys from Paul Whiteman's band as a feature attraction, and his nightly two-hour radio broadcast helped Bing Crosby to become widely known. Records made at this time – *Wrap Your Troubles In Dreams* and *I Surrender Dear* are typical – feature impeccable arrangements (usually by Jimmie Grier, who later became a well-known bandleader himself), assured musicianship and a pleasantly individual sound, but apart from *One More Time*, an unusually spirited performance, are now sought after mainly for the Crosby vocals. Working at the Coconut Grove meant that Arnheim was called upon to accompany singers and other acts in lavish floor shows, and he also appeared in several films. During the mid-'30s Arnheim rather

surprisingly switched his musical allegiance and organised a band in the swing style that became popular in Chicago and New York. In 1937 he used arrangements by Budd Johnson – an outstanding jazz tenor saxophonist who was chief arranger for the Earl Hines band for many years – and his then un-known young pianist Stanley Kenton, and he produced some musically impressive versions of *Exactly Like You, High, Wide And Handsome* and *Schubert's Serenade.* Considering the

Above: Leo Reisman, one of the most flamboyant of bandleaders. Right: the late Hal Kemp, who on several occasions led excellent bands.

quality of his personnel and arrangers, however, it seems likely that the full potential of the band was not realised on record. At this time a featured trumpeter with Arnheim was Charlie Spivak, who himself fronted a band in later years, and

68

is today still active as a leader in Greenville, South Carolina. Arnheim retired from music after the war years and died in 1955 at the age of 57.

A popular leader during the '30s was Ted Weems, who had a proficient band in the late '20s but reached his musical peak around 1933. As early as 1923 Weems co-led, with his trombonist brother Art, a band that secured an important engagement at the Trianon Ballroom in Newark, N.J. Prior to this he had worked with Paul Specht in Reading, Pennsylvania, but a few years passed before he came to national prominence. Because Weems, particularly in his later years, prominently featured vocalists and the whistling solos of Elmo Tanner, it is easy to overlook his achievements during the '30s, but *When The Morning Rolls Around, Lonely Park* and *My Baby Just Cares For Me* (all on Victor) reveal an unusually well integrated ensemble sound and a rhythmic drive that was impressive for the period. Unfortunately Weems did not succeed in gaining public acceptance at this time and soon turned to featuring novelty numbers in profusion. The titles mentioned above and such '20s recordings as *Big Boy, Savannah* and *Somebody Stole My Gal* suggest that there was a potential within the band that was never fully realised. Further commercial success came to Weems in 1947 when an old recording of *Heartaches* became one of the industry's most surprising million-sellers.

The fact that the late Leo Reisman wrote a column of jazz in a trade paper during the late '20s, and once engaged in a dispute with Henry Ford on its supposed immoral influence, would seem surprising to anyone familiar with his music, for up to the time of his death, on 18 December 1961, his forty-four years as a leader had been spent mainly in the area of smooth society dance music. Reisman, who, in his earlier years at least, was a flamboyant and flashy leader, was born in Boston on 11 October 1897, and by the age of twelve was earning a dollar a day in a music store plugging hit songs. He emigrated in 1917 to Baltimore, where he doubled as a violinist with the local symphony orchestra and as leader of a salon orchestra, but returned to Boston within a short while and commenced to build a reputation as a dance band leader. By the mid-'20s he was the organiser of more than twenty bands.

On 19 February 1928 he followed the Paul Whiteman tradition by presenting a Symphony Hall concert, under the title of 'A Programme Of Rhythm'. The repertoire included the première of Ferde Grofe's *Three Shades Of Blue*, Gershwin's *Rhapsody In Blue*, Rube Bloom's *Soliloquy* (played by the composer), and *St Louis Blues* and *Aunt Hagar's Blues*, both featuring Johnny Dunn. Because of Dunn's colour some of the audience walked out when he played.

In 1929 Reisman went to New York, as a result of a $60,000 contract, to play at the Central Park Casino, and two years later he headed the bill at the Paramount Theater. In 1934 he was resident at the Wedgewood Room of the Waldorf-Astoria Hotel and played there each season until 1947. That Reisman's musical conservatism was not pervasive is shown by the fact that he hired the former Duke Ellington trumpet star Bubber Miley during 1931; in the same year he made RCA Victor's first LP record, which featured Fred and Adèle Astaire. He also made the first 'binaural' (stereo) records (which were never issued), for his recording career extended over two decades.

Reisman's peak years as a recording artist were the early '30s, and a few titles such as *Without That Gal* and *What Is This Thing Called Love* offer an unexpected bonus in the shape of outstanding plunger solos from Miley, which contrast rather oddly with the string-laden surroundings; the latter also has the bizarre juxtaposition of a backing to the vocal by Miley and Eddie Duchin. Reisman's real forte was his performance of show tunes, examples being *Time On My Hands, Night And Day* and *Stormy Weather*, with vocals by Lee Wiley, Fred Astaire and composer Harold Arlen respectively. At their best Reisman's records reveal proficient musicianship,

an ability to highlight the melodies of the more durable show themes, and an overall smoothness that at times veers into blandness. By the later '30s Reisman's music sounded increasingly dated, though to the end he remained a favourite of the clientele of several of the more sedate hotel ballrooms.

Hal Kemp had a period of success in the mid-'30s when he led perhaps the most musical of the sweet bands. Its style had been set by arranger John Scott Trotter and was built around the use of muted trumpets and clarinets in unison playing sustained notes, sometimes through megaphones. The lead trumpeter, Earl Geiger, was a key member of the band and his departure proved an unsettling event, but Kemp scored a great success with records like *Got A Date With An Angel*, *The Touch Of Your Lips* and *It's Easy To Remember*, largely as the result of the intimate vocal style of Skinnay Ennis. Most sweet bands were content to hit upon a personalised style that pleased the less demanding listeners and continue with it, but though Kemp pushed his individual sound strongly there were attempts by his arrangers to achieve some musically interesting sounds within the format.

Kemp, who was born in Marion, Alabama, on 27 March 1905, organised his first band, The Merrymakers, at high school in 1919, subsequently becoming a member of a college band at the University of North Carolina. In 1927 he led his first professional group and three years later came to London, where he played at the Coliseum and the Café de Paris. In these early years Kemp's band was a hot unit, including in its personnel such musicians as trumpeters Bunny Berigan, Mickey Bloom and Jack Purvis. Records like *Navy Blues*, *Fraternity Blues* and *Them There Eyes* prove it to have been highly efficient if not startlingly original within this idiom.

After he achieved prominence with his sweet band he fell into a period of stylistic uncertainty towards the late '30s, veering between his familiar sound and a not very impressive attempt to emulate the swing groups. It is from this time that records like *Jazz Me Blues*, *Dodging A Divorcee* and *Serenade For A Wealthy Widow* date. Kemp's band was declining in public favour when he was killed in a car crash in December 1940, but throughout the years his fans have remembered him with gratitude for the bland, sophisticated approach he brought to a kind of dance music that has too frequently been exploited by musical charlatans and tricksters.

The final bandleader to be discussed in this chapter is Isham Jones who, by any critical standards, can be considered to have had one of the finest all-round dance bands in the history of the music. It is in one sense arbitrary to include him in a chapter on the '30s for his career stretches back to pioneer days, but I do so because I consider his band at this time was the greatest that he ever led.

Jones was born in Coalton, Ohio, in 1894, and his earliest years as an important innovator in defining the instrumentation and direction which dance bands were to follow have been

Isham Jones, leader of one of the finest American dance bands.

dealt with in the first chapter of this book. By the early '20s he had established himself as a popular favourite in Chicago, a town with a demanding dancing public that sometimes reacted poorly to big-name leaders such as Paul Whiteman, whose music, they felt, substituted showy effects for solidity of rhythm. In 1922 the Jones band recorded *Wabash Blues*, which is reported to have sold close on two million copies, and around this time his bandsmen were said to have been fervent admirers of the great Joe 'King' Oliver's Creole Jazz Band, then playing at Chicago's Royal Gardens and Lincoln Gardens. In 1924 Jones brought his band to London, where it had a successful engagement at the Kit-Cat Club, and upon his return he was resident for a while at a club in Miami. However, although his great popular success meant that he often worked in New York and undertook many profitable theatre tours, there is no doubt that he was most happy when he was playing in Chicago, and that the audiences there regarded him as one of their own. He retired briefly around 1928, returned as a leader in the following year, and by 1930 was riding high once more as a result of his record of *Stardust*.

During the '30s Jones led a superb band, one that the late Ziggy Elman, who became famous as a featured soloist with Benny Goodman's orchestra, described as having 'the greatest sound of any of the dance orchestras. No one else came close.' He retired from music once more in 1936, when a number of his sidemen became the nucleus of the Woody Herman Orchestra; made an unsuccessful attempt at a comeback in the '40s; and died in 1956. He must have made a great deal of money in his career, for as early as 1923 the American Brunswick company announced that it had already paid him over $500,000 in royalties, and in the following years his royalties from his many song hits must have been considerable.

Many prominent bandleaders were poor instrumentalists – some indeed could hardly even be considered as practising musicians at all – but in his early years Jones was an excellent performer on both C-melody and tenor saxophones, and when he turned to conducting with a baton he was no figurehead brought in to add a personality to the orchestra. Throughout his career Jones – who by all accounts was a taciturn individual, not given to displays of showmanship (contemporary reports described him as looking like a country attorney, a bank manager or a farmer) – stubbornly kept to his chosen path of presenting music that was ideal in tempo for his dancing public yet at the same time interesting for listeners as well. He seemed impervious to fads of the moment, but used what was valid for his needs in any innovations that arose. Sometimes he changed the role of an instrument, such as the tuba for instance, which he replaced with a string bass in his rhythm section but retained for its melodic and harmonic possibilities. A disciplinarian by nature, Jones was hardly beloved of his musicians, but whatever they thought of him as an individual did not interfere with their playing on the stand. In later years most of them echoed the views of his one-time arranger, Gordon Jenkins, who termed his early '30s orchestra 'the greatest sweet ensemble of that time or any other time'.

Jones's records of the '20s include many that are first-rate, with an unusually rich ensemble sound for the period and a much more flowing rhythmic quality than was normal for white bands at the time. His '30s band, however, was a great one and more fully reflected his mature style, largely owing to the presence of first-class arrangers, the chief of whom was Gordon Jenkins, and a personnel that included some outstanding instrumentalists. Apart from Jenkins, whose scores were superior to almost any being turned out at that time, and called for a high degree of technical expertise in their performance, the three key members of the band were probably Joe Bishop (tuba and brass bass), Saxie Mansfield (tenor saxophone) and Johnny Carlson (trumpet). Bishop, who went on to become an important figure in the first Woody Herman bands, played his cumbersome instrument with a unique skill and

tonal flexibility, laying down the foundation for the group to build upon. Johnny Carlson is considered by most musicians to be one of the greatest lead trumpeters in the history of dance music; his beautiful relaxed phrasing and broad warm tone imprinted themselves on almost every record the band made, and he was also an excellent soloist. Mansfield, a bustling tenor player, had a full rounded tone and he frequently doubled the lead an octave below Carlson's trumpet, adding to the richness of textures that was so much a part of Jones's style. Fortunately, two LPs are currently available from the band's peak period and these include many outstanding performances.

The first LP, of recordings made between May 1930 and March 1931, is titled 'Swingin' Down The Lane' in celebration of the presence of Jones's composition of this name. It includes one of the band's most famous performances, Hoagy Carmichael's *Stardust*, which was the first recording of this number to be played in ballad style. Previously the tune had been treated as a hot item, but Jones realised its immense potential as a melodic ballad and his version, which features some splendid muted trumpet playing by Carlson and a violin solo by Victor Young, must have helped Carmichael amass a con-

The late Victor Young, arranger for the Isham Jones band.

siderable sum in royalties. Another well-known Jones recording, *Trees*, is also contained on the LP, but the sentimental lyrics, as sung by a mediocre vocalist, make this a far less rewarding listening experience than the instrumental *Stardust*. The hot tracks on the LP, including a version of Don Redman's *Miss Hannah* (the composer had taken part in a superb recording of this with McKinney's Cotton Pickers), have their moments, but indifferent vocals and a certain rhythmic stiffness make them less interesting than the ballad performances. *My Ideal*, *I'll Be Blue Just Thinking Of You* and *Goodnight, Sweet Dreams*, despite period vocals of slight merit, show the Jones band at its best, with interesting scores, assured section playing, and a crisp sound that was impressive for the period.

The second LP, titled 'The Great Isham Jones And His Orchestra', is from the 1932–4 period and is consistently outstanding. The jazz-styled performances, on such numbers as *Dallas Blues*, *China Boy* and *Darkness On The Delta*, show an improvement in rhythmic quality and there are some reasonable solos, but in general the Jones band was precise and alert in this idiom without equalling the efforts of the more jazz-oriented orchestras. Once again it is in the ballad numbers that the band really shows its exceptional worth, and though the vocals by Eddie Stone, Joe Martin and Frank Hazzard are indifferent, the inventiveness of the scoring and the impeccable section work provide ample compensations. The opening number is the attractive *Blue Prelude*, written by Joe Bishop and Gordon Jenkins, and the performance is notable for superb section interplay and sensitive individual playing. *Georgia Jubilee*, written by pianist Arthur Schutt and Benny Goodman, is also outstanding for the smooth precision of the section work; one of the secrets of the success that this band achieved lies in the legato phrasing of the sections with the matched vibratos. The richness of sound in such typical ballad performances as *For All We Know*, *You've Got Me Cryin' Again* and *It's Funny To Everyone But Me* is readily identifiable, and Jones joins the limited group of leaders who found a formula for pleasing audiences on both functional and artistic levels. Many other recordings by the Jones band are worthy of reissue and no doubt at least some of these will appear on microgroove releases in the future.

Just before the Jones band broke up in 1936 a group from within it recorded eight jazz-oriented performances, the personnel including Woody Herman, Saxie Mansfield and Chelsea Quealey. The results were pleasant and proficient rather than inspired, but are interesting for introducing Woody Herman as a vocalist to jazz audiences who at the time would have been likely to dismiss the full Jones band as of little merit. By the autumn Herman had formed his first group, 'The Band That Plays The Blues', with various colleagues from the Jones orchestra in its line-up. One particularly welcome ex-Jones musician must have been trumpeter Clarence Willard, for he had learned many of the arts of leading a section from the redoubtable Carlson.

Before leaving Jones we must consider an aspect of his work that has not been touched upon: his songwriting. Over the years he wrote more than 200 songs, of which forty or so became hits, the most famous being *On The Alamo*, *Swinging Down The Lane*, *It Had To Be You*, *I'll See You In My Dreams*, *Spain*, *The One I Love Belongs To Somebody Else*, *There Is No Greater Love* and *Why Can't This Night Go On Forever*. Upon being given a piano by his wife on his thirtieth birthday, Jones stayed up all night and by the morning had completed *Spain*, *The One I Love Belongs To Somebody Else* and *It Had To Be You*, partly because he was aware of the cost of the piano and was determined to make it pay its way! This frugal, aloof man seems in many ways an unusual personality to have played such an important part in the development of dance music, but, adhering rigidly to his own high standards, he left an indelible impression on the scene and is remembered to this day with great respect by audiences and musicians alike.

Several all-female bands were formed in the '30s. The most successful was led by Ina Ray Hutton, shown here during a stage show. Right: Ted Fio Rita and his band, from the film 20 Million Sweethearts.

Without doubt, the Isham Jones band was the most musical and inventive of the American dance orchestras of the pre-swing '30s and in some respects was a spiritual forerunner of such groups as the Claude Thornhill band of a later period. Above all it proved that popular success need not be attained at the expense of musical integrity, a fact that can so easily be overlooked in the hurly-burly of the popular entertainment industry.

From 1936 the more conservative bandleaders were pushed to the sidelines as the triumphant swing bands gained their dominance, though many continued to flourish economically in the ballrooms of the more staid hotels. To sum up, the American dance bands of the '30s appear, with a few exceptions, to have been content to rest upon successful formulas. Only a minority achieved the overall versatility that distinguished their British

counterparts, and the pioneering in arranging techniques and exploration of instrumental and textural possibilities that had characterised the '20s was consolidated rather than extended.

The jauntiness and extrovert quality of the typical '20s number was replaced by more introspective material, expressive in the main of private wish-fulfilment. It has been claimed that *Buddy Can You Spare A Dime* is the archetypal song of the American depression years, but in fact it stands out by its very atypicality, in comparison to the average number performed by dance bands of the period. Certain songs – *Ten Cents A Dance*, even *I Can't Give You Anything But Love* – offer an oblique commentary on the social and economic ills of the time, but in general dance music has never indulged in direct social criticism. The 'race' and 'country' releases contained many items that spoke directly of harsh conditions and poverty, for these forms of music draw their strength from mirroring the attitudes, prejudices and hopes of their audience, but dance band musicians and leaders – if they thought about their social role at all – were more concerned with helping their public to forget, briefly, the problems of their everyday existence. Folklorists and music scholars may regret it, but at certain periods in time the 'June moon' song may as strongly reflect the hidden yearnings of the 'folk' as one with a rousing social message, escapism being as commonplace a reaction to stress situations as social commitment. If it were otherwise the history of popular music during the depression years would have been very different.

Right: Art Kassel, a popular '30s leader who headed the 'Kassels In The Air'. Below: Anson Weeks and orchestra, 1932. Note in front row Xavier Cugat and Bob Crosby (2nd and 4th from left).

BRITAIN—
THE
THIRTIES

W. H. Auden described the '30s in a famous phrase as 'a low dishonest decade', an apt enough summary of its social and political climate. Yet by a curious paradox these were the golden years for the British dance bands, both economically and musically, and some of the leading groups benefited from the very inequalities that disturbed economists and sociologists. Amongst the general population economic distress might be widespread and unemployment figures reaching an all-time high, but the society clientele who nightly wined, dined and danced at the leading London hotels and night-clubs preferred to ignore such realities. Sometimes they even ascribed them to the shiftlessness of the working class, who, some right-wing newspapers assured their readers, were so unfamiliar with rules of hygiene that they regarded baths as convenient receptacles for storing coal. There is a further paradox in the position of the musicians who formed the leading dance bands, many of whom came from a working-class or lower middle-class background. Night after night they played in surroundings of tawdry luxury and witnessed spending on a scale that must have shocked the more socially conscious amongst them, but there is some evidence that many came to accept, in part, the attitudes of their social superiors.

Ambrose was a particular favourite of the society crowd. Not long ago, interviewed about his former career, he provided some fascinating insights into the social milieu within which the major hotel bands operated. He described the Embassy Club first, reminiscing about the days when the audience would include the Prince of Wales (later King Edward VIII, now the Duke of Windsor), the Duke of Gloucester, King George VI and King Alfonso of Spain. He returned to the club from New York in response to a telegram from the Prince of Wales, which read 'Come back, we need you – Edward. P.' The rigid class structure of '30s society is underlined in his comments on his residency at the Mayfair Hotel:

Well, we used to get all these people at the Mayfair. But we ruined it for ourselves. For 5½ years we had a regular Saturday night broadcast. We used to attract people from the provinces, not the hoi polloi, but nice people. It was their big night out. But, unfortunately it drove away the other people – high society – away. We were over-popular.

The King thought nobody could play a waltz like Ambrose. Of course, he wasn't a very good dancer. I used to start off very slowly – all wrong of course – and then I would watch him like a hawk until he got into the swing of things and then I would increase the tempo until he went whirling away. The other bandleaders didn't do it that way.

Perhaps more than any other bandleader of the period Ambrose became enmeshed in the social conventions of his clientele, losing vast sums of money in gambling, including a reputed £28,000 in one night at Monte Carlo. In his own words 'It was all part of show business. But I overdid the show part.' It is as well to recall that he and the bandleaders resident at the leading hotels and night-clubs were the privileged members of the dance band profession, and that others reacted to their surroundings in a far less flamboyant manner, through either caution or personal temperament. But it must have been hard for musicians who worked in such an environment to escape completely the social attitudes which prevailed within it.

To the vast listening audience whose only contact with the dance bands was their radio sets, and possibly an occasional concert or visit to a theatre, it was a matter of academic interest how the leading bands achieved economic stability. Most people, if they thought about it at all, were probably glad that hotels and night-clubs were able to afford to engage the bands. From the standpoint of the leaders, broadcasts, even more than records, continued to be their means of securing a national following, and by the early '30s the BBC had established a late-night dance band formula that was immensely popular. With odd exceptions each night of the week, apart from Sundays, saw 10.30 to midnight allocated to a single band – Lew Stone on Tuesday, Harry Roy on Friday, Ambrose on Saturday – so that followers of the various bands knew exactly when their favourites were broadcasting. Though the bandleaders who were excluded from these schedules might feel a sense of grievance, the plan worked well, primarily because the most imaginative and skilled bands did in fact get the regular weekly opportunity to display their talents; but inevitably these were the groups that built up the largest followings. It says much for the quality of the bands that they could, by carefully planning their programmes to achieve as much variety as possible of repertoire and mood, continually sustain these long broadcasts. The late Lew Stone once said that the three-minute length of an average number was of considerable help in this respect, for, if a band played an item that some of the listeners did not appreciate, they were prepared to tolerate it, knowing that it was short and that something more to their taste was likely to follow.

Having established the pattern of regular bands on regular nights it was not too long before the BBC began to have doubts about the wisdom of its policy, presumably reasoning that it was vulnerable to charges of showing gross favouritism to the leaders selected for the weekly broadcasts. In due course a new schedule was introduced, substituting feature programmes built around a variety of bands, but the public outcry against the discontinuance of the old format forced the BBC to reintroduce a modified late-night dance band pattern that retained many characteristics of the earlier days. Not all leaders were on the side of the public in this matter, and Jack Payne subsequently wrote:

The public demanded to know why it had been denied its soporific of the unbroken weekly chain of Carroll Gibbons, Roy Fox, Harry Roy and so on. The public kicked up hell and won. Late-night music came back to stay. On the whole I think the public was wrong: dance music should not just become a habit; there must be something else worthy of concluding each day's task – conversely I never saw any obvious reason for putting the bulk of dance music right at the end of the day.

Other dance band leaders viewed the process of having the same bands broadcasting on a regular night in a less favourable light than the public. A 1938 *Melody Maker* carried the somewhat melodramatic headline 'BBC Plotting Against The Dance Bands', referring to the supposed collusion between the BBC and the governments of Britain and France to suppress Continental radio stations which were beaming sponsored programmes at this country. The article claimed that the BBC was planning to reintroduce the old pattern of late-night broadcasts, with the bands of Joe Loss, Syd Lipton, Jack Jackson, Jack Harris and Ambrose on regular nights. It went on:

Why has the BBC – if it has – decided to revert to the fixed band per night policy? The answer here is not difficult to find when one is told that all these five bands are to be confined to actual Outside Broadcasts at Outside Broadcast rates. Those rates are cheaper than those for studio broadcasts, and the schedule of terms for broadcasting of dance music provides that there shall be a further reduction when broadcasts are regular and continuous!

It all looks very strange, it all looks very unnecessary, and it all looks very fishy.

Important as broadcasts were to the dance bands during the '30s, the relations between the BBC and bandleaders had been anything but smooth from the earliest days of dance band transmissions, and such papers as the *Melody Maker* carried many news stories which indicate the strained attitude existing between the two sides. We have already seen the almost bizarre lengths to which the BBC went to stamp out songplugging in the '20s, and throughout the '30s it continued to grapple

The Ray Noble Band upon their arrival in Holland, 1933. From left to right, Tiny Winters, Nat Gonella, Al Bowlly, Mrs Noble, Ray Noble, Harry Berly, Lew Davis, Bob Wise, Mrs Gardner, Freddy Gardner and Alfie Noakes.

ineffectually with the problem. Although right could not always have been on the side of the bandleaders, it would certainly appear that several of the BBC's restrictions were hardly the result of rational thinking; in early 1935, for instance, it banned the term 'hot music' and the employment of scat singing. Nat Gonella was one of the victims of the latter ban, and his request for information on the reason for the ban elicited only vague responses about listeners' objections. A cartoon in the *Melody Maker* showed a grim-visaged Auntie BBC larruping a youngster labelled 'listening public', the caption reading 'There, brat! Whether you like it or not, your mind's got to be elevated!' This was clearly a reference to the well-known views of the BBC's Director, General (later Sir) John Reith; to the extent that his thinking dominated the BBC during this period, its attitude to the dance bands and popular entertainment in general was never free from ambivalence. On the other hand the BBC and the bandleaders were to a great extent dependent on each other, neither side being in a position to take up too dictatorial an attitude in their mutual bargainings. Though leaders might fulminate against the BBC, either individually or collectively, none could be unaware that the establishment of a national reputation depended on at least a reasonable relationship with the broadcasting authorities. In the last resort, this situation gave the latter a position of strength in negotiations, and they were not always unwilling to exploit it. In the later '30s most of the popular bands took part in commercially sponsored programmes, relayed to this country from Continental stations, and it is very probable that these outlets delighted many

leaders who had over the years felt frustration or resentment at the BBC's monopolistic invulnerability.

During the '30s every town in Britain with a population sufficient to maintain a variety theatre had at least one, and by the middle of the decade more and more bandleaders were well enough established to risk leaving location jobs for the theatre circuit. Some did so on a full-time touring basis; others during slack periods at hotels and night-clubs, in the summer months. Invariably such a band was the main attraction on a variety bill, occupying the stage for most if not all of the second half of the show, and generally the productions played towns a week at a time. Most of these bands had built their reputations on the strength of regular broadcasts – an exception was Jack Hylton, who was not a prolific broadcaster during many of the peak years of his career – but records were certainly next in importance as a means of gaining a nation-wide following.

Record sales during the '20s and '30s were a far cry from those that are commonplace today, but, despite the economic recession in Britain, during most of the '30s some artists still racked up impressive sales figures. Cheap records, some with an eight-inch diameter rather than the conventional ten-inch, appeared in profusion, and chain stores such as Curry's and Woolworth's marketed their own products. Several of the most active leaders concentrated almost solely on recording work, and amidst much that is mediocre there are occasional outstanding items, but the widespread habit of giving studio groups a variety of pseudonyms sometimes makes certain identification difficult.

Amongst the most prominent studio band directors were Harry Hudson, Bert Firman and Jay Wilbur. Hudson was particularly active on the staff of Edison Bell's Radio label from 1928 to about 1931, when his line-up often included such musicians as Sylvester Ahola, Lew Davis, Sid Phillips and

George Melachrino. His later career is obscure; he died on 27 July 1969 and had been working for some years beforehand as musical director at a holiday camp. Many of his Radio recordings are excellent, including some issued under such pseudonyms as the Blue Jays, the Radio Rhythm Boys and the Deauville Dance Band. Bert Firman, who led regular bands in London clubs during the '30s, also produced a number of good jazz-inclined titles when he was Zonophone's MD at about the same time as Hudson was with Edison Bell. Most prolific of all was Jay Wilbur, at first as staff director for Dominion, subsequently in the same role for the Crystalate Company, with their Imperial, Eclipse and Rex labels. However, interesting though they may often be, studio-assembled bands are in a special category and space does not permit more than a passing reference to them. An exception must be made for Ray Noble's studio bands during the period from July 1929 to August 1934, when he was musical director for the HMV label, for historically they are important in the annals of British dance music, and they produced many recordings of high quality.

Ray Noble was born in Brighton in 1907, the son of a London neurologist, and at the age of ten commenced studying the piano. In his teens he became interested in dance music, and he came to prominence in 1927, when he won a *Melody Maker* contest for arrangers, his winning score being recorded by Bert Firman for Zonophone. Shortly afterwards he joined the music publishing firm of Lawrence Wright as a staff arranger, working in 1928 with Jack Payne at the BBC. When Carroll Gibbons, then director of HMV's house bands, was offered a contract with MGM in America he suggested Noble as his replacement, and in July 1929 the latter took over. Late in 1934 he moved to the United States, taking with him vocalist Al Bowlly and

drummer-manager Bill Harty. He finally returned to Britain in the '50s and retired to Jersey, where he now lives. Apart from his bandleading and arranging career Noble is well known as a popular song composer; his most famous hits include *Goodnight, Sweetheart, Love Is The Sweetest Thing, By The Fireside, The Very Thought Of You* and *Cherokee*.

Noble did not remain in the United States uninterruptedly from 1934 onwards; in May 1938 he went to Britain as the nominal leader of a Canadian band – Jimmy 'Trump' Davidson's, from Toronto – and toured for several months, filling a two-week engagement at the London Palladium. Apparently Davidson's band was considered the only Canadian equivalent of an American swing group, but this aspect of its style was not apparent during its British tour and reviews in the musical press were lukewarm. It was said that, while the stage programme of the band was notable for its high degree of technical proficiency, it lacked any individual character, and the attempt to blend Noble's arrangements with its normal style was unsuccessful. By contrast, Noble's HMV recordings of the early '30s are the most personal and musically rewarding of his whole career.

When Noble assumed his position as house band director for HMV he found that the titles considered the most commercially desirable were assigned to Jack Hylton and Ambrose, and he

Below, and opposite: two photographs, taken on the same occasion, of the Ray Noble Band in Holland in the summer of 1933; left to right – Lew Davis, Harry Berly, Ray Noble, Freddy Gardner, Al Bowlly, Cecil Norman (back row), Bill Harty, Alfie Noakes, Tiny Winters, Nat Gonella and Bob Wise (front row). This was the only occasion that Noble led a band in public prior to going to the U.S.A.

was left to select the best of what remained. His skill as an arranger, and the fact that he was able to draw upon a regular team of top instrumentalists from the leading bands of the day, soon led him to establish an individual style, due in no small measure to the close rapport between himself and his musicians. Max Goldberg, Norman Payne, Nat Gonella, Harry Hines, Freddy Gardner and Harry Jacobson were amongst those featured regularly on these recordings, while the vocalists included Val Rosing, Pat O'Malley, Sam Browne, Elsie Carlisle and Jack Plant, though without a doubt the most important of his singers was the late Al Bowlly. Today the reissue LPs from this period invariably highlight Bowlly's vocals, even to the extent of giving his name more prominence on the sleeves than Noble's, but initially Bowlly's role was not considered any more important than that of any other singer.

For a while after he commenced recording Noble did not get any special billing; his titles were issued as by the New Mayfair Orchestra or the New Mayfair Novelty Orchestra. But their success led to a change of policy and in due course all records were released as by Ray Noble and his Orchestra. Noble's output was prodigious and some of it is of slight interest, yet, despite a prevalent rhythmic stodginess and lacklustre string passages, a reasonable number of the records has survived the passage of almost four decades remarkably successfully. Because Noble's was a studio band and this book is concerned primarily with groups which played in public, I shall discuss only its better recordings, but it can be said that all the reissue LPs by the orchestra are well worth obtaining.

Maybe It's Because, *How Could We Be Wrong*, *Close Your Eyes*, *Time On My Hands*, *Here Lies Love* and *Lazy Day* are examples of the Noble–Bowlly combination at its best. The excellent vocals are set within sympathetic and apt arrangements which include a variety of neat individual touches, such as the contrasting dynamics on *Here Lies Love*, the switching of lead parts on *Lazy Day*, the richness of the ensemble on the final chorus of *Close Your Eyes*, and the contrasts between reeds and brass in *Time On My Hands*. Benny Carter's well-known *Blues In My Heart* is sensitively interpreted by Noble, and includes rich saxophone scoring and a pleasant alto passage, while *You Ought To See Sally On Sunday* is in semi-hot vein and features good tenor and ensemble work. *The Very Thought Of You* and *Love Locked Out*, both Noble compositions, receive definitive treatments in versions which combine excellent scores and outstanding Bowlly vocals; the smooth blend of the sections and the varied ensemble textures are hallmarks of the leader's distinctive approach to ballads.

The popularity of Bowlly has led to a bias in the selection of material for reissue LPs; this has both a good and a bad side, on the one hand eliminating titles on which indifferent vocals by other singers lessen the value of the overall performance, but also excluding some of the better jazz-influenced performances. Five titles in a jazz vein have appeared on the anthology 'Jazz In Britain – The 30s', four of which were originally issued as by the Night Club Kings. Of the latter, *Allah's Holiday* and *Whispering* have the disadvantage of fairly dreadful vocals by Jack Plant, but there are more than adequate compensations in the excellent lyrical solos from trumpeter Norman Payne and the concise and rhythmic scores. Even better is *Who Walks In When I Walk Out* (released under Noble's name), which features good solos by Lew Davis and Freddy Gardner and spirited ensemble playing which in the last chorus employs call-and-response patterns.

Though Noble's considerable output of the 1929–34 period

includes its fair share of ephemera, at its best it achieved an alliance of individual scoring and sympathetic interpretation that makes it unique in the annals of British dance music. Ironically Noble was never able to obtain the same results from any regular band that he led, and he must be one of the very few personalities of the dance band era whose reputation was established solely on the basis of studio recordings.

Whether Ray Noble had any long-term influence on British dance band developments, other than in the most oblique manner, must be open to doubt, but the importance of Lew Stone both historically and musically cannot be questioned. Stone was born in London in 1898 and developed an interest in music from an early age. His first professional job of any importance was as pianist with Bert Ralton's band. Ralton, facing an imminent recording session, and lacking special arrangements, persuaded Stone to write some scores, an assignment he enjoyed and one that soon led to his recognition as one of the most inventive and advanced arrangers of the day. From

1927 he contributed a number of outstanding arrangements to Ambrose's book, but by 1931 the calls upon his service had become so extensive that he temporarily retired from his arranging activities to work as pianist with the Roy Fox band. A few months after his arrival Roy Fox was taken ill and Stone found himself both the band's unofficial leader and its arranger, a situation recognised by the Monseigneur Restaurant management when, in September 1932, they invited him to form his own band.

I said I'd need several days to think it over but the Monseigneur owner said he'd give me as long as it took to walk round the block. I'd got half way round when I found myself thinking what I might do with a band of my own so I went straight back and said yes.

The Lew Stone band opened at the Monseigneur on 24 October 1932 and remained in residence until November

Left: Al Bowlly, the outstanding British dance band vocalist of the '30s. Thirty years after his death in an air-raid a cult has grown around him. Below: on the back of this photo is 'Up at the Rainbow Room with financier Mr Morris of New York, Anna Neagle, Ray Noble, producer Herbert Wilcox and myself . . . Al Bowlly'.

Maniac's Ball and *Black Jazz*, put over with every ounce of the verve and precision for which his star personnel is already famous.

The personnel of Stone's band at this time was unquestionably

1933, sometimes doubling at variety theatres. The famous Tuesday night broadcasts commenced and 'Detector' of the *Melody Maker* (probably the late Edgar Jackson) wrote ecstatically:

In any case, I am certain that the most prejudiced listener will not disagree with me when I say that the broadcasts of the new Monseigneur Band have been, in a sense, staggering. Naturally everyone expected something extra good, but I doubt if many were prepared either for the extraordinarily high degree of instrumental finesse or the really intelligent selection of programmes which is being evinced.

The leaders of our broadcasting bands have always been shy of modern or futuristic music, and have usually played for safety all the time where the selection of programme is concerned. Now Lew Stone has come along and with one bold sweep cast all this prejudice aside by showing everyone that he is not afraid to feature such classic compositions as *Blue Ramble*,

an all-star one, and within its ranks could be found trumpeters Nat Gonella and Alfie Noakes, trombonists Lew Davis and Joe Ferrie, saxophonists Joe Crossman and Ernest Ritte, bassist Tiny Winters, drummer Bill Harty, and vocalist Al Bowlly. From late 1931 until 1935 Lew Stone was also working as musical director for British and Dominion Films, and it has been estimated that he was responsible for the music of some forty films, in some of which he and his band made personal appearances.

For the remainder of the period up to World War II Lew Stone led a hectic existence, his activities embracing club and theatre engagements, recording, further film work, broadcasting, directing musical shows and, in 1935, having the first edition of *Harmony And Orchestration For The Modern Dance Band* published. In November 1933 he moved to the Café Anglais, but four months later returned to the Monseigneur and remained there until the summer, when it closed and was sold for use as a cinema. He then went out on a provincial tour, but in the autumn lost Al Bowlly and Bill Harty, who left to join Ray Noble in the United States. In November 1934 he severed his connection with Decca and signed a contract with Regal Zonophone. The connection was not an altogether happy one for him and a year later he returned to Decca and recorded for them well into the '40s. On 14 February 1935 the Stone band opened at the Hollywood Restaurant, and in the following summer began an extensive theatre tour, which lasted until early 1936, when with a smaller personnel it became resident at the Café de Paris. In October of that year Stone became the musical director for the Rodgers and Hart musical 'On Your Toes', which opened in London's West End four months later. He remained with his band at the Café de Paris until 31 July 1937. During the next year he worked mainly as musical director on various films for the British National Company and on the show 'Hide And Seek', starring Bobby Howes and Cicely Courtneidge, but he continued to broadcast with pick-up groups. One such broadcast was reviewed in a 1938 *Melody Maker*, and the enthusiastic comments make it clear that he had lost none of his skill as a leader.

Lew Stone no longer has a dance band. His time is taken up with film work and directing the pit orchestra in 'Hide And

Seek' at the London Hippodrome. So he just picks up a bunch of lads, the same lads who are available to any other leader, has a brief run through the arrangements with them, and then goes into the studios and plays the heads off practically all the regular bands. How is it done?

The answer seems to be that we have the musicians, and that most of the shortcomings of our bands is due entirely to the inadequacy of our leaders. There is hardly a band in town that is as good as it ought to be on the ability of its rank and file, but the leaders get away with it by hiding behind the contention that they are giving the public what it wants. The sooner they realise that they are kidding themselves the better for all.

Left: Joe Crossman, member of several major British bands. Right: publicity material for Lew Stone and the Monseigneur Restaurant.

This broadcast was notable for the return of Al Bowlly, who had recently undergone an operation on his vocal cords, which, the *Melody Maker* reviewer assured his readers, 'has enriched the quality of his voice most noticeably'. Bowlly took part in broadcasts and personal appearances with the Stone band until shortly before his death in 1941.

Dance band fans rejoiced in the news that Stone would be assembling a twelve-piece band on the lines of the Monseigneur unit to play at the Trianon Restaurant from late April 1938; the musicians named to play in it included such ex-Stone

LEW STONE
& the
Monseigneur Band

ALL COMMUNICATIONS TO
Dan S. Ingman (MANAGER)
85 LONG ACRE, LONDON, W. C.
TEMPLE BAR 2468 (EXTENSION 58)
MAIDA VALE 5261 (PRIVATE)

MONSEIGNEUR
Luncheon
Theatre Dinner
Dinner
Supper Cabaret
LEW STONE AND
THE MONSEIGNEUR BAND
and
MANTOVANI'S TIPICA
ORCHESTRA
Extension of License
every Thursday until 2 AM

MONSEIGNEUR

MONSEIGNEUR

stalwarts as Alfie Noakes, Lew Davis, Joe Crossman, Ernest Ritte and Jock Jacobson. It was not long before Stone discovered that the company controlling the Trianon was in financial difficulties and that a receiver had been appointed to look into its affairs. He wisely decided that in the circumstances it was better to seek a more stable engagement. Shortly afterwards he was selected by Billy Butlin to provide one of the two bands – the other was Mantovani's – for the opening of his new holiday camp at Clacton, and he followed this with a week at another Butlin camp at Skegness, but of greater long-term importance was an offer to lead a band at London's Café de Paris. Stone opened there in September, leading a nine-piece band which, with additions, was to broadcast frequently

in the months ahead. In October he once more became musical director for a musical show – 'Under Your Hat', featuring Jack Buchanan – and held the job throughout 1939.

Once hotels resumed their entertainment policies during the war years a number of leaders, now faced with difficulties in maintaining good bands because of the call-up, settled into residencies. Stone opened at the Dorchester Hotel in June 1940, directing a seven-piece group which he led on the novachord; for broadcasts he used a large band and a smaller jazz group called the Stonecrackers. He remained at the Dorchester until June 1942, when he formed a large band, which toured military camps, ballrooms and theatres for the remainder of the war years. From January 1945 he was at a Southampton

hotel, leading a nine-piece group, the Novatones. He returned to London nine months later to play at the Embassy Club. From 1947 to 1949 he led the theatre orchestra for the show 'Annie Get Your Gun', in the autumn of 1948 resuming broadcasts, with a large band, which continued through most of the '50s. From 1951–3 he was resident at the Pigalle Restaurant, London, following which he moved to Oddenino's Restaurant until May 1955. For the next three years he did seasonal engagements for Mecca ballrooms in the north of England and Glasgow. In 1959 Lew Stone formed a sextet for broadcasting and was heard with this group until 1967, but his main activities were now devoted to an agency which supplied artists for private functions. In the last years of his life he became aware that interest in his earlier career was growing, and despite poor health he proved an unfailing source of help to researchers of his own activities and British dance music in general. His death on 13 February 1969, in his seventy-first year, came as a great blow to an extensive circle of friends and acquaintances both within and outside music.

The Lew Stone Band. Below (1933), left to right: Ernest Ritte, Albert Harris, Jim Easton, Lew Stone, Monia Liter, Harry Berly, Tiny Winters, Joe Ferrie, Joe Crossman, Lew Davis; seated, Nat Gonella and Alfie Noakes. Lower left (1933): Easton, Bill Harty, Winters, Al Bowlly, Noakes, Ferrie, Nat Gonella (standing), Davis; Stone has his back to the camera. Upper left (1935, on tour): (back row) Liter, Winters, Jock Jacobson, Stanley Black; (front row) Berly, Don Barrigo, Ritte, Crossman, Archie Slavin, Noakes, Ferrie, Tommy McQuater, Don Macaffer. Stone is by the microphone.

Because of Lew Stone's importance in the history of British dance music I have given a fuller description of his activities than I have generally been able to do for other bandleaders. It is easy to read the outline of his remarkably varied career, but less easy to understand what this sometimes meant in human terms. An article in a 1936 *Radio Review* detailed a week in Stone's career at the time, the most striking fact being that on no single day did he sleep for longer than seven hours; working days of sixteen to eighteen hours were not uncommon. Success on those terms was indeed hard earned, and, indeed, activity on such a scale was not uncommon for bandleaders during their peak years. Its effect on their health scarcely needs to be underlined.

Earlier in this chapter I mentioned that both leaders and musicians were sometimes influenced by the social attitudes of their club patrons, but Lew Stone certainly was not. Throughout his life he remained a socialist, acutely aware of the contrast between the lives of the average hotel and club frequenters and those of the population at large. If some reports are accurate, this awareness led him at times to minimise the value of his own activities, but he was also conscious of the high standards which he attempted at all times to maintain in his music. He was greatly respected by other musicians, and Joe Crossman reminisced not long ago:

I found Lew communicative and eager to discuss among the boys the arrangements he so ably planned. He was clever at discovering and developing hidden talent within the band. With his very imaginative orchestrations, we presented a stage show, which is remembered by a large and grateful audience.

The sax section was soon co-ordinated into a team which was the envy of many bandleaders, and together with the flexibility of the brass, presented a front line which made no demands on the rhythm section to carry them, and indeed the 'rhythm' provided plenty of inspiration.

Lew Stone was an innovator in several aspects of dance band orchestration, but his innovations did not stop there, for, amongst other developments, he pioneered – in Britain – the use of a female band-vocalist (Ella Logan) and the employment of the accordion in regular dance band instrumentation. Over the years he recorded prolifically, starting as early as September 1929 with some now rare titles for Duophone. In discussing a number of his better recordings it must be stressed that here,

as in similar instances throughout this book, only a fraction of the whole is covered, and the selection is very much a matter of personal choice.

Though some good titles were made for Regal Zonophone, as a whole they do not compare with the best of Stone's Decca output, and all titles mentioned below were originally made for the latter label. If, particularly in the later years, some of the material that Stone recorded seems trivial, it should be remembered that he did not have a free hand in its selection, often being sent a list of titles for his next session by the company recording director. Today the Lew Stone band is remembered by many of its former listeners chiefly for its hot recordings, amongst them many of the famous Gene Gifford numbers for

Nat Gonella.

Lew Stone and his band.

Lew Stone and his Band.

the Casa Loma Orchestra. These scores call for a high degree of ensemble precision and skilled individual musicianship, and the Stone band certainly possessed these virtues in abundance. Versions of *White Jazz* and *Blue Jazz* follow the Casa Loma performances in outline but include solo variations, Lew Davis and Joe Crossman (on clarinet) being heard to particular advantage. While the Casa Loma influence was present in a number of Stone recordings, it should not be given exaggerated importance.

Serenade For A Wealthy Widow and *Garden Of Weed*, two compositions by that singular and somewhat enigmatic musician Reginald Foresythe, received idiomatic treatment from the Stone band, the latter in particular capturing the emotional ambiguity of Foresythe's writing. On *Serenade* only the clattering drums behind Liter's piano seem out of place; before this passage Liter has a solo that is almost Thelonious Monk-ish in its stark harmonic structure. Of all the orchestral versions of Foresythe's compositions – excluding those which Foresythe himself directed – Stone's are by far the most sympathetic and skilfully performed. Of other jazz-inclined recordings *Milenberg Joys*, with its beautifully precise section work and good solos by Crossman and Davis; the extrovert *Tiger Rag*, with solos by Crossman, Davis, Gonella and Harry Berly; and Stone's excellent score of Paul Barbarin's *Call Of The Freaks* (made famous by the Luis Russell band), with solo space given to Crossman – a really splendid clarinet soloist with a distinctive, full, reedy tone – Davis, Berly, and a muted trumpeter I assume to be Noakes, are worthy of note.

It would be wrong to single out Stone's jazz-styled recordings, for, while he was noted for such performances, they form only a fraction of his output. In the '30s many listeners enjoyed the comedy performances, *Annie Doesn't Live Here Any More* and *Little Nell* being typical, but of considerably more lasting worth are the recordings of popular ballads of the day which featured Al Bowlly. In the course of listening to hundreds of records of the period I have encountered all the leading band singers, many of whom, it must be said, are exceedingly mediocre, and I am left with the impression that in his day Bowlly was virtually in a class by himself. Though a versatile singer, able to interpret a rhythmic number with competence, he was at his best in sentimental ballads, and the combination of Stone's arranging and Bowlly's singing on such numbers resulted in uniquely effective recordings. Above all, Stone was a subtle arranger, particularly able in writing backgrounds for Bowlly that employed textural, melodic and rhythmic variation. It is noticeable, when one compares recorded versions of numbers which Bowlly made with both Stone and other leaders, that the former are almost always superior. I suspect that the reason for this is that, while Stone was sensitive to the nature of the number being recorded, a basic astringency in his arranging style prevented sentiment descending to bathos. The results are shown in such performances as *Just Let Me Look At You*, *Easy Come Easy Go*, *How Could We Be Wrong*, *With My Eyes Wide Open I'm Dreaming* and *I'll Never Be The Same*, which to a large extent summarise all that is best in one aspect of the popular music of the '30s. Many recordings other than those I have named reflect the musical integrity and considerable skill of Lew Stone, as both leader and arranger, and of all the bandleaders of the peak years of British dance music he was the most consistent in avoiding the commonplace and encouraging what was inventive and musically satisfying. Consequently his place as one of the truly major figures in the history of popular entertainment remains indisputable.

Lew Stone and his Band, c. 1944: left to right – Chris Curtiss, Art Williams, Jim Easton, Stanley Flaun (saxes), Norman Burns (drums), Arthur Devy (piano), Teddy Wadmore (bass), Kip Heron, George Harper (trumpets), Bert Cooper, Gwyn Evans (trombone). Lew Stone spent most of the war years touring.

Roy Fox has already been mentioned in Lew Stone's career summary, and this dignified, immaculate figure was one of the most prominent and successful leaders of the '30s. He was born in Denver, Colorado, on 25 October 1901 but his parents moved to Hollywood when he was only a few months old, and it was here, at the age of eleven, that he first became interested in playing the cornet. Five years later he took his first professional job with an obscure band at Santa Monica, California, soon afterwards joining Abe Lyman. In 1920 Fox led a band for the first time – at the Club Royale in Culver City – and in the ensuing years he had resident engagements in Los Angeles, Miami and New York. One such location job, at the Montmartre Café in Hollywood, led to his being noticed by the executives of the Fox Film studios, who offered him a position as musical director. It was while working in this capacity that he received a cable inviting him to play an eight-week season at London's Café de Paris, and after slight initial hesitation he accepted, forming an eight-piece band consisting of American musicians.

Fox opened at the Café de Paris on 29 September 1930, but the reaction to his group was not enthusiastic. Matters were complicated by the management of the café regarding him as a solo attraction – at this time he had gained the sobriquet of 'The Whispering Cornetist' – and the other musicians as relatively unimportant. At the end of the engagement Fox remained in England, helped by the fact that Decca awarded him a contract to form a recording band; his work-permit from the Ministry of Labour was granted comparatively swiftly. He commenced recording in January 1931 and used the pick of the leading musicians and arrangers of the day, also directing a large orchestra for stage shows. His big break came in the spring of 1931, when he was invited to become resident bandleader at the newly-completed Monseigneur Restaurant, and he opened there on 27 May with an excellent personnel that included Nat Gonella, Sid Buckman, Joe Ferrie, Billy and Micky Amstell, Harry Berly, Lew Stone, Al Bowlly and Bill Harty. The band was at once recognised as outstanding and the BBC scheduled it for regular weekly broadcasts, but in the following October Fox was taken seriously ill and had to spend a spell in a sanitorium. In his absence the musical direction of the group fell to Lew Stone. After Fox's return the band continued as before for a while, but in October 1932 he and the Monseigneur management parted company by mutual agreement, all of the musicians except Sid Buckman remaining at the restaurant under Stone's leadership.

Fox's second band, which opened at the Café Anglais in Leicester Square, London, on 24 October, was built around a nucleus of five musicians who played at a club called the Spider's Web, and once more it was an immediate success. When he received an offer from the Kit-Cat Club the management of the Café Anglais released him from his contract, and he opened there with additional personnel on 16 January 1933. In the years that followed, this band, with inevitable personnel changes, remained immensely popular with audiences throughout Britain, undertaking club, stage, radio and recording engagements in profusion. After just over a year at the Kit-Cat Fox returned to the Café de Paris (the size of the bandstand necessitating a reduction in personnel), but he was only there from 5 March to 19 May 1934, when he undertook a nationwide theatre tour, a pattern which continued until the final break-up of the band in August 1938. While touring the Fox band broadcast from provincial studios and made recordings as schedules allowed, also appearing in a film titled *Radio Pirates*. In common with many leaders of the period, Fox made transcriptions for Continental radio stations – which, incidentally, show the band in a somewhat different light from that of its commercial recordings for Decca and HMV.

The years of touring affected Fox's health and in 1938 he

Lew Stone in the recording studio, 1934.

" Here is ROY FOX and his Band - - "

Now meet all the boys of the band. George Rowe and Freddie Welsh (trombones), Jack Nathan (pianist), Syd Buckman and Les Lambert (trumpets), Maurice Burman (drums), and Denny Dennis (vocalist) on his right. On his left is George Gibbs (bass). Immediately in front of the drums is Ivor Noirants, while Roy himself, of course, is at the microphone. The four saxophones in the front row (from left to right) are Rex Owen, Art Christmas, Hughie Tripp and Harry Gold, while Peggy Dell, of course, is at the piano on the extreme right

decided to go to Australia, where he fronted a band that was actually Jay Whidden's, unsuccessfully on all counts. Unable to return to Britain in the war years, he led small bands in

Roy Fox bands. Top: a mid-'30s line-up. Bottom: later in the '30s, with singer Mary Lee sitting on the bar. Right: a postwar combination.

New York, but in 1946 received permission to work in Britain once more and set about forming a new band, which included only Sid Buckman and Bobby Joy from the pre-war days.

This band toured during 1946–7, apart from a short residency at a London club, and spent the latter summer in the Isle of Man; then Fox led a smaller group at the Potomac Club in

NAT GONELLA AND
HIS GEORGIANS

TO THE "MELODY MAKER":
Here's Hoping We'll All "Swing" Together!

London for a while. Popular entertainment was in a state of flux and, in common with most of his fellow bandleaders of the '30s, Fox shortly afterwards decided that it was time to bow out. He devoted his energies from then on to an entertainment agency, which he still heads at the time of writing.

In considering some representative Fox recordings one can ignore the eight titles made with his 1930 American group – he had also recorded for American Brunswick before going to Britain – and the eight titles made with his post-war band, for these do not compare with the best of his output from 1931–8. In its personnel the Monseigneur band of 1931–2 was the most distinguished that Fox led, and, though not musically outstanding, the August 1931 version of his famous signature tune *Whispering* is interesting for a spoken introduction by him and a chorus of his cornet in the 'whispering' style later taken over by Sid Buckman. *Georgia On My Mind* is a number associated with Nat Gonella and the 1932 Fox recording features him effectively as vocalist and soloist, but in a hot vein *How'm I Doin'* and *Old Man Of The Mountain* are better overall performances and give an indication of the drive of the ensemble. A title such as *You're My Everything*, with its smooth scoring and impeccable playing, is probably more typical of Fox's basic approach, and has the advantage of a Bowlly vocal. The chief problem in assessing the band of this period is the often lamentable recording quality, and friends who heard the band in person at the Monseigneur assure me that the records do it scant justice.

Of the later recordings, some of the more overtly commercial are the most successful. *Blue Moments*, with a vocal by Jack Plant, is well scored and has such interesting touches as the use of baritone saxophone and clarinets on the theme and a passage by soprano-led saxophones. The soprano is again used neatly on *Maybe I'm Wrong Again*, at one point in conjunction

Above: after working with many leading bands Nat Gonella led his 'Georgians' for several years, mainly on theatre tours. Right: a '30s Ambrose line-up, with Sid Phillips (extreme right), Danny Polo (4th from right), Ted Heath (extreme left) and Max Goldberg (4th from left). Behind Ambrose stand Elsie Carlisle and Sam Browne.

with a muted trumpet. In 1935 Fox added the fourteen-year-old girl singer Mary Lee to his ranks, but though she was highly regarded by many listeners I find her style on such recordings as *It's Been So Long* and *Rhythm Lullaby* very affected. From late 1933 until the break-up in 1938 Fox's main vocalist was Denny Dennis, a stylist who at times owed much to Bing Crosby, and on such titles as *June In January*, *May I* and *Everything I Have Is Yours* his singing is well integrated into the sophisticated, rather bland approach of the band. Andy Hodgkiss's accordion and a soprano saxophone are used well in the score of *May I*, and despite their unadventurousness such performances as these probably best reflect the impeccable musicianship for which Fox was noted. There is, however, another side to the Fox band that is poorly represented on commercial records, and that is its swing style. *Londonola*, though a theme of crushing banality, has passages where the bite of the ensemble and its rhythmic drive come nearer to that of American swing bands than one would believe likely, and some versions of swing numbers from 1937–8, made for Continental radio programmes, are even more successful in this vein. Though Fox's records, of which nearly six hundred were made between 1930 and 1938, are very uneven, there can be no doubt that the best of them fully entitle him to be considered one of the three outstanding leaders on the British dance music scene during the '30s.

The third of these top three leaders is of course Ambrose. (His earlier career and some of his '20s recordings were discussed previously.) In the autumn of 1933 Ambrose returned to the Embassy Club, remaining there until 1936, when, on 14 September, he once more took up residence at the Mayfair Hotel. Six months later, in partnership with bandleader Jack Harris, he took over the management of Ciro's Club and led his band there, but the arrangement was unsatisfactory and by the autumn he had temporarily disbanded. Spring 1938 saw Ambrose leading his band at the Café de Paris, after which it went on a tour that included an engagement at the Paris exhibition. For a year, from autumn 1937, the band did not record, since Ambrose refused to renew his Decca contract on the terms offered. (The terms called for a reduction in fees, on account of the depressed state of the recording industry.) Early in 1938 he took a firm stand about his musicians taking outside engagements without his permission, and told a *Melody Maker* reporter that he fully intended to dismiss any member who defied his instructions.

I am certainly not going to maintain the best possible instrumentalists in my band just so that a lot of West-End orchestrators can gather them up from time to time, and snatch engagements at a cheaper price because they don't have to pay out weekly salaries.

I have already issued my ultimatum because I understood that some of my band were going to do a broadcast with Lew Stone who has no dance band available. I am sorry I have had to take this step in a case in which a so well respected and right-thinking fellow as Lew Stone is concerned, and I wish it were anyone else, but I have delayed my decision too long, and now I will make no exception in anybody's favour.

That he meant what he said was soon obvious, for a week later he dismissed trombonist Eric Breeze for disobeying his instructions. This action resulted in a hurried meeting of many of the musicians who undertook session work, and under the chairmanship of trombonist Ted Heath they issued a statement presenting their viewpoint, but the outbreak of war seven months later made the whole subject of purely academic interest.

For much of 1938 and 1939 the full Ambrose orchestra was inactive, but an octet toured the variety theatres in support of such leading Ambrose personalities as Max Bacon and Evelyn Dall. In August 1938 the full band did go out for a two-month tour, and a report of its appearance in Birmingham referred to 'eight curtain calls . . . tumultuous applause that could only be silenced by *God Save The King* . . . a rousing, roaring reception that took even the performers by surprise.' By October, however, the full band was again laid off and the octet resumed its theatre tour, now supporting Denny Dennis, Vera Lynn and Les Carew in addition to Bacon and Miss Dall. The following month the BBC claimed it could not afford to use the Ambrose band for studio broadcasts – location broadcasts led to a 25% cut in fees – but it must have relented or found some extra money by March 1939, when Ambrose led a pick-up unit on several occasions, presumably overcoming his objections to the use of star instrumentalists from other bands when he himself was not the one suffering raids!

On 22 December 1939 Ambrose finally led a resident band once more, at the Mayfair Hotel, his personnel including Tommy McQuater, Alfie Noakes, George Chisholm, Les Carew, Billy Amstell, Joe Jeannette, Andy McDevitt, Stanley Black, Tiny Winters and Ivor Mairants. This was probably the last really outstanding band that Ambrose led, and in March 1940 he lost many of its key members to the RAF, where they became part of the Squadronaires. Subsequently, in common with other wartime bandleaders, he struggled to maintain a stable personnel, and used the best of the remaining studio musicians to augment his group for recording sessions. The band played at the Mayfair throughout the

orchestra was noted for its high standards of musicianship and its discipline. The latter quality was emphasised by Joe Crossman when he compared the band to Lew Stone's:

On the other hand, the Ambrose band was more stringent, and a sense of discipline could be felt, which in turn was reflected in the style of clip phrases and a tight rhythmic background, but indeed it was just right for the Mayfair Hotel.

On a number of occasions Ambrose himself made far from complimentary remarks about the musical taste of the average patron of the clubs and hotels at which he played, and about the restraints imposed by such venues. He commented ironically that, while playing in Monte Carlo, 'if I couldn't hear the surf, I knew we were playing too loud'. Considering such factors, the ability of the better location bands to maintain outstanding musical standards is even more creditable than one might at first think.

Looking at some of Ambrose's more interesting '30s recordings, we may start with two performances from an HMV session of March 1930. Both *Moanin' For You* and *Cryin' For The Carolines* are smooth and well played, with reasonable vocals by Sam Browne. Sylvester Ahola takes a pleasant solo in *Moanin'* and clarinettist Danny Polo has a good eight-bar passage in *Cryin'*, but overall the most impressive qualities of both performances are the cohesion of the ensemble and the skilful arrangements, which make use of varying instrumental blends to effect tonal and textural contrasts. In many ways I myself enjoy Ambrose's records of the early '30s more than his later output, primarily because there is a balance between

blitz, but in September Ambrose himself had to hand in notice terminating the engagement and miss the final fortnight of its stay, as a result of ill health. By July 1941 a revised Ambrose octet, now including Carl Barriteau, Dave Wilkins, Aubrey Franks and Max Abrams, went back to touring the theatres, the stars of the act including only Anne Shelton and Les Carew of former Ambrose associates. Throughout the war and into the mid-'50s Ambrose continued to lead a band, but in 1956 he turned his attention to artist management, and he remained in this field until 18 June 1971, when he collapsed in a TV studio in Leeds and died in hospital a few hours later.

Throughout the years of its pre-eminence the Ambrose

musical discipline and freedom of individual expression that was later partly lost. This balance is obvious even on commercial titles like *Nevertheless* and *Free And Easy*, both of which have vocals by Sam Browne, who was at this time an uneven singer, but never more so than on one of Ambrose's classic recordings, *'Leven Thirty Saturday Night*. The number was brilliantly arranged by Lew Stone and the quality of the ensemble playing and solos is impressive, creating a performance that represents one of the peaks of early '30s dance band music. That Ambrose enjoyed a great popular success at this time is shown by the fact that in 1932 alone he had sixty-two records issued, or, in modern terms, the equivalent of about ten LPs.

From November 1934 to May 1949 Ambrose recorded for Decca, the best of this output being made in a period up to about 1943. With one exception – 'Tribute To Cole Porter' – the reissue LPs have tended to concentrate on the well-known instrumental performances, many featuring compositions and scores by Sid Phillips. A few of these – *Tarantula*, *Hick Stomp* and *B'Wanga* for example – are basically novelty numbers, though their interpretation leaves nothing to be desired, but on titles like *Cotton Pickers' Congregation*, *Night Ride*, and particularly the more relaxed *Early Morning Blues* and *Plain Jane*,

Top left: Ambrose and his orchestra with vocalists Sam Browne, Elsie Carlisle and the Three Rhythm Sisters. Bottom left: Danny Polo (2nd from right) at a 1938 recording session, with George Chisholm (5th from right) and guitarist Albert Harris. Below: Max Bacon, who also used his comedy talents on the halls. Right: Billy Amstell, a mainstay of Ambrose's reed section.

AMBROSE'S TIGER RAG !
SENSATIONAL RECORD OF THE YEAR

Phillips achieves real individuality, in such touches as the use of wordless vocal passages in *Cotton* or his reworking of traditional methods of dance band scoring in *Night*. *Early* and *Plain* have the advantage of excellent solos from trombonist George Chisholm and trumpeter Tommy McQuater, but while the Ambrose band over the years invariably included its jazz contingent it never really succeeded in swinging as a group. A slightly out-of-character recording is *Tootin' Around*, a Billy Amstell theme arranged in a Dixieland style, which has good solos from the composer, Chisholm and McQuater. The smooth, technically impeccable Ambrose ballad style is heard on such numbers as *I Get A Kick Out Of You*, *After You* and *Dinner At Eight*, which all have nostalgic vocals by Sam Browne, but the comedy duets of Elsie Carlisle and Sam Browne, immensely popular with radio listeners during the '30s, have not been reissued to date, and American vocalist Evelyn Dall is only heard on an occasional track. Though Ambrose was responsible for a good deal of ephemera during his years as a leader, his overall concern with high musical standards justifies his reputation as one of the major figures of the dance band era.

Whereas Lew Stone, Roy Fox and Ambrose produced the most impressive recorded work in Britain during the '30s, the premier European show band was that led by Jack Hylton. It was formed in 1924, and from New Year's Eve of 1927 until 1938 it undertook no fewer than sixteen European tours, playing in almost every country and recording at different times in Czechoslovakia and Germany. These tours were interspersed with lengthy appearances throughout Britain, and just how successful Hylton became is made clear by the fact that in July 1928 he declined an offer of £40,000 for the exclusive services of himself and his band for one year at the Empire Cinema in London's Leicester Square. In May 1929 he was to have led his band at the Roxy and Paramount theaters in New York City for a fee in the region of £1,100 a week, but a threatened strike by the pit musicians at these venues resulted in the cancellation of the projected engagements. It has been calculated that in 1929 alone the Hylton band gave no fewer than 700 performances and travelled over 63,000 miles, in addition to which its sales of records for the year totalled a staggering 3,180,000.

Elsie Carlisle (above) and Sam Browne (opposite, top left) became immensely popular during the 1930s as a result of their singing with the Ambrose Orchestra. Jack Hylton (opposite, top right) has famous guest star Maurice Chevalier on a broadcast, and below, leads his band on one of many stage engagements.

To list only a few of the Hylton highlights of the '30s will give a fair indication of the band's popularity. In August 1930 Hylton himself was decorated at Deauville for has services to France and music, and in the following year he played a concert at the Opera House, Paris, which included excerpts from Stravinsky's operetta 'Mavra', in the presence of the composer. It was also in 1931 that Hylton's became the first British band to broadcast direct to the United States; previously it had presented radio programmes in Nice, Prague and Vienna. Its arranging staff at the time comprised Billy Ternent, Paul Fenoulhet, Leighton Lucas and Peter Yorke. In 1932 Hylton was refused an entry permit to play in the USSR but still covered 30,000 miles of Europe in his touring, while 1933 saw him negotiating the successful British tour of Duke Ellington, with whose orchestra he shared the bill on part of a Continental trip. The tenth anniversary of the Hylton band, in 1934, was celebrated with a special programme at London's Holborn Empire, and in the same year it appeared on film for the first time. The fourteenth European tour, in 1935, saw Coleman Hawkins added as a solo attraction. This was the tour in which the band had a great triumph in Germany, despite the objections of a writer in the Nazi magazine *Kultur*, but when in the autumn it arrived in the United States for a series of engagements it ran into a ban from the American Federation of Musicians and returned minus Hylton and some key personalities to play a few British dates prior to disbandment.

Hylton retained the services of arrangers Billy Ternent and Melle Weersma, and speciality acts Alec Templeton, Peggy Dell, Eve Beck and Pat O'Malley, and triumphed in the United States with an American personnel, undertaking regular broadcasts and theatre and hotel engagements. When he returned to England in July 1936 he set about forming a new band and the previous pattern of touring continued, the final European trip being undertaken in 1938. In 1939 the Hylton band appeared in the film *Bandwaggon*, and after the

outbreak of war it broadcast frequently, leaving Britain on a single occasion in April 1940 to present concerts at the Paris Opera House. At the end of that month the band broke up, but some of its personnel broadcast in the war years as 'The Dance Orchestra', under Billy Ternent's leadership. On 13 November 1950 Hylton himself conducted a show band for a Royal Command Performance at the London Palladium.

With his vast knowledge of staging shows it was only natural that Hylton should turn to the role of impresario, and from the late '30s this occupied more and more of his time. He was associated with a string of successful shows, perhaps his most famous being ITMA, which he presented as a stage revue, and the Crazy Gang, which ran in one form or another for over twenty years until 1963. In 1964 Hylton fulfilled a personal ambition when he put on the musical show 'Camelot' at the Drury Lane Theatre – it achieved a run of several years – but the following winter he became ill, and he died three days after admittance to hospital, on 29 January 1965.

Hylton once set down his ideas on music in an article entitled 'The British Touch', and though it reads rather oddly today it does afford an interesting insight into his method of working. After referring to the need to achieve a balance of rhythm, melody and harmony, and describing his music as symphonic syncopation, he says:

Shall I be giving away a secret if I confess that I receive weekly all the latest music from America which is arranged and scored precisely in the same manner in which it is played in America? I examine all the music in detail and have tried much of it live, but it has not appealed to the public. Before it can be played here it must be modified, given the British touch, which American and other foreigners never understand. In the dance halls or gramophone record alike it makes a subtle appeal to our British temperament, it is in fact becoming a truly national music.

It is unfortunate that Hylton was not more explicit in defining the 'British touch', and did not tell readers exactly what changes the numbers underwent before being accepted by the British public, but the consistency of his record sales and his drawing power as a theatre attraction suggest that he did have a great understanding of what that public liked. Of all the major leaders of his day Hylton relied least upon broadcasting,

Hylton led the most famous, and largest, show band in Europe for over a decade, and is shown above with his line-up of the mid-'30s. Opposite, top: Jack Hylton and his band outside the Monte Carlo Opera House. Bottom: some of 'Poggy' Pogson's instruments.

though this was obviously counterbalanced by the frequency of his nation-wide theatre appearances. The musical parallels with Paul Whiteman need no stressing; Hylton too had a repertoire of light classics, popular hit songs and more ambitious works; but there were also definite differences in presentation and programming. To some extent Hylton remains something of an enigma as a musician, for his sponsorship of Coleman Hawkins, his bringing over Duke Ellington to Europe, and his use of jazz musicians such as the excellent French trumpeter Philippe Brun suggest an interest in jazz that was far from opportunist. Spike Hughes made a revealing comment about the period when he worked with Hylton: 'I don't think Jack will mind my saying that I was bored to hell playing at his sessions, but there I think he was too and anyway, I could do with the money.'

Hylton recorded for HMV until the autumn of 1931, then switched to Decca, then returned to HMV in March 1935 and stayed with it until the end of his bandleading career. An LP of his HMV period from 1926–31 includes such eminently forgettable trivialities as *Shepherd Of The Hills, Rhymes, Me And Jane In A Plane* and *Ain't That A Grand And Glorious Feeling*, also a curiosity in Sam Browne singing *I Must Have That Man* without changing the last word of the title, but Billy Ternent's arrangements of *Tiger Rag* and *Limehouse Blues* are excellent and these performances include some agreeable solos and splendid playing from the trumpets. The April 1926 version of *Oh Miss Hannah*, despite its jerky rhythm, has very assured section work for the period, while Leo Vauchant's score of *Diga Diga Doo* is well conceived, though the solos are generally better than the somewhat turgid ensemble passages. A further LP of 1932–3 Decca recordings is more commercial in selection, and, while the overall musicianship cannot be faulted, there is little to be heard that can be considered particularly individual or creative. Pat O'Malley, who returned to the United States in the '30s to become a well-known radio and later TV personality, takes nostalgic vocals in *Love Is The Sweetest Thing, We Just Couldn't Say Goodbye, By A Waterfall, Moonstruck* and *Auf Wiedersehen, My Dear*, all examples of

the better type of melodic songs commonplace during the '30s.

That Hylton's band of this period was nevertheless the most satisfying he led is clear from a reissue which contains some splendid performances. Billy Ternent's *Black And Blue Rhythm* is an attractive exercise in Ellingtonia, while the medley of *Black And Tan Fantasy*, *It Don't Mean A Thing*, *Mood Indigo* and *Bugle Call Rag*, though perhaps a pastiche, is very skilfully performed. *Dinah* is in the take-off routine which was to become familiar; the artists impersonated are Lombardo, Tommy Dorsey, Louis Armstrong (atrociously!), Whispering Jack Smith and Crosby. It gives the mood of a Hylton show speciality, but, though amusing, cannot match *St*

Edward Pogson was much in demand as a sideman and recording artist during the peak years of the dance band era.

Louis Blues and *Hylton Stomp*, which display the band at its best. Such performances as the latter, and the spirited backings to Coleman Hawkins on *Darktown Strutters' Ball* and *My Melancholy Baby*, are examples of the Hylton band realising its potential, and demonstrate beyond doubt its versatility and assured musicianship.

From January 1933 to June 1937, with only occasional breaks, Mrs Jack Hylton, the former Ennis Parkes, led a touring variety band whose itinerary was generally confined to Britain but included one European trip during February–

March 1934. Mrs Hylton, who met her husband-to-be at a concert party, made her debut as a bandleader in the mid-'20s, when she fronted the Metro-Gnomes, a group that included Ted Heath, E. O. Pogson, Al Starita and Phil Cardew. Despite the presence at different times of such musicians as Philippe Brun, Jimmy Macaffer and Jack Raine, and the fact that it backed Coleman Hawkins for a brief period in the summer of 1934, her band was not distinguished in any way – as its records bear out rather too clearly. It does not seem that Jack Hylton had any direct control of the band or its musical policy; if he had, one suspects that its contributions would have been less undistinguished.

Hylton's only real rival in the show band/variety area was Jack Payne. Payne was born at Leamington Spa, Warwickshire, on 22 August 1899, and an early ambition to be an aviator was realised when he served in the Royal Flying Corps during World War I. While in the RFC he organised small dance bands and became sufficiently interested to consider following a career in the field, and after the war he led a variety of groups at different venues. In 1925 he approached the management of the Hotel Cecil, situated in the Strand, London, and secured an engagement there with a six-piece group, enlarging it to a ten-piece when the BBC commenced relays from the hotel in December of that year. In February 1928 Payne was appointed Director of Dance Music to the BBC, and with seven broadcasts a week, records for Regal and later Columbia, and stage appearances that commenced at the London Palladium in April 1930, he became a national figure.

His line-up at the BBC included such outstanding musicians of the day as trumpeter Jack Jackson, multi-reed man E. O. Pogson, and violinist Eric Siday. This personnel was contracted to him, not to the BBC, so when he finally decided to leave and concentrate on touring he was able to take his sidemen with him. In 1932, the year in which he decided on this course, ten of his musicians broke away after a dispute and formed a co-operative group called The Barnstormers, which billed itself as 'Pleasure Without Payne' – until Payne won an injunction forbidding the use of the description.

Payne replaced the errant musicians and continued to be immensely popular as both stage attraction and recording artist; his Rex records from 1934 were encased in a sleeve that showed a picture of himself and the band. In 1936 the band had a very successful tour of South Africa, and its chief vocalist Billy Scott-Coomber sang a few choruses in Afrikaans on some numbers. In May 1937, however, Payne dismayed his followers by announcing that he was retiring from personal stage appearances to take over the direction of his stud farm in Buckinghamshire, though he would continue home and Continental broadcasts and occasional Sunday concerts. He was, by this time, also a very active impresario with numerous road shows under his control, but, unable to resist tempting offers for personal appearances, he recommenced touring in February 1938, leading a twenty-piece band as part of a show titled 'Round The Dial'.

At some time in 1939 Payne again temporarily disbanded, but he re-formed in time to become the first leader to take his band to play for the troops in France, commencing with a concert on Christmas Day. By February 1940 he was back touring in Britain, but not before engaging in a verbal battle with the head of NAAFI about the poor quality of the entertainment offered to the troops. In the following year he took over from Billy Ternent as the BBC's resident dance band leader, a position he held until 1946. After this he returned to theatrical management once again, but during both the '50s and the '60s he worked as a compère and disc jockey on a number of BBC programmes. It appears that his role as an impresario was not always successful, and on several occasions he became involved in litigation. His last years were plagued by the ill health that led to his death at Tunbridge Wells on 4 December 1969. He appeared in one film, *Say It With Music*

(1935) – the title of his signature tune and of one of the two books which he wrote.

Between 1927 and 1936 Payne was a prolific recorder, but afterwards he took part only in occasional sessions. Between June 1928 and March 1932 he averaged 96 titles annually, an average which dropped to 60 when he switched to the Crystalate Record Company, for whom he recorded between 1932 and 1936. Many of his releases were comedy numbers, medleys from musical shows and period ephemera, but occasionally he produced a proficient instrumental performance like *Choo Choo, Hot And Heavy* and *Hot Bricks*. The last-named, written by the Belgian brass instrumentalist and arranger Peter Packay, includes a remarkably accomplished trombone solo from, presumably, Jesse Fuller, but such titles were not normal for Payne, and his average recordings now have little to recommend them other than nostalgic appeal. A session of April 1935 produced a surprise in the shape of a version of *My Dance* which featured a piano solo by the black American artist Garland Wilson, but most people now recall Payne for such performances as *Say It With Music* (his signature tune), *My Brother Makes The Noises For The Talkies* and *You Can't Do That There 'Ere*. For many, his name brings back memories of their earliest days of radio listening. On the somewhat undemanding musical level at which he operated, Jack Payne was, without doubt, eminently successful.

When Payne decided to leave the BBC in 1932 the Corporation was faced with the prospect of finding a replacement within a few months, and the choice fell on Henry Hall. Hall was born at Clapham, London, in 1898 and in his youth was associated with the Salvation Army in its musical editorial office. Later he undertook musical studies at Trinity College and the Guildhall School of Music. After World War I he worked in variety, as a cinema pianist, and then in 1924 became a bandleader for the first time at the Gleneagles Hotel in Perthshire, Scotland, fronting a six-piece group that made its initial BBC broadcast on 4 June. In 1930 Hall's success was such that he was the musical director for all the hotels owned by the London, Midland & Scottish Railway, controlling altogether thirty-two bands. This wide experience was probably the main reason for his selection by the BBC. His first broadcast with his BBC Dance Orchestra took place on 15 March 1932, and within a short while he had established himself as a nation-wide favourite. The band was at Radio Olympia during August 1933 and after this made stage appearances as schedules permitted, the almost obligatory starring role in a film taking place in 1935 when *Music Hath Charms* was produced. From 1934 until the end of his BBC tenure Hall featured a weekly 'Guest Night' show, introducing stars from the theatre, the variety halls and the musical world, and his regular broadcasting schedule was heavier than that of his predecessor.

In the late summer of 1937 Hall gave in his notice to the BBC and announced his intention of forming a touring unit; it opened at the Birmingham Hippodrome on 25 September. The band toured the provinces for two months before making its London debut on 29 November by doubling at the Finsbury Park and Holborn Empires. The *Melody Maker* suggested that no great musical heights were attained, but commented: 'there is no doubting the fact that, as far as his immense public is concerned, he can do no wrong.'

In February 1938 the Hall band went to Germany to play at the National-Scala Theatre in Berlin, Hall arousing understandable ire in British critics by his decision to remove all songs by Jewish composers. He later explained:

In eliminating Jewish tunes from our programme for Germany, we do not want to appear to approve of the racial prejudice existing in that country.

On the other hand, we are not going over there to make trouble, and common sense tells us that it is only reasonable that we should formulate a programme that will be acceptable to people who are going to listen to us there.

In fairness to Hall, who is, I imagine, an apolitical figure, it may be mentioned that his position was no different from that of many other British visitors to Nazi Germany during the '30s. At least his band did not follow the example of certain British sportsmen, who on one occasion even gave the Nazi salute.

The Hall band continued touring the theatres until the outbreak of war, when, in common with many other groups, it concentrated on playing to the troops in ENSA shows and making frequent broadcasts. Soon after the war Henry Hall retired from bandleading and became an impresario, producing such popular shows as 'Annie Get Your Gun' and 'High Button Shoes', but for a period from 1953 was involved in a popular BBC-TV series titled 'Face The Music'. He has lived in semi-retirement for some years but still has an interest in a theatrical agency.

Henry Hall first recorded in 1924 and during 1931 and 1932 made some titles for Decca, but from February 1932 until May 1939 appeared on the Columbia label. It has to be remembered that his role as official BBC resident dance band leader limited his freedom of choice in the presentation of adventurous material. In a conversation with me he made the point that in late-morning or afternoon broadcasts the younger listeners had to be catered for, and in general jazz-inclined numbers were out, but on late-night shows the more interesting scores were played – if only, in his own words, 'to stop the musicians going to sleep'. In 1936 he engaged the famous American bandleader, arranger and multi-instrumentalist Benny Carter,

but through union restrictions Carter only made a couple of guest radio appearances with the band. However, he contributed over three dozen arrangements to its book. Unfortunately only five of these were recorded and none have been reissued, but there are a few characteristic Carter touches on such titles as *One, Two, Button Your Shoe* and *What's The Name Of That Song*.

Other Hall recordings of interest include *East Wind* and *Wild Ride*, both written by the leader and arranged by Benjamin Frankel, and the two-part *Southern Holiday*, which features its composer Reginald Foresythe on the piano, but the one available LP reissue concentrates on such popular favourites as *Little Man You've Had A Busy Day*, *The Man On The Flying Trapeze*, *Butterflies In The Rain* and *Here's To The Next Time*. The anthology 'Jazz In Britain – The 30s' includes an ingenious Burton Gillis arrangement of an old Original Dixieland Jazz Band favourite, *Eccentric*, featuring a well played clarinet duet. Though not in the same class as the leading bands of the '30s, Henry Hall's BBC Dance Orchestra is still remembered with affection by thousands who regularly listened to it during its heyday.

Below and lower right: Henry Hall and his BBC Dance Orchestra during broadcasts. Upper right: Benny Carter leads an all-star jazz group in the recording studio, 1936. The saxophonists are Harry Hayes, Buddy Featherstonhaugh (hidden) and George Evans; Leslie Thompson and Tommy McQuater are in the centre of the brass group. The rhythm section is Al Craig (drums), probably Wally Morris (bass), Eddie Macaulay (piano) and Albert Harris (guitar).

To the public at large the name of Harry Roy was as big in the '30s as those of Ambrose, Roy Fox, Jack Hylton and Lew Stone, and his Friday night broadcasts were considered amongst the entertainment highspots of the week. Harry Roy was born in London on 12 January 1900, and after a training in business management worked for a time in his father's box-manufacturing company. The firm lost money in World War I, and after the Armistice Harry joined his brother Sidney and organised a dance combination, known as the Darnswells, which played at the Fitzroy Galleries in Oxford Street. When the Original Dixieland Jazz Band left the Hammersmith Palais they were replaced by the Roy brothers with their Original Lyrical Five, and up to 1926 their group, now called The Original Crichton Lyricals, played engagements at the Café de Paris, Oddenino's, Rector's Club and the Cavour Restaurant. On 20 December 1926 they opened at the Alhambra in Leicester Square, doubling at the London Coliseum, and they switched to the Café de Paris in February 1927. In March 1928 the brothers went with their group to South Africa and later Australia, and upon their return to England appeared in a show titled 'Variety Pie'. In January 1930 they toured Germany, recording in Berlin, but in the following year Harry Roy went out under his own name and led a band at a Leicester Square theatre. Sidney Roy continued for a while, as a stage and recording artist, subsequently becoming Harry's manager.

In 1932 Harry Roy and his band played at the London Pavilion, moving in January 1933 to the Café Anglais, where it commenced its successful broadcasting career. Roy's big break came in March 1934, when he secured an engagement at the Mayfair Hotel. It lasted until his decision to return to theatre work in June 1936, ten months after his much-publicised marriage to Miss Elizabeth Brooke, daughter of the Rajah of Sarawak. The Harry Roy band proved a popular stage attraction, and on 16 April 1938 it left London – serenaded by Bram Martin's band in appropriate showbiz style – for a three-month tour of South America. Just before leaving Roy organised a juvenile band under the leadership of Johnny Green for a tour of variety theatres, and while Green himself later worked with the main Roy band and Harry Parry, the history of the juvenile orchestra is obscure. When Roy returned to Britain the following August he reported that his tour had been a great success, adding that his most popular number had been a now forgotten opus titled *Rita The Rhumba Queen*! For the greater part of a year it seems that Roy was inactive, but just after the onset of war he re-formed a band that went into the Café Anglais on 16 October 1939, and in the following month he was featured in the show 'Eve On Parade' at the Garrick Theatre, the first London stage appearance he had undertaken in four years. Four months later the band was part of a new show at the Stratford Empire, and the *Melody Maker* reported a

greater concentration on music than in previous Roy stage presentations. After ten months of touring it became resident at the Embassy Club on 6 October 1940, at which point it lost the services of Joe Crossman to the RAF.

The remainder of the war years saw the Harry Roy band alternating between resident jobs – one was a return to the Embassy Club in September 1942 – and tours, including one to play for the forces in the Middle East. At around the same time as the second Embassy job, a small group led by Reg Owen and billed as Harry Roy's Tiger Ragamuffins was playing at Prince's Restaurant, Piccadilly, its personnel including the excellent jazz tenor saxophonist Jimmy Skidmore. In 1948 Roy went to the United States but was refused a work permit, so he rebuilt a band in the following year to play at the Café Anglais. He achieved a temporary success with his version of *Leicester Square Rag*, but as the '50s went by drifted out of full-time music and at one point was managing a restaurant. Early in 1969, only a year short of his seventieth birthday, he led a quartet during intervals of the show 'Oh Clarence' at the Lyric Theatre in London, and in a couple of TV interviews he gave the impression that he had fallen on difficult times. His health was failing and after a short illness he died in London during February 1971, survived by his second wife.

The early records of the Sid Roy group, released as by Sid Roy's Crichton Orchestra, the Crichton Lyricals, and The

Left: Syd Roy's Lyricals; Syd is sitting on the piano, Harry Roy is on the right.

Lyricals, are not very common and none have been reissued, but a few I have heard contain solos of value. Roy's own records are not on the whole of great musical interest; the earlier ones are marred by the square piano duets of Ivor Moreton and Dave Kaye (who left to go into variety in January 1936) and the clattering drumming of Joe Daniels, and frequently by the novelty material. When Stanley Black and Norman White replaced Moreton and Kaye, and Ray Ellington took over from Daniels, the position improved, but not, generally, the material. The two-piano team often recorded with a bassist, a drummer and Roy himself on clarinet, as Harry Roy's Tiger Ragamuffins, and some of their titles have quite pleasant low-register work from the leader. In fairness to Roy one has to remember that the record companies were anxious to maintain his 'King Of Hot-cha' image and pressed him to use as much as possible of the bowdlerised rag material with which he was associated, but even on such numbers there are surprises like the excellent alto solos by Nat Temple on *Twelfth Street Rag* and *Roy Rag*, the latter a Roy composition which at one point uses a comparatively advanced harmonic sequence. *Limehouse Blues* and *Spanish Shawl*, apart from the two piano passages, are good band performances and include several

creditable solos. To those familiar only with Roy's novelty records *Clarinet Marmalade* and *When A St Louis Woman Comes Down To New Orleans* will come as a great surprise. The former has assured ensemble work and good solos, including one on clarinet by Roy himself in a distinctly New Orleans vein, while the latter, with its driving brass, pleasant clarinet solo and modern-sounding score, is one of the best items Roy ever recorded.

In the minds of many listeners Roy is thought of as a vaude-villian, and certainly his vocals are in that idiom, but while realistic about his clarinet playing he could on occasion perform ably enough. One of his idols was Larry Shields of the Original Dixieland Jazz Band, whom he had heard at the Hammersmith Palais; a less fortunate influence was Ted Lewis. Given a free hand Roy might have chosen to record less in a novelty vein, and perhaps it is irrelevant to judge most of his output by strict musical standards, for to his public he was above all an entertainer and in that capacity his achievements entitle him to consideration as one of the major figures of the dance band era. Like most of his contemporaries he appeared with his band in films during the '30s, the two in which he was featured being *Everything Is Rhythm* (1935) and *Rhythm Racketeers* (1936).

The late Carroll Gibbons always gave the impression of being a modest man, in both a personal and a musical sense, yet within presumably self-imposed limitations he achieved standards that are not to be lightly dismissed. He was born at Clinton, Massachusetts, on 4 January 1903. He went to Britain as a young man with the intention of furthering his piano studies at the Royal Academy of Music, and it was almost an accident that caused him to take up a career in dance music. His association with the early Savoy bands has been outlined earlier, and in speaking of Ray Noble in the present chapter it was mentioned that he was musical director for the Gramophone Company during 1928 and part of 1929. Upon his return to Britain after spending 1930 and 1931 in Hollywood as a staff composer for MGM, he became joint director with Howard Jacobs of the Savoy Hotel Orpheans, assuming sole leadership when Jacobs moved to the Berkeley Hotel. While working at the Savoy he also broadcast frequently, made numerous records for Columbia and wrote the music for such films as *Rookery Nook* and *Calling All Stars*.

Just prior to the outbreak of World War II Gibbons went to the United States for a holiday and had difficulty in returning, but he managed to do so in November 1939 and at once formed a sixteen-piece touring band with a personnel that included trumpeters Laurie Payne and Frenchie Sartell, trombonist Paul Fenoulhet and vocalist Anne Lenner. The *Melody Maker* reported of one appearance that it was 'musicianly and tasteful in the extreme, with Carroll's own piano playing, of course, a

Left: Ivor Moreton and Dave Kaye grew so popular as members of Harry Roy's band that they became vaudeville and recording artists in their own right. Above and upper right: Carroll Gibbons, with his vocalist Anne Lenner and with his Savoy Orpheans in the recording studio. Lower right: interior of the London club 'The Bag O' Nails', popular during the '30s.

highspot of the performance'. One member of Gibbons's Savoy personnel of 1939, Ian Stewart, is now leading the resident band there. From mid-January 1940 Gibbons was back at the Savoy, leading an eleven-piece band, and during the war years he was a frequent broadcaster. At the same time he continued to compose music for films and also branched out as a writer for stage shows, such as 'Gaiety' and 'Big Boy'. In 1950 he was made director of entertainment for the Savoy Hotel, a position he held until his death after a short illness on 10 May 1954.

Gibbons's most famous composition was his band's signature tune *On The Air*, and he recorded it with Dorothy Stedeford's precise musical-comedy vocal and passages by the American violinist Matty Malneck. Although largely functional and unadventurous, such titles as *A Nightingale Sang In Berkeley Square*, *Room 504* and *Home*, the first two with pleasant vocals from Anne Lenner, are played in a polished manner and have an agreeable nostalgic quality about them. *When Day Is Done* was an unaccompanied piano solo, and though there was a simplicity in his style it was at base a deceptive simplicity, for his embellishment of the melody on this number and others revealed numerous highly personal touches. Gibbons was above all the embodiment of the skilled professional musician, and a man whose talent was greater than his somewhat self-deprecatory manner suggested.

Dance bands proliferated in Britain during the '30s to the same extent as rock groups do in the '70s. While the London-based hotel and club bands received most of the publicity, every provincial city of any size possessed one well-established

dance orchestra. To list them all would call for a work of encyclopaedic proportions, so I shall discuss them only briefly – a task made easier by the fact that, with only a few exceptions, their musical contributions were not significant.

The longest-term bandleader of all was the late Billy Cotton. He was born in London on 6 May 1899, and became a drummer boy in the army as a youth; during the latter years of World War I he joined the Royal Flying Corps. He led a band while a member of the RFC and in the post-war years formed several groups, including one for the 1924 Wembley Exhibition, but his real breakthrough came in 1928, when he was booked to appear at the Astoria in London's Charing Cross Road and organised a band which included a nucleus of musicians who stayed with him for many years. After the Astoria residency the

band moved on to the Locarno, Streatham, and Ciro's Club in both London and Paris, but by the mid-'30s it had become a touring stage unit. It survived the passing of the dance band era, and the Billy Cotton Band Show became a popular TV programme up to the time of Cotton's death on 25 March 1969, though the band itself had a strictly subsidiary role in its latter years. During the '20s Cotton was a talented footballer, and in the '30s he became a well-known racing driver. For part of the '30s the Cotton band was a reasonable unit, employing such musicians as Nat Gonella, Teddy Foster, Jack Doyle and the black American trombonist Ellis Jackson, who was also an energetic tap dancer. (As late as 1969 he was reported to be still active in British variety, at the age of eighty. One of my fondest boyhood memories is of Ellis Jackson cavorting about the stage during a number titled *Skirts*.) Such early Cotton recordings as *New Tiger Rag*, *St Louis Blues*, *Truckin'* and *Shine* are quite creditable hot performances, but to the public at large Cotton will always be remembered as a showman and entertainer, a role in which his warmth of personality was well displayed.

Any reader who recalls Maurice Winnick's band will be surprised to learn that it took part in a 'Jazz Jamboree' in 1940, for Winnick was a fanatical admirer of Guy Lombardo and modelled his own group on similar lines. Born in Manchester in 1902, Winnick studied the violin at that city's College of

Below: Billy Cotton and his band, with Teddy Foster (2nd row, 2nd from right) and Ellis Jackson (front row, 2nd from right). Left: Cotton in a '30s musical film. Upper right: at Ciro's Club, late 1930. Lower right: Maurice Winnick and his vocal quartet.

Music, and his first professional work was in cinema orchestras. In 1928 he organised an eight-piece band for the Plaza, Manchester, shortly afterwards taking over as director of Jan Ralfini's orchestra at the Nottingham Palais. By the early '30s he was in London, with residencies at the Hammersmith Palais de Danse, the Carlton Hotel and Ciro's, among others. In November 1934 he opened the San Marco Restaurant in Piccadilly, and first broadcast from this location the following January. Later in 1935 he replaced Harry Roy at the Mayfair Hotel. After similar resident engagements in the next four years Winnick opened at the Dorchester Hotel on 20 April 1939, and after a temporary reduction in his eleven-piece band surprised the music world during December 1939 and January 1940 by engaging trombonist Ted Heath, trumpeter Bill Shakespeare, pianist-arranger Bert Barnes and tenor saxophonist Don Barrigo, followed in February by Joe Crossman. At this time Winnick's vocalists for broadcasts were Al Bowlly and Dorothy Carless. Rather than reduce his personnel, as the Dorchester management requested, Winnick terminated his engagement there on 31 May 1940. His band became quite popular during the remainder of the war years, but when popular entertainment moved away from the dance orchestras he disbanded and became a contractor for television shows.

He died at some time in the '60s. The Winnick band made a number of records, and while some have the merit of Al Bowlly's presence they are generally undistinguished.

The pianist Charlie Kunz, born at Allentown, Georgia, around the turn of the century, first went to England in 1922 with an all-American group and played at various London restaurants. He later formed a local band and was resident at the Chez Henri Club from 1925 to 1933, switching in March 1933 to the Casani Club, where he became known for his broadcasts. Later in the '30s Kunz commenced work as a stage attraction, though he once admitted that he preferred playing in small clubs, and on 16 October 1938 he made history by becoming the first dance band musician to broadcast over the BBC on a Sunday. His popularity rested on his simple, melodic piano playing, and increasingly he recorded as a soloist on medleys of popular hit material. He remained in Britain until his death in 1960. Though his band recordings are mediocre, the Casani Club Orchestra was by all accounts a proficient functional dance unit.

Sydney Lipton made his debut at London's Grosvenor House Hotel in July 1932 and is still there in 1971 as its director of music, though now seldom actually taking the stand. He was born in London in 1905, and his first professional engage-

ment took place in Edinburgh. Prior to opening at the Grosvenor he had played with Billy Cotton and Ambrose, forming his first band of any size in 1927. He did not do a great deal of theatre work during the '30s, preferring his Grosvenor residency, but he became reasonably popular as a result of twice-monthly broadcasts and recordings. Although seldom very venturesome in repertoire or performance he always had a thoroughly proficient band, and the musicians who played with him include George Evans, Archie Craig, Max Abrams, Ted Heath and Max Goldberg. In 1937 he dispensed with a guitar and added a third trumpet to his personnel so that Tommy Heath could switch from trumpet to flügelhorn, then a very unusual instrument in a dance band. Perhaps his best band was that of 1938–9, in which Ted Heath, Harry Hayes, George Evans and Billy Munn were featured. Sydney Lipton's daughter Celia was at one period a popular vocalist in her own right.

Unlike Cotton, Kunz, Lipton and Winnick, all of whom were indifferent instrumentalists, Jack Jackson was a good soloist with a background in brass band music. Born at Barnsley, Yorkshire, in 1907, he studied trumpet at the Royal Academy of Music in the early '20s. His first professional jobs were with small bands on ocean-going liners. During the rest of the decade he worked with a variety of bands, including Bert

Left: Sydney Lipton and his band at the Grosvenor House Hotel, c. 1939. The trombonist on the far left is Ted Heath. Above: Jack Jackson and his Dorchester Hotel Band, 1935. Note the Js forming the centres of the music stands.

Ralton's, Ambrose's, and Jack Hylton's; he accompanied Ralton on the South African trip which resulted in his death. From 1931 to 1933 he was with Jack Payne, then he decided to form his own band, which opened at the Dorchester Hotel on 1 August 1933 and remained in residence until 1 April 1939.

Jackson's earliest records are commonplace, though some 1934 titles have pleasant vocals by the black American singer Alberta Hunter, but as a result of increasing popularity, derived from regular broadcasts and recording, in the late '30s he pursued a more ambitious musical policy. Upon leaving the Dorchester – basically because of a disagreement with the management over salaries – he went out on tour with a line-up of two trumpets, trombone, clarinet doubling alto, two pianos, guitar, bass and drums, but by the end of June had added vocalist Mary Lee and an additional two trumpets, trombone and three saxophones, and was even featuring jam session performances in his stage act. In December the band returned to London to play a six-week engagement at Rector's Club in Regent Street, following which it again resumed a touring schedule for eight months before going into the Mayfair Hotel on 7 October 1940.

The last engagement that Jackson undertook as a bandleader was in 1947, and thereafter he followed a successful career for

many years as a TV personality, disc jockey and solo variety act, prior to his retirement in the Canary Islands. Over the years Jack Jackson the musician gradually became superseded by Jack Jackson the entertainer, but, while few of the records issued under his own name are other than mundane, his early playing with such groups as Spike Hughes's reveals him as a competent jazz stylist, clearly influenced by Red Nichols.

Reading the trade press of the '30s one is often intrigued by reports of bands which receive high praise and are said to be mounting challenges to the major figures, but sink back into obscurity within a short while. Around 1938 Arthur Rosebery led a band at the Paradise Club which, according to the *Melody Maker*, was 'steadily becoming known as one of the best swing outfits in town'. It attracted the attention of the Music Corporation Of America (MCA), which booked it to double at the Dolphin Square Restaurant. A further *Melody Maker* review commented that Rosebery had trained virtually unknown musicians to a point where only Ambrose and Jack Harris had superior bands. Unfortunately the Paradise closed in May 1939, Rosebery was forced to disband, and little more was heard of him. Another leader, Stanley Barnett, gets fleeting mentions in the '30s press, but there are at least records by which we may judge one of his bands. They were made for the Edison Bell Winner label in 1933 and were issued as by Madame Tussaud's Dance Orchestra, since Barnett was resident at Tussaud's restaurant at the time. The nine-strong personnel included the fine guitarist Albert Harris, who later made his name in the United States. What is most impressive about the band's recordings is the interpretations of such Duke Ellington numbers as *Rocking In Rhythm*, *Stevedore Stomp*, *Lightning* and *Echoes Of The Jungle* which, though largely derivative, are brave attempts in a challenging idiom. Barnett led other bands in London for many years, holding down a residency at the Café Anglais in 1938 and broadcasting from there in September of that year.

Bert Firman has already been mentioned in this chapter in connection with the period when he was musical director for Zonophone. Prior to this he had been active in dance music for several years. On the termination of his Zonophone contract in 1930 he went to the United States and spent a year doing radio work for NBC. In 1932 he was leading a band at Ciro's, switching to the New Sporting Club, Monte Carlo, for the 1932–3 winter season with an impressive three-saxophone line-up of Buddy Featherstonhaugh, Harry Hayes and Sid Millward. Early in 1938 he was at the London Casino with a personnel including trombonist Bill Mulraney and saxophonists Freddy Gardner and Harry Gold, but upon leaving early in 1939 he announced that he was again going to the United States because 'a good band does not appear to be wanted here'. He did not in fact leave Britain, for on 27 September 1939 he opened at the Café de Paris with a group that had Freddy Gardner, George Melachrino and Ivor Mairants within its ranks, but he resigned soon afterwards as a result of a dispute with the management over their allocating the key times of 9–10.30 pm and midnight–2 am to his fellow bandleader Ken Johnson. Reviews of Firman's 1938 band were quite enthusiastic but unfortunately it never recorded.

The final bandleader who always promised rather more than he produced is Jack Harris. Harris left the United States in 1927 for a six-week residency at the London Embassy Club, but decided to remain, and in the following years built up a large society following as a result of being heard at such venues as the Embassy and Grosvenor House. His band was at Ciro's from August 1936 and included good musicians like Alfie Noakes and Lew Davis. A *Melody Maker* reporter a year later claimed that 'musically, Harris's band is the equal of Ambrose's'. Harris was by all accounts a man not beloved of his musicians; in March 1938 he demanded that they should both give him their exclusive services and accept a salary cut because of the depressed state of the dance band business. A *Melody Maker*

Above: Jack Harris (front, 2nd from right) with his band, c. 1939. Max Goldberg is immediately behind Harris. Left: Buddy Featherstonhaugh, who, after years as a prominent sideman, led a highly successful sextet in the '40s. Right, top: Freddy Gardner, a brilliant reedman and, apparently, an enthusiastic photographer. Bottom: Ken Johnson and his band on stage, 1937.

review of a Harris broadcast during November 1938 still praised the band's musicianship, but went on to add tartly that 'like so many English bands, Jack Harris's lacks guts'.

In February 1939 Ciro's, in which Harris had an interest, was closed as the result of a lawsuit, but by 12 April he was at the London Casino with a sixteen-piece band numbering amongst its members Max Goldberg, Eric Breeze and Billy Amstell. In June Harris was back in the *Melody Maker's* favour after a London Palladium appearance; its reporter enthusiastically claimed that 'Harris stands in front of fourteen of the best musicians in England while they play half an hour of jazz'. The London Casino contract was terminated on 22 July and the band went out on tour; in August Harris said that he hoped to take it to the United States. December saw Harris leading an eight-piece group including Arthur Mouncey, Laddie Busby and Andy McDevitt at the El Morocco Club, and a larger unit at the London Casino, though occasional stage appearances were also fitted in. On 4 May 1940 Harris announced that he was going to the United States on a five-week holiday to see his wife; he left his pianist Jack Penn in charge of the London Casino band. He did not return, and by July had formed a new band in his own country.

Unlike Firman and Rosebery, Harris did record quite extensively. Of his HMV output, the titles I have heard are performed with great proficiency. There is no doubt about the technical expertise of the band, but the records do not support the more extravagant claims made on its behalf. However, tapes of fragments of Harris's broadcasts are said to be a great deal more impressive than his commercial recordings, so it could well be that his was a band which failed to realise its potential under recording studio conditions.

In another chapter I commented on the lack of British swing bands, outlining some reasons why they were not likely to flourish. There were attempts at building such groups, however, one of the first involving the pianist Eddie Carroll. Carroll had worked with Lew Stone's Monseigneur band, once the leader found the strain of playing as well as arranging and directing too great, and after a variety of jobs he formed a band in February 1935 for a residency at the Empress Rooms, London. Carroll's earliest records, including a number of piano duets with Bobby McGee, are entirely commercial and gave no indication of what was to follow. In 1938 he was given the opportunity to lead a fourteen-piece band in the swing manner to play before and during intervals of the show 'Choose Your Time'. His musicians included George Chisholm, Bennie Winestone and Jimmy Macaffer, and a broadcast of 19 April featured Chisholm's very first arrangement, *Dinah*. In September of the same year Carroll went on a short theatre tour with his 'Swing Orchestra', and in the following January opened at the Chez Henri Club with a nine-man line-up, featuring his discovery Pat Barnett on trumpet and mellophone, and a three-piece reed section. His broadcasts received lukewarm reviews, but in August he was still persisting with a large swing-styled band that was heard in a radio programme titled 'Let's Go To Town'. Carroll enjoyed a minor success with a tune he wrote called *Harlem* – in fact based on a familiar riff used much earlier in the tune *Moten's Swing* – but the recording of this (included on the LP 'Jazz In Britain – The 30s') and other would-be swing performances released on Parlophone during 1937–8 signally failed to capture the real sound or spirit of a swing band. There is no doubt of Carroll's sincerity in wishing to capture the essence of the swing idiom, but unfortunately in practice it proved to be beyond him.

The West Indian leader Ken Johnson was another who attempted to follow a swing policy, initially with some success. Born in Georgetown, British Guiana, in 1911, Johnson went to Britain in 1929. By the mid-'30s he had turned to bandleading and in 1937 he was leading a mainly West Indian band at London's Old Florida Club. In the following year he gained some national recognition as a result of broadcasts and theatre appearances. One broadcast of July 1938 presented his band in an uncompromising swing manner, with specially commissioned arrangements from Adrian de Haas, who at the time was writing for Gene Krupa, Lucky Millinder and Fats Waller. Two soloists added for the occasion were the late Leslie 'Jiver' Hutchinson and the brilliant altoist Bertie King. Early in 1939 it was reported in the musical press that he was to make a film for a prominent British company, probably based on his life, but unfortunately nothing came of this. Soon after the outbreak of war he was resident at the Café de Paris and under-

Opposite, top: Sam Browne (left) and Sydney Lipton. Bottom: Howard Jacobs with his band, as they appeared in the British Lion film In Town Tonight. Above, top: the popular Provincial band-leader Billy Merrin, with his Commanders at Ramsgate, 1936.

Below: the only known photograph of The Heralds of Swing: left to right – Bert Barnes, Tommy McQuater, George Firestone, Dave Shand, George Chisholm, Norman Maloney (back row), Tiny Winters, Benny Winestone, Sid Colin, Archie Craig (front).

"We shall have Music: Wherever She goes" REGD.

The value of a gramophone depends upon the use you make of it. If it is too big to be easily moved from room to room, if too heavy and cumbersome to be taken with you when you go up the river, on the Broads, to the Seaside or in the Country, then you miss musical pleasure you might otherwise enjoy You are tied down to time and place for gramophone entertainment.

But if your gramophone is a Decca you can have music when and where you like. You can take your Decca with you anywhere. It is wonderfully light and compact, is virtually weatherproof and it has the musical quality of instruments many times its size and price· Many hundreds of Deccas have been supplied to purchasers who already own a gramophone of the larger variety. And so delighted have they been with their new possession—with its beautiful tone, clear musical definition and high standard of acoustic performance—that in many cases the Decca has superseded its bigger brother even in the home.

So whether you already possess a gramophone or not, a Decca is a most desirable acquisition. Recent improvements have greatly added to its quality and convenience and prices have been considerably reduced.

Prices from
£3 : 12 : 6
to
£9 : 9 : 0

THE DECCA
THE PORTABLE GRAMOPHONE

Of Music Dealers, Stores, etc.

New Decca Book "3-G," containing unique photographs, received from Decca enthusiasts, post free from
"DECCA," 32, Worship Street, London, E.C.2
(Proprietors: Barnett Samuel & Sons, Ltd.)

taking fairly regular broadcasts, but he complained to a *Melody Maker* reporter about the compromises in musical policy he was forced to make, remarking that 'I determined I'd make them like swing at the Café, or die in the attempt, and, boy, I nearly died'. The Café de Paris closed temporarily in the summer of 1940 but when it re-opened on 5 November the Johnson band was once more in residence, broadcasting on some Sundays during the next few months. In March 1941 a bomb struck the

Above: a Decca advertisement of 1923, showing a new range of portable gramophones. Opposite, top left: a 1939 Decca supplement: prices were down from 1923! Bottom left: a November 1939 supplement introducing the first batch of wartime-slanted songs, most of them still light-hearted. Top right: Nat Gonella and his Georgians, a popular touring unit in the '30s. Bottom right: poster for the song-publisher Herman Darewski, who also led a dance band for some years.

117

Café, and Johnson and his tenor saxophonist Dave Williams were killed.

The Johnson band is best heard on its one Decca session of September 1938, sounding almost Lunceford-like in a version of *My Buddy*, which, like *The Sheik Of Araby*, is well scored. The section work is excellent, particularly as the band could sometimes sound rather rough, and there are good solos on both titles. The band's HMV output, other than an only partly successful *Tuxedo Junction* and *Ida*, was much more commercial and does not do it justice. That the Johnson band had the potential to become a first-rate swing group is not in doubt, but it was ultimately forced to compromise its musical policy as a result of the conservatism of its night-club audiences.

On 11 February 1939 the *Melody Maker* announced with banner headlines the formation of the Heralds Of Swing. This was a co-operative unit, the brainchild of a group of ex-Ambrose

Top left: Joe Loss (left) and Monte Rey (right) in 1938 with Charles Arnold, who claimed at 108 to be the world's oldest crooner. Top right: composer Jose Norman (at piano) gives tips to Harry Roy's 1938 juvenile band. Above: a '30s musicians soccer team: front row, left to right, Fred Stone (Lew's brother), Tiny Winters, unknown, Billy Ternent, Jack Hylton and Lew Stone. Right: Claude Bampton's late-'30s all-blind band, with pianist George Shearing.

musicians. It was fortunate enough to secure a residency at the Paradise Club from 20 February. The line-up on the opening night was Tommy McQuater, Archie Craig (trumpets), George Chisholm (trombone), Dave Shand, Norman Maloney (alto saxophones), Benny Winestone (tenor saxophone), Bert Barnes (piano), Sid Colin (guitar, vocal), Tiny Winters (bass) and George Fierstone (drums), and the *Melody Maker* reported that they received an enthusiastic reception, with 'the amount of

applause given to the musicians from the tables particularly remarkable'. The Heralds appeared in the annual Jazz Jamboree concert, and then on 2 April at the first of a series of Sunday Night Swing Club Concerts sponsored by Geraldo. The *Melody Maker* enthused over a performance where it claimed the band had struck brilliant form and George Fierstone gave a drum display that would not have disgraced Gene Krupa. A month later the idealistic venture was almost over, for the management of the Paradise asked for a reduction in personnel which the band members were not willing to make, and with no other work in sight the close of the Paradise engagement marked the end of the band. The members did come together after ceasing to work regularly as a unit, appearing at a highly successful concert at the First Avenue Hotel on 12 June and broadcasting on 19 June and 29 August. I recall hearing the latter two broadcasts and at the time found the

band disappointing apart from Chisholm, but it may be that studio conditions did not suit it. The outbreak of war five days after the Heralds' last broadcast banished any lingering hopes of a possible regrouping, though some of the personnel later found themselves together once again in the Squadronaires.

The '30s may have been the peak years of the British dance bands, but a recurring theme in the trade papers was the depressed state of business, and several leaders complained of inflated salaries. (A rather unexpected note of alarm was sounded in a 1938 *Melody Maker* under the headline 'Irish Dance Craze Alarms Bolton Danceband Men'; it was reported that *ceilidh* bands were becoming popular in that town and as a result orthodox dance band musicians were finding work hard to come by.) The fans of the bands complained about the three-shilling (60-cent) price of some records, which they considered exorbitant, though in fact many records cost less.

Above: Bertini and his band of the Tower Ballroom, Blackpool, 1934; left to right – Jack Knowles, Norman Vickers, Billy Brakewell, Dick Moir, Jack Pilney, Lucas, Jimmy Heritage, Jack Llewelyn, Frank Maddox, Jack Overdon, Charlie Barlow, Charlie Farrell, George Ashwell. Bertini himself stands under the large B.

In 1938 a chauvinistic note was sounded in the *Melody Maker* when it complained that there was a 'refugee menace still rife' and went on to assert that refugee musicians were taking jobs which could be done equally well, if not better, by British musicians. At the time of the international crisis in September 1938, P. Mathison Brooks, editor of the *Melody Maker*, wrote that, if war came, 'to the flippant strains of jazz, marching troops would forget their fatigue, recover their humour and see the brighter colours of the clouds' lining'. He did not, however, say if marching troops who were averse to jazz would find alternative music available to them. When war did come in 1939 the tone of the musical press was a great deal more sober, and there were forebodings of what lay ahead for the entertainment industry.

The complex factors that brought about the decline and ultimate collapse of the dance bands will be detailed in a later chapter. While dance bands continued to flourish, some as never before, in the World War II years, in retrospect we can see that the war marked the end of an era in popular entertainment that can never be repeated. It is to the credit of the British dance band musicians that they made it a memorable one.

THE
SWING ERA

Whereas many historical events in the annals of dance music are shrouded in confusion and doubt, it would not be unreasonable to pinpoint the beginning of the swing era to the evening of 21 August 1935, at the Los Angeles Palomar Ballroom. Benny Goodman decided the chances of his band remaining in existence much longer were minimal and, after a set or two of stock dance scores, turned to the Fletcher Henderson arrangements in his book, reasoning that if all was lost he might as well go down in a blaze of musical glory. To the amazement of both himself and his musicians this was what the audience had been waiting for, and from this point in his career Goodman went on to become a popular idol and the catalyst of a new era in big band music.

Most jazz writers have been less than just to Goodman. Their cool attitude has been based, in part, on a puritanical attitude towards anyone who achieves great popular success, but also on resentment that he and one or two other white bandleaders gained most of the publicity and reward while superior black bands were denied such recognition. It is certainly true that by strictly musical standards the three most creative bands of the swing era were undoubtedly Duke Ellington's, Count Basie's and Jimmie Lunceford's, but it is unfair to blame Goodman for circumstances that arose from social conditions and prejudices in which he himself did not acquiesce. A more tolerant climate of critical opinion towards the swing bands has been evident amongst many critics of late, and phrases like 'degenerate swing' are now used only by a few of the more eccentric diehards, but it is worth stressing the fact that the pioneer swing leaders initially had an uphill fight to gain acceptance, and made considerable personal sacrifices to maintain their musical integrity.

Goodman himself had striven hard to keep his band in exist-

ence. His big break came when he won a contract to appear as one of three regular bands on a coast-to-coast programme, sponsored by the National Biscuit Company, titled 'Let's Dance'. (The others were Xavier Cugat's Latin-American group and Ken Murray's bland society unit.) The programmes ran from 1 December 1934 to 25 May 1935, but the Goodman band's first booking after this proved a total disaster when their agency miscalculated by getting them an engagement at the Roosevelt Hotel in New York, generally the home territory of Guy Lombardo. To patrons of Lombardo's music the sound of the Goodman band must have sounded uncouth if not positively riotous, and the management of the Roosevelt fired them after one night. A road tour that followed was only partially successful and it was a rather disillusioned group of musicians that took the stand at the Palomar Ballroom.

In his autobiography, *The Kingdom Of Swing*, Goodman unhesitatingly gave much of the credit for his success to the arranging ability of Fletcher Henderson. In particular he mentioned Henderson's flair for scoring not only jazz standards but also melodic tunes such as *Can't We Be Friends*, *Blue Skies*, *I Can't Give You Anything But Love* and *Sometimes I'm Happy* to the formula of the band. He wrote many scores in this vein, and Goodman stated that 'There were the things, with their wonderful easy style and great background figures, that really set the style of the band'. It is of course ironical that Henderson should have been such an important figure behind Goodman's success, for many of the first batch of arrangements he sold to Goodman were precisely those he had been using for his own band during the past two years, and the fortunes of that band were at a low ebb. Henderson remains to this day an enigmatic

Left: Benny Goodman at the height of his reign as 'The King of Swing'. Above: jitterbugs dance to Goodman's music at the Paramount Theater, New York.

figure; he led a band in the '20s that helped formalise the role of big band jazz, and at different times included in its ranks some of the greatest figures in jazz, but he then followed with various personnels which almost invariably included major soloists but produced a bewilderingly uneven recorded output. In his early bandleading years he did little arranging himself, leaving this to the brilliant Don Redman, but once Goodman achieved national prominence his methods became the norm of big band scoring, except among a few arrangers who followed their own paths. Through success and failure Henderson maintained a striking detachment, while at the same time drawing a loyalty from his musicians that certainly transcended, at times, any concern with their own economic security. That Henderson resented the success of Goodman is unlikely, in the light of what we know of the man, but even he could not have been unaware of the contrast in the public reaction to his scores when performed by Goodman's rather than his own band, and he may have ruefully reflected on the inestimable commercial advantages to be gained from the possession of a white skin.

In this chapter I shall not go into any great detail concerning individual bands and performances, primarily because I consider that the bulk of the so-called swing bands were in fact large jazz units. While Count Basie, Duke Ellington, Jimmie Lunceford, Earl Hines, Red Norvo, Charlie Barnet and Artie Shaw, for example, frequently played for dancers, theirs were not dance bands in the sense in which the term is used throughout this work. The objection can immediately be advanced that Paul Whiteman and Jack Hylton also did not lead dance bands, but in the public mind they are indelibly associated with the dance band era, whereas Basie and Ellington are rightly considered jazz performers. There are, I will readily admit, inconsistencies in such terms of reference – King Oliver's Creole Jazz Band and the Fletcher Henderson band were dance bands on occasions – but readers with some knowledge of the subject will

accept that the categories I am following have at least the advantage of being commonly accepted. What I hope to offer in this chapter is an explanation of what the swing era represented to the musicians who came to the fore as a result of it, at the same time pointing out that generalised criteria will not be applicable to all of the swing bands. I shall also take the opportunity of drawing attention to one or two of the lesser-known bands, whose recorded output suggests that they have not received their fair quota of recognition.

As the '30s progressed, the straight dance bands in the United States did not, except in a very few cases, reveal much indication of musical progress. Conservatism and a willingness to remain tied to successful commercial formulas seemed hallmarks of most of the bands, and with the exception of Isham Jones and possibly the Casa Loma Orchestra there were not many American bands with the all-round versatility of such British counterparts as Ambrose, Roy Fox or Lew Stone. The moment was ripe for a breakthrough from more adventurous leaders, and in this sense Goodman's arrival on the scene was well timed. Quite apart from musical considerations, this was a period when a new spirit of optimism was abroad in the United States; the election of Roosevelt and the determined attempts to break out of the depression through the New Deal programme were convincing people that a better time was possible here and now. In such a climate of opinion the type of dance music commonplace during the early '30s might well have seemed lifeless and inappropriate, for, whatever their faults, the swing bands did offer music that was exciting, buoyant, and optimistic in mood. In *The Kingdom Of Swing* Benny Goodman makes the point that styles in dancing follow the styles in music, except when a song is specifically written to put across a certain dance. As if to illustrate his statement the swing era was not long under way before new dances such as the 'Lindy Hop' and 'Shag' arose that gained nationwide acceptance, as often as not emanating from such favourite haunts of Harlemites as the Savoy Ballroom. These were energetic dances calling for a high degree of physical effort, and not unnaturally were the preserve of the young. They drew, incidentally, the same type of unthinking condemnation from older people as beat groups do today from, all too often, dance band devotees of an earlier generation.

Just who it was that coined the word 'swing' is not known, but, though it was useful in defining a specific era in music, what it described was in a real sense nothing new. The antecedents of swing were already evident in some of Fletcher Henderson's '20s recordings or in many of the performances of such bands as McKinney's Cotton Pickers or Luis Russell's. Certainly the Goodman band never evinced any greater degree of swing than did Bennie Moten's in its remarkable 1932 recordings (which were also noteworthy for their sophisticated reworking of popular song material). What in fact distinguishes the swing bands from the straight dance units of the immediately preceding era is the emergence of jazz as a major rather than secondary element of their music.

From almost the beginning of dance music many bands had within their ranks a contingent of jazz musicians. Even the most commercially inclined leaders were mindful of the fact that amongst their public was an element that enjoyed 'hot' performances, and, with varying degrees of success, they attempted to cater for this clientele. Jazz musicians within the bands were allocated the occasional 'hot' solo; now and then they were even allowed to organise smaller groups to play specifically jazz performances. These musicians were frequently in conflict with their leaders, and the history of jazz performers is replete with stories of individuals who lost their jobs with commercial dance bands through overstepping the jazz limits the leaders considered commercially viable; the commonest is the one in which the leader leaves the stand for some reason or other and returns to find that the jazz contingent has taken over, to the displeasure of the hotel or ballroom management. The swing era might be said to have been a period when the jazz musicians got their

own backs on their former tormentors. It would be wrong, however, to assume that all the more overtly commercial bands packed up and left the scene, for many just went on churning out their music as before, to the vast satisfaction of the clientele of the stuffier hotels and more conservative radio audiences.

Writers unsympathetic to the swing era, particularly those jazz critics who see it as an unfortunate break in the dominance of 'pure' jazz (represented on the one hand by New Orleans music and on the other by bop and later avant-garde stylists), tend to write of the swing bands as though it were quite impossible to tell one from the other, and dismiss their music as computerised and lacking in creativity. It would be unrealistic to go to the other extreme and claim that there were no mediocre swing bands, for indeed success on the scale achieved by a Goodman, Tommy Dorsey or Artie Shaw inevitably attracts second-rate copyists, amongst whom must be considered a number of leaders who dropped their normal styles almost overnight and became suspiciously swiftly devoted to the new music. As the swing era progressed, the search for something new to say or for new methods of presentation led some leaders to fall back on gimmicks, ranging from the shuffle rhythm of Jan Savitt – whose band was, apart from this, quite a reasonable secondary swing group – to the commercial exploitation of the boogie woogie craze by Will Bradley. Possibly the most barren of all the bands was that led by Larry Clinton, Gene Gifford's replacement as chief arranger for the Casa Loma Orchestra. Clinton seemed to be able to use all the clichés of the period, and he employed them as the basis of an endless series of Victor recordings whose only saving grace was the level of execution.

There were also bands which, though good on many levels, and possessing first-rate soloists, never really succeeded in establishing a personal identity, with the result that, while they turned out numerous highly enjoyable records, they always seemed to be reflecting what was contemporary without attaining any degree of creativity. In this category one might include several led by star soloists, including Bunny Berigan (whose own playing, when he was in good health, is certainly exempted from the above criticism), Harry James and Gene Krupa.

When one considers that at the height of the swing era dozens of bands had achieved some national fame, and probably hundreds of lesser-known ones worked within the broad swing tradition, it is not surprising that a fair number should be found uncreative or unoriginal. In popular music of any period or style, the percentage of really creative artists does not vary greatly from decade to decade; the continuation and health of any development is dependent on the existence of a reasonably large number of secondary performers, whose important role it is to use the discoveries of the major creative figures to establish wide public acceptance. Amongst these secondary figures there are sure to be individuals who will jump on the bandwagon of contemporary fashion. But it is wrong to equate 'secondary' with 'second-rate', for many of these performers will have their own contributions to make. There were indeed several indifferent swing bands around in 1935–45, but proportionately they were no more numerous than the indifferent dance bands of the '20s, or the indifferent bop groups of the '50s, not to mention the indifferent beat groups active today. To condemn an era or style of music because of its less talented performers is the oldest critical gambit of the disenchanted.

If one takes an objective look at the swing era bands – even at those which it is common to damn with faint praise – it is clear that, despite the paucity of really original arrangers, a considerable diversity of styles can be found within a common framework. Confining oneself to the white bands, one need only consider the widely differing approaches used by, for example, Benny Goodman, Bob Crosby, Woody Herman and Charlie Barnet. Goodman's earliest band might be considered the archetypal swing outfit, but in fact he was to undertake a personal stylistic evolution that resulted in a very different band in the early '40s, when his chief arranger was Eddie Sauter, and this to a considerable extent set the pattern for such bands as those led by Tommy Dorsey and Artie Shaw. In total contrast, Bob Crosby's band attempted, with a fair degree of success, to incorporate elements of traditional jazz within a big band framework, and though on commercial ballads this approach was dropped in favour of a much blander and more

Left: one of the greatest big bands of all time – Jimmie Lunceford's, shown here during a stage presentation. Above: Bob Crosby in a scene from a film.

conventional sound, the presence within the group of such soloists as Sterling Bose, Yank Lawson, Eddie Miller, Irving Fazola and Matty Matlock gave it an authenticity of style that many later, earnest, traditionalist bands utterly failed to capture.

Woody Herman came to lead his most famous and creative bands near the close of the swing era, but his earliest 'Band That Plays The Blues' pursued an individual course for some years, and though any large band playing blues smooths out the emotional content of the genre, Herman's compromises in this respect were generally effective. In Neil Reid, Cappy Lewis and Joe Bishop, Herman possessed a trio of soloists who played with conviction in the blues idiom; it must be added, however, that his own vocals on blues numbers were totally unconvincing, if generally inoffensive. He eventually dropped his blues policy – one of his less agreeable experiences was a notice from a hotel manager insisting that he stop playing that 'nigger music' – and for a while led a more orthodox band, which still produced excellent music, but was in essence a transitional group prior to the first 'Herd'. Charlie Barnet might on the surface be open to criticism of lack of creativity, in as far as he made no secret of the fact that he was greatly influenced by Duke Ellington and, to a lesser extent, Count Basie, but his records of Ellington material and numbers in that vein show that he had assimilated his influences well and went on to create an individual style for the band. Barnet led one of the three best white bands of the swing era, the others being Red Norvo's and Goodman's '40s group. When one considers that during the late '30s both the Count Basie and Jimmie Lunceford bands reached their peaks, and that in the early '40s the Duke Ellington band reached what many consider to be the highpoint of big band jazz, it is hard to deny that the '30s and early '40s were halcyon days for all the bands.

One result of the popularity of the big swing bands was the emergence of personality soloists. When the public went to hear the Goodman band it expected soloists such as Harry James, Ziggy Elman and Jess Stacy to be well featured, and in due course many of these musicians formed their own bands, with or without the blessing of their former employers. Among the best known of the second wave of bandleaders are Bunny Berigan, Gene Krupa and Harry James; James is one of the few men who has kept a big band in existence to the present day. Generally the bands led by ex-sidemen of Goodman, Tommy Dorsey, and so forth leaned heavily on their leaders' popularity, and consequently the cult of the personality was further extended. If few of these bands achieved any great height of creativity, it was not always because their leaders were unwilling to follow new paths, but sometimes because they adopted an economic caution, which led them to concentrate on the safe and familiar, and lacked really individual and imaginative arrangers.

Of all the figures who helped to make the swing era, the arrangers are the least publicised. Most people familiar with the more successful bands are vaguely aware that Fletcher Henderson contributed a great deal to the early book of the Goodman orchestra, or that Sy Oliver was responsible for some of the best scores used by Tommy Dorsey; they may possibly be able to name, in the latter category, *Opus 1* and *On The Sunny Side Of The Street*. Yet few will know the names of the chief arrangers for Artie Shaw, Bob Crosby, Woody Herman or Bunny Berigan – despite the fact that a first-class arranger who could set an individual style for a band was probably even more important than its soloists. Unfortunately, while craftsmen arrangers are frequently met with in the history of large dance and jazz bands, creative arrangers who can mould the style of a band are very few and far between. Excellent as Fletcher Henderson's arrangements were for Goodman, the lack of individual arrangers meant that all too soon they became the norm of big band writing, and were slavishly copied on all sides.

Henderson made considerable use of call-and-response patterns, in which phrases were passed around from one section to another, and on the whole this is a proved and effective method

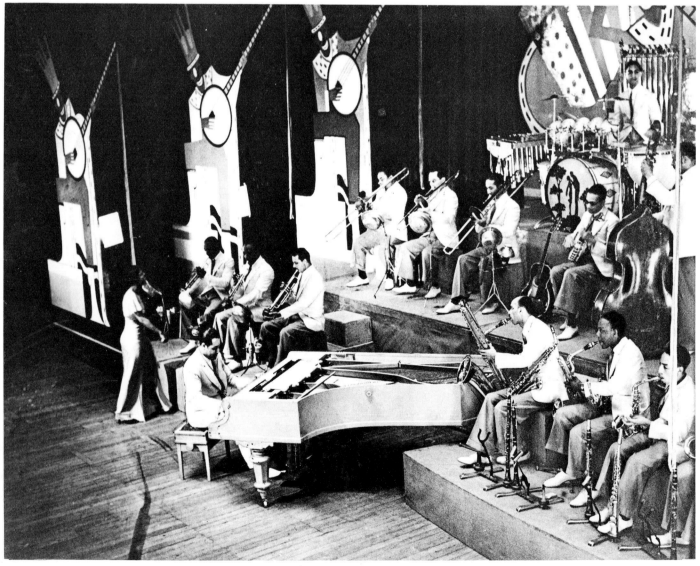

of scoring for a big band. On the other hand there is another type of arranger, represented by such figures as Duke Ellington, Don Redman, Sy Oliver and Eddie Sauter, who eschew call-and-response scoring in its simplest form and favour unusual voicings, blending instruments not tied to conventional sections, and creating interesting and varied ensemble textures. Duke Ellington is in a class by himself, as one of the few great jazz composers, for he conceives a composition and arrangement as a whole; in addition, he has led for close on half a century a band which is a unique interpreter of his own material. Don Redman, first for Fletcher Henderson and McKinney's Cotton Pickers and later for his own and other bands of the '30s, worked in a more conventional style to enormous effect, as did Sy Oliver with Jimmie Lunceford and later Tommy Dorsey, and Eddie Sauter with Red Norvo and Benny Goodman. But they were exceptional figures, compared with the dozens of arrangers who turned out scores that were efficient and work-manlike but, in the last resort, insufficiently distinctive to rise above the commonplace. In the decades since the decline of the big band era the absence of really creative arrangers has become even more marked. One of the very few exceptions is Gil Evans, who has been responsible for a handful of records remarkable for the intensely personal nature of the scores. A number provide settings which perfectly complement the sombre emotional climate of Miles Davis's trumpet-playing.

Much of the literature on popular swing band leaders gives an impression that they led virtually the same band for the greater part of their careers, rather than a number of quite different bands. Over a decade line-ups normally undergo con-siderable transformation – few achieve the stable personnels of an Ellington or Lombardo – and in some instances these amount to the formation of totally new bands, embracing musical policies that might be quite different from that pre-viously followed. Not all leaders were content to work indefi-nitely with proved, successful formulas; some attempted to enlarge the horizons of their music, quite frequently to the dismay of their more conservative followers. During 1947-9, for example, Benny Goodman led what was to be his last regular band – after this he formed bands for specific engage-ments or tours – and called on the services of bop-influenced arrangers like Chico O'Farrill and Tommy Todd to provide fresh material and, more significantly, to update the scores of such familiar numbers as *King Porter Stomp*, *Jersey Bounce* and *Don't Be That Way*. His band at the time included numerous young musicians intensely sympathetic to bop, but unlike the bop flirtations of his former drummer Gene Krupa, whose records using elements of the style were both commercially acceptable and often musically interesting, Goodman's releases were generally unsuccessful. Probably his embracing of the idiom resulted less from a deep sense of personal involvement than from a desire not to sound out of date. When this band broke up Goodman returned to his familiar swing style and never afterwards evinced the slightest interest in bop or any subsequent jazz development.

Prior to this, however, Goodman had already on one occasion more subtly altered the character of his music. When his Victor contract ended in 1939 and numerous stars departed from his ranks, he refurbished his personnel, and while retaining

Popular sidemen often became bandleaders in their own right during the swing era. Sonny Dunham (top left), a featured soloist with the Casa Loma Orchestra, later led his own unit. On the other hand, Bobby Hackett (top right), who became well known after soloing on a few Glenn Miller records, had previously led his own big band. Bottom: Duke Ellington's band at the London Palladium, 1933: Sonny Greer (drums), Joe Nanton, Juan Tizol, Lawrence Brown (trombones), Fred Guy (guitar), Wellman Braud (bass), Freddy Jenkins, Cootie Williams, Arthur Whetsol (trumpets), Otto Hard-wicke, Harry Carney, Johnny Hodges, Barney Bigard (hidden) (reeds), Ivie Anderson (vocal), Ellington (piano).

Fletcher Henderson as one of his arrangers introduced others of a more modern bent. One of these newcomers was Mel Powell, also the band pianist, and another Eddie Sauter, and between them these two moulded the early '40s Goodman band, probably the finest he ever led. Eddie Sauter was one of the truly individual arrangers of the big band era, and his scores revealed a searching preoccupation with the creation of unusual textures and instrumental blendings, even on the more overtly commercial numbers such as the backgrounds for vocalist Peggy Lee.

Some four years before he commenced to write arrangements for Goodman, Sauter had been the principal arranger with one of the finest and in some ways most neglected white bands of the swing era, that led by xylophonist Red Norvo. Norvo him-self is a subtle stylist, and his band – initially, at least – reflected this facet of his personality, achieving a relaxed type of swing far removed from the frenetic music of many contemporary outfits. Mildred Bailey, one of the greatest of all jazz singers despite her light, high voice, which superficially seems ill suited to a jazz stylist, was at the time Norvo's wife and she came into the band as its regular vocalist. Because of her com-mercial potential a high proportion of Norvo's records feature vocals by her, but Sauter's instinctive bent towards rich textures and unorthodox harmonies enabled him to write arrangements that were not only rewarding in themselves but drew the best from the singer. Such records as *Smoke Dreams*, *Remember*, *I Would Do Anything For You* and *I Let A Song Go Out Of My Heart* combine beautiful arrangements by Sauter, sensitive playing by the band and some of its soloists – including trum-peter Stew Pletcher, clarinettist Hank D'Amico, tenor saxo-phonist Herbie Haymer and primarily Norvo himself – and superb, musicianly vocals from Mildred Bailey. Norvo refuted the view that all swing bands were noisy and unsubtle, but eventually he was forced to compromise and, excellent as some of his later records were, they lack the qualities of his output of 1936-7. In the '50s Sauter teamed up with another arranger, Bill Finegan, and formed the Sauter-Finegan Orchestra, but while his arranging was often striking it began to pursue effects for their own sake, and lacked the disciplined quality and sensitivity of his work with Norvo and Goodman.

Artie Shaw, who for years has been in the limelight as much because of his matrimonial problems as because of his music, may seem singularly ill fitted for the role of leader of an under-rated band, in view of the enormous success of *Begin The Beguine*, *Nightmare*, *Frenesi*, *Concerto For Clarinet* and many others; yet his first group, formed in 1936, does entitle him to consideration in this respect. Its instrumentation was unusual, consisting of two trumpets, trombone, tenor saxophone, clarinet (Shaw himself), a conventional rhythm section, and a string quartet of two violins, viola and 'cello. In the history of jazz and dance music, the successful use of strings is a rarity; even the most extrovert arrangers produce an effect poised between a large restaurant ensemble and Mantovani. While it would be untrue to claim that Shaw solved this problem, he was more successful in integrating strings with conventional dance band instrumentation than most. Such titles as *Thou Swell*, *Sobbin' Blues*, *Copenhagen*, *Streamline* and *Sweet Lorraine* have Shaw in far less bland mood than was often the case subsequently, and his arrangements make clever use of the strings in a reasonable astringent manner. Shaw expressed his dismay at having to drop the strings for commercial reasons, and with his large string-laden groups of 1940 onwards we are back, as far as the writing for the strings is concerned, in Mantovani territory.

Charlie Barnet led the most consistently rewarding of all the white swing bands, but, while he was not without a fairly large public following, he never attained the success of a Goodman, Dorsey or Shaw. His admiration for Duke Ellington is clear in the reworking of such familiar Ellington material as *The Gal From Joe's*, *Echoes Of Harlem*, *Ring Dem Bells* and

Artie Shaw and his band, at a dance in the late '30s (bottom left) and in the Paramount film Second Chorus *(top left and above).*

The Sergeant Was Shy, as it is in numerous original numbers in the Ellington vein. Barnet achieved his greatest success with a version of Ray Noble's *Cherokee* and some commercial titles featuring vocals by Lena Horne, but he also produced many band performances on the lines of *The Reverie Of A Moax*, *Phylisse, Lois*, and Billy May's *Wings Over Manhattan*, which remain to this day outstanding examples of their kind. Barnet soloed on alto, soprano and tenor saxophones, on tenor using a type of jump phrasing that is curiously effective; in a number of recordings the scores make good use of his soprano as a lead instrument in richly textured saxophone passages. In Bob Burnet, Barnet possessed one of the most versatile trumpet soloists of the swing era, and in guitarist Bus Etri one of the first musicians to use an amplified instrument with taste and imagination in a big band setting. Nowadays Barnet, reputedly a wealthy man whose activities have always been governed by a love of music rather than economic necessity, occasionally forms a band for specific engagements; one such group in late 1966 and early 1967 produced an exceptional record.

The factors that led to the decline of big bands in general, including of course the swing bands, will be discussed in the succeeding chapter, but it is worth noting here that a number of musicians were by the mid-'40s showing signs of disenchantment with their lot. Swing had resulted from an unprecedented drawing together of jazz and dance music, but virtually all the jazz soloists came from big band backgrounds and looked upon them as the working norm. Initially they were delighted at their release from the bondage of commercial bands, but after a while they hankered after further increases in freedom. Virtually all the bop pioneers came out of a big band tradition, and as bop gained ground there arose younger musicians who saw big bands as hangovers from a past of which they wanted no part, and who felt that real musical freedom could only be achieved in small groups. Jazz and dance music drifted apart and the schism has been with us ever since.

In retrospect one can say that, despite all the valid criticisms of the swing bands, they lifted popular music to a level of technical accomplishment that remains unequalled. The saccharine sentimentality of much pre-swing dance music was replaced by a more lively, vital, and emotionally diversified music, and within certain conventions there was a great deal of experiment. The technical advances that accompanied the development of swing have left a lasting mark on subsequent generations of musicians; more important, what is best in swing remains valid music to this day. It is impossible to resist the conclusion that the breakthrough of the first swing bands foreshadowed one of the most exciting periods in the history of popular music.

As a postscript, one might speculate why European countries, which up to this point had generally followed American models, did not produce their own equivalents of Goodman, Tommy Dorsey, Barnet and so on. The reason, I think, lies in the very different social and economic conditions prevailing in most European countries during the '30s. In Germany, Italy and Russia political factors prevented any such development, though several other Western European countries might have offered good opportunities for swing bands to be organised and gain public acceptance. (One such attempt in England was mentioned in the preceding chapter.) But quite apart from considerations of public taste there is the question of the different emotional climate that prevailed in Western European countries. Swing music mirrored the optimism of a people emerging into a happier economic future after a catastrophic depression, whereas optimism was at a premium in a Europe over which the shadow of fascism and war hung large. It is doubtful, too, whether the Western European countries possessed enough star instrumentalists to maintain any significant number of swing bands. Above all, secure economic bases were lacking. Though the United States had its share of exclusive and conservative hotels, there were still many others which welcomed a young clientele willing to spend money to dine, dance and listen to the swing bands. The locations of the major dance bands in England, by contrast, were hotels like the Savoy

and the Mayfair, bastions of a class society, with a clientele that was conservative in both politics and taste, and unlikely to extend a welcome to an influx of younger people from the lower orders. The aftermath of the war, despite all its chaos and hardship, could provide an emotional climate more favourable for the growth of an extrovert music like swing, and for a brief period it did so. But developments in popular music in the

Benny Goodman in a scene from the 20th Century-Fox film The Girls He Left Behind. *The pianist on the left is Jess Stacy.*

United States soon saw the big band era pass into history, and this time, with some local variation, the European countries were swift to follow the lead of the American popular music industry.

EUROPEAN
DANCE MUSIC

Not infrequently during the '30s the BBC relayed programmes of dance music to Britain from other European countries, the bands most often selected being Ray Ventura's from France, Kai Ewans's from Denmark, Fud Candrix's from Belgium, and The Ramblers from Holland. Reviews of these transmissions were usually kind but condescending; the most frequent criticism centred on the rhythmic ponderousness of the Continental bands. Such comments were not entirely the result of chauvinism; although, during the late '30s, the majority of British bands compared unfavourably with their American counterparts on rhythmic grounds, the best of the local bands – Ambrose's and Lew Stone's for example – possessed an individuality and stylishness that no other European groups quite equalled. By the closing years of the decade, however, the Continental bands had made great strides in rhythmic flexibility and technical expertise, and the leading groups were well able to hold their own with most of their British counterparts.

Except in Germany, the reawakening of interest in the dance bands of the '30s does not appear to be so widespread in most European countries as it now is in the United States and Britain; hence only a trickle of reissues of local dance bands has so far appeared in such countries as Belgium, France, Holland and Sweden. Most of the records that have been released are strongly jazz-slanted, which can lead the listener unfamiliar with the overall recording output of the featured bands to gain a somewhat distorted view of their style. It is as if all the reissue LPs of Paul Whiteman and Lew Stone contained only their jazz-inclined performances and their purchasers assumed that those bands always performed in that manner. Further, adequate documentation of the histories of the many excellent Continental dance bands is sparse. National studies published in Belgium and Germany in the past few years, for instance, concentrate on the jazz qualities of the bands without necessarily concerning themselves with their more commercial output.

By the mid-'20s American-derived dance music had become firmly established in all western European countries with Czechoslovakia and Poland soon following suit, and it was not long before locally organised dance bands became popular within these countries, a number gaining recognition on a continental scale. No writer or follower of the subject could honestly claim to know the complete story of dance music in over a dozen European countries, and in any case an authoritative study, whether historical or critical, would require every page of the present book. For these reasons, what follows is a vignette on some of the European bands which I have heard on record or on long-past broadcasts, with no pretensions to completeness. It is hoped that, despite its limitations, the chapter will lead some readers to listen to the less ephemeral recordings by the bands mentioned, and even more that it may stimulate researchers in the countries concerned to present us with detailed information on the artists who contributed to the spread of dance music in Europe.

Partly because of the intransigent attitude of the British Musicians Union, and partly through smug assumptions of the superiority of the British bands, few Continental units played in Britain during the pre-war years. Without doubt the best-known European band, to British ears, was that led by Ray Ventura, known throughout its career as Ray Ventura's Collegians, which performed in Britain on a number of occasions. Ventura commenced leading a band in the '20s and by the early '30s was well established in both his own country, France, and its neighbours. He visited London for the first time in 1931, his group at that period including the American bass saxophonist Spencer Clark, but four years later he completely reorganised his band. In March 1938 he made a flying visit to England for a concert at the Odeon Theatre, Guildford, a broadcast the following day, and then a recording session for the Parlophone label. His personnel at the time included trumpeters Philippe Brun and Gus Deloof, trombonist Guy Paquinet, and bassist Louis Vola, the latter a long-time member of the famous Quintet of the Hot Club of France. The *Melody Maker* reported enthusiastically of the concert: 'Ray's boys are quite up to the finest standard of the best British band acts.' Brun was featured in a number titled *A Study In Brown*, and Deloof (a Belgian) in his own *Easy Going*, but the most popular number with the audience was Vola's display piece *Tiger Rag*. A broadcast of a year later was received far less happily by the *Melody Maker's* reviewer, who concluded: 'Ray Ventura's hesitating and rather pointless announcements put the finishing touches of unimaginativeness to a broadcast which for all its superficial contrasts was as dull as music as it was unenlightened as jazz.'

Undeterred by such criticism – if indeed he even read it – Ventura returned to England just prior to the outbreak of war, subsequently spending some of the war years in Argentina leading his band. His career lasted into the '50s and apart from another British tour in 1946 he was featured in a film built around his band. In many ways Ventura was the French equivalent of Jack Hylton; his group was essentially a show band, and among its specialities were arrangements of numbers like *St Louis Blues* as Ventura imagined Mozart, Chopin, Wagner and Ravel might have conceived them! Despite the nature of his band Ventura usually included a jazz contingent within it, the fine tenor saxophonist Alix Combelle being featured with him in the late '30s. Over the years the band occasionally

recorded quite interesting titles like *Margie, I Got Rhythm, Can't We Be Friends, Button Up Your Overcoat* and *Blue Prelude,* the cream of which would make a worthwhile LP.

Though Ray Ventura became the best known of all French dance band leaders, the most musically interesting band from that country that I have heard is Gregor and his Gregorians. I know little of the history of the band, whose recording career covered the years 1929–33, other than that it was playing at the Olympia in Paris during the early '30s, undertook a South American tour in 1931 and had a residency at Nice in 1932. Gregor was a vocalist-leader who apparently did not play an instrument. At various times during these years the personnel included Philippe Brun, trombonists Leo Vauchant and Guy Paquinet, alto saxophonists Roger Fisbach and Charles Lisee, and Stephane Grappelly. I have heard only a proportion of the band's recorded output but such titles as *Put On Your Old Grey Bonnet, Ev'ry Day's A Lucky Day, Harlem Madness* and *Puttin' On The Ritz* offer good arrangements, spirited ensemble playing, and a variety of excellent solos. One reissued title is *Tiger Rag,* and this has outstanding hot solos from several musicians and is rhythmically quite remarkable for the period. If the latter is at all typical of what Gregor and his Gregorians sounded like in the flesh, the band must be rated one of the finest European groups of its day, and indeed equal to quite a few of the leading American bands.

One European band that did gain some respect in Britain during the '30s was The Ramblers, a Dutch group which became known to jazz followers for its sympathetic support on record to the late Coleman Hawkins. The Ramblers has an unusually talented arranger in Jack Bulterman who, in later years, worked in one of the major Hollywood film studios. Bulterman wrote several numbers for Hawkins which were singularly well suited to show-casing the great jazz musician's rhapsodic style, but while The Ramblers always included jazz-styled numbers in their programmes they were basically a versatile dance band with an extensive repertoire.

The band was formed by Theo Uden Masman, a pianist with wide experience, in 1926, and under the name of the Original Ramblers the seven-piece group, including the subsequently well-known trumpeter Louis de Vries, opened at a cabaret in Amsterdam on 1 September. The band soon became well established and by the end of the '20s had toured Germany, Denmark and Switzerland, had a resident engagement at the Kurhaus at Scheveningen and was broadcasting and recording frequently. In 1932 The Ramblers were signed to a recording

contract by Decca, the first sessions taking place in London. Their regular engagements consisted of appearances at the most lucrative locations in their own country. In October 1936 The Ramblers became the resident dance band of the VARA radio station at Hilversum, broadcasting frequently, sometimes relayed by the BBC, from 1937–40; one such transmission took place on 9 May 1940 at the moment that the Germans invaded Holland. The size of the band had doubled since the original 1926 engagement and for stage appearances further additions were made, but musical progress was brought to a halt by the invasion and by the Germans' insistence that all Jewish musicians in the band should be discharged. Despite many restrictions the band continued to be active throughout the war, appearing with success in Belgium, where a greater degree of freedom in musical programming was permitted, and after the liberation playing for American service personnel.

Upon settling down again in his own country Masman re-organised the band and resumed the previous schedule of regular broadcasts, recordings and personal appearances, including a tour of British theatres in 1957. By this time the band's popularity was on the wane and though it continued to broadcast regularly it ceased to make records. In the early '60s Masman had to bow to the demands of broadcasting executives to introduce rock 'n' roll elements into his music. Completely out of sympathy with his directive, he finally decided to disband The Ramblers after a farewell broadcast on 17 April 1964, and he himself died at The Hague on 27 January in the following year at the age of 63.

Initially The Ramblers were heavily committed to a jazz policy and their first recordings are almost solely in this vein. In later years the demands of regular broadcasting and stage appearances caused a broadening of their repertoire, but at least until the final years of the band's existence its professionalism won it the deserved acclaim of dance band musicians throughout Europe.

Although he was virtually unknown in Britain, the Dutch leader Ernst Van t'Hoff led a popular swing-style band during the '40s which, on record at least, shows a strong Glenn Miller influence. Van t'Hoff worked in Germany during the early war years, recording there in 1941 and 1942, paradoxically enough at a time when jazz and swing was officially frowned upon by the Nazi authorities. The Nazis did not allow their antipathy to 'decadent Western music' to blind them to its value as a propaganda medium, and, as well as allowing swing bands to be heard in broadcasts beamed at Allied service personnel, they used some of the Dutch and Belgian musicians who were working in Germany as members of the notorious 'Charlie and his Orchestra'. The records made under this name often included

Left: Ray Ventura and his band, 1938. Below: Gregor and his Gregorians in the early '30s. Gregor is with the show girls.

special lyrics of an anti-British nature, and, understandably, in the post-war years the foreign musicians who took part in the sessions have been anxious not to become identified. Van t'Hoff, some of whose records reveal an impressive level of technical facility in the swing idiom, moved to Brussels in late 1942 and took part in sessions there during the remaining war years. These later recordings, featuring a Belgian personnel, are more overtly commercial, but still include a proportion of swing-styled instrumentals. Van t'Hoff's post-war career is somewhat obscure but it seems that he remained in Belgium, for he died in Brussels on 17 May 1955.

On 27 June 1927 a recording session took place at the Edison Bell studios in London that has historical interest as the first jazz date with an exclusively Belgian personnel. The leader was the alto saxophonist Charles Remue, who subsequently organised numerous bands over the years, including one in 1929 and another in 1930 that are spoken of with considerable respect by Belgian musicians and collectors. Although he continued to work as a musician until his death in 1971, Remue's later career was a chequered one that took him to various European countries, but one musician who was present on his pioneer 1927 recording date proved more successful in establishing himself during the following decade. This was the pianist Stan Brenders, who, from 1 January 1936, led the Belgian radio band known as 'L'Orchestre Jazz de l'INR'. Brenders became well known in several western European countries as a result of his many broadcasts and recordings, and was referred to in the *Melody Maker* as the 'Belgian Henry Hall'. Musically, the earlier recordings by the Brenders band are more adventurous than those of Henry Hall – the linking of names being occasioned by the fact that both leaders led official radio orchestras – and even the first sessions undertaken during the war years include a fair proportion of swing instrumentals. In common with bandleaders in various European countries at this time, Brenders disguised many well-known American titles to escape the Nazi censorship. The excellence of his band is clearly revealed on eight May 1942 performances in which it backed the brilliant French guitarist Django Reinhardt. As the

'40s progressed Brenders increasingly used string sections on his recordings and broadcasts, and though well performed his later recordings do not have the quality of his earlier ones.

Perhaps the best known Belgian band of all was that led by Fud Candrix, who as early as 1928 had made his recording debut in Berlin as a tenor saxophone soloist. In 1936 Candrix formed a big band and was active in this role for over two decades, recording extensively for Telefunken and other labels. In February 1939 one broadcast by the Candrix band, relayed by the BBC, caused 'Detector' of the *Melody Maker* to report with alarm that 'Fud Candrix and his orchestra showed once again that the Continental bands are getting uncomfortably ahead of us in this little matter of swing'. Candrix's records include many that reflect the influence of several of the popular American swing bands, a number featuring very professional scores by his pianist Raymond Colignon, and though the approach is at times highly derivative the level of ensemble playing and solos is generally excellent. Candrix was able to achieve a degree of commercial success during the '30s on the basis of his swing-oriented policy.

An important year in establishing big bands in Belgium appears to have been 1936, for in addition to Brenders and Candrix a third well-known Belgian leader launched his band at this date, the saxophonist and clarinettist Jean Omer. The full Omer band did not record until the latter part of 1940 but was then very active in the studios for the next three years, after which sessions again became few and far between. Such titles as *Dry Gin*, *Porte De Namur* and *Rhythm Indien* offer further proof that Belgian musicians had achieved considerable facility in playing in the swing manner. Omer's band had a number of excellent soloists, and his arrangers included the talented Peter Packay, though, interestingly enough, in the late '30s he was also featuring scores written specially for him by Benny Carter.

The early '40s saw various highly professional-sounding big bands recording in Belgium, fronted by such leaders as Gus Deloof, Gene Dersin and Jack Kluger, the latter using the name of Jay Clever, but the group that has impressed me most from this period is that led by Emile Deltour, who for profes-

Left: Charles Remue (3rd left, seated) and His New Stompers Orchestra in a London recording studio 1927. Above: Håkan von Eichwald and his Orchestra, 1930.

sional purposes used the name Eddie Tower. Deltour first recorded in 1939, his initial output being notable only for its technical facility. Though his post-1944 recordings become increasingly mundane, a number made in April 1940 include spirited and well performed versions of several titles associated with the Count Basie band and are outstanding of their kind.

The personal position of musicians in Europe during the war years was made difficult by the German occupation of so many countries. The only possibility of bands remaining in existence was for them to agree to play for the occupying forces, and several of the most prominent groups worked and recorded in Germany during the '40s. In the immediate post-war years quite a few musicians were consequently imprisoned as collaborators, though political naïvety, a desire to remain active in the only profession known to them and fear of the consequences of their refusal to agree to German demands, rather than sympathy with the Nazi cause, were probably the chief reasons for musicians compromising themselves in this manner.

Because of its size Switzerland is not a country which has produced many well-known dance bands, but an exception was The Original Teddies. This was a group organised by Teddy Stauffer, born in Berne in 1907 and a student of classical music during the '20s. In 1927 he formed his first band, its personnel including drummer Paul Guggisberg, who was to be associated with Stauffer for many years, and then in 1929 he took a group to Berlin. Until 1939 he led a roving existence with his band, for apart from various summer engagements in his own country he worked frequently in Germany and went as far afield as the United States, Cuba and the USSR, at one point during 1938 playing in London in support of a British singer. With the deterioration of the political situation in 1939 Stauffer and The Original Teddies returned to Switzerland, opening at the Swiss National Exhibition in Zürich in June. Stauffer himself left his home country in March 1941 and embarked on an American

career in the night-club business that he still follows; he handed over the direction of the band to the talented tenor saxophonist Eddie Brunner. During the remainder of the war, The Original Teddies became popular in their own country, and, as a result of regular broadcasts, in neighbouring countries, their musical policy stressing a versatility highlighted by their arrangements of hits of American swing bands.
hits of the American swing bands.

The many recordings that the band made for the Swiss Elite Special label during the '40s reveal impeccable technical expertise, with a number of special scores showing a marked individuality of approach. Apart from Brunner, a good soloist who was prominent in his country until his death in 1956, the band also featured an excellent clarinettist in Ernst Hollerhagen – who had chosen to exile himself from Germany rather than serve in its armed forces – and a rhythm section that was striking by European standards. In common with many other dance bands The Original Teddies did not long survive the end of the war, declining economic opportunities forcing it to disband. Although little known in Britain or the United States, the better recordings of The Original Teddies would no doubt surprise followers of dance bands in those countries by their general excellence.

The developments in jazz and dance music within the Scandinavian countries followed an unequal course, with Finland, for reasons outlined in a previous chapter, lagging behind Denmark, Sweden and, perhaps to a lesser degree, Norway, in the creation of nationally popular bands. It is generally considered in Sweden that the three finest local bands were those led by Håkan von Eichwald Arne Hülphers and Thore Ehrling, all of whom are fortunately to be heard on available reissues.

Håkan von Eichwald commenced his musical career by leading theatre orchestras, a role to which he returned during the war years, but is best remembered for the dance bands he organised and fronted between 1930 and 1939. During this period he made over 300 recordings, a few of which were in the jazz manner. Titles such as *The Snake Charmer, Nagasaki, Limehouse Blues* and *Alabamy Bound* give an impression of a

well organised dance band, though one in which the quality of the soloists is uneven. The playing of the saxophone section comes across more crisply than that of the brass, a not unusual aspect of virtually all European bands of the '30s. Unfamiliarity with much of von Eichwald's large output makes it dangerous to draw conclusions from what may be slightly atypical performances. Recalled with respect and affection for his adherence to strict musical standards and for his pioneering role in Swedish dance music, von Eichwald spent the remainder of his musical career in the post-war years leading a symphony orchestra in Hälsingborg, in the southern part of Sweden, up to the time of his death at Malmö in 1964, at the age of 55.

Arne Hülphers, a pianist who later became a front man, commenced to lead his big band in January 1934, in fact taking over von Eichwald's current personnel. At the time von Eichwald was conducting both his regular dance orchestra and a pit band for an operetta; the direction of the former fell to Hülphers when the owner of a dance hall at which it played became enraged at von Eichwald's constant preference for the theatre. Hülphers led a band until at least the '40s, and a 1939 session that resulted in performances of *Swingin' In The Promised Land*, *Baltimore*, *Don't Be That Way* and *I'm Coming Virginia* proves it to have been an excellent one. Trombonist Julius Jacobsen's arrangement of the first title is skilful, and the sections are heard to advantage in well played and spirited passages that are underlined by a good rhythm section. The assurance of the section work is also notable on Miff Görling's arrangement of *Baltimore*, a performance that includes worthwhile solos by tenor saxophonist Erik Eriksson and a trumpeter who is probably Gösta Törner. It is only on *I'm Coming Virginia* that the swing approach suffers from a degree of stiffness in the execution of the call-and-response patterns.

Thore Ehrling was certainly the most successful Swedish dance band leader, directing various personnels from 1938 until the mid-'60s. Ehrling was an excellent all-round musician, playing trumpet, arranging and composing as well as leading his band, and over the years he recorded quite extensively on various Swedish labels. One 1939 session had Nat and Bruts

Above: Arne Hülphens's big band, Berlin, 1938. Below: poster for Hülphens's summer tour of Sweden, 1936. Right: Harry Arnold directed a large jazz-influenced group which made regular broadcasts. Here he leads it at a Stockholm concert.

Gonella present as guests. On occasions Ehrling recorded with smaller groups, among them a Dixieland-style unit, but while his regular big band records include a fair amount of ephemera and some undistinguished vocals, such performances as *Meditation*, *My Buddy*, *Blues On Strings*, *Kansas Jump* and *Mississippi Mood* are first-class. Ehrling's technical standards were high, and he always had a number of worthwhile soloists, so many of his records still make very good listening.

There were other highly competent Swedish dance bands in existence during the '30s and '40s, one being directed by Harry Arnold, who was to make his greatest impact during the following two decades. Arnold, whose full name was Harry Arnold Persson, was born at Hälsingborg on 7 August 1920. He studied alto saxophone and clarinet during the latter part of the '30s and became an outstanding arranger. After a period with local bands he led his own twelve-piece group at a dance hall in Malmö in 1942–9. After this he worked as a saxophonist and arranger with Thore Ehrling for a while, returning for weekend engagements at Malmö during 1952–4. His subsequent career was a brilliant one; he worked as an arranger-composer for a film company and led a star seventeen-piece radio band, whose records attracted attention throughout Europe and in the United States. Although the peak period of Arnold's career is outside the scope of this book, he was an example of a musician whose success was founded on dance band work from an earlier decade. He died at the age of fifty in Stockholm on 11 February 1971.

The story of Danish dance music is dominated, for other Europeans at least, by Kai Ewans. Ewans was born in Copenhagen on 10 April 1906, and from 1924 to 1926 worked with the important pioneer dance band leader Valdemar Eiberg. After this he appears to have travelled around Europe and the United States before returning to his own country and accepting a job with Kai Julian's band during 1931 and 1932, switching to Erik Tuxen's band the following year and replacing Tuxen as leader in 1936. For most of the next decade Ewans, who himself played clarinet and alto saxophone, regularly led his band at important locations. His band recorded with such visiting American stars as Benny Carter and Adelaide Hall, thus coming to the attention of European jazz fans, but its own output includes a great deal that is meritorious, owing partly to the scores provided by Kai Moller and Leo Mathiesen. Reviewing a broadcast relayed by the BBC in October 1938, 'Detector' of the *Melody Maker* commented that Ewans 'has achieved for Denmark the one thing no one here has yet succeeded in achieving for us – a swing band whose music is a true reflection of what, rightly or wrongly, is today considered to be the millennium in jazz'. In fact 'Detector' was not strictly correct, for though the Ewans band strongly featured swing material, which its arrangers and soloists interpreted with a degree of individuality, it was by no means confined to this repertoire, but was a versatile all-round dance band. During the late '40s Ewans dropped out of music, a decade later emigrating to the United States, where today he lives in retirement in California.

Erik Tuxen, born at Mannheim on 4 July 1902, was another important figure in Danish dance music history, his band from 1932 to 1936 including such prominent musicians as Peter Rasmussen, Kai Moller, Kai Ewans and Leo Mathiesen. Tuxen's recorded output is not large and, though well played, does not have the impact of Ewans's, despite the fact that the

Left: Eric Tuxen and his orchestra. Above: Kai Ewans and his band. Top right: Frankie Witkowski's society band, Warsaw, 1937. Centre right: the Polish trumpeter Ady Rosner and his 1939 touring band which visited several European countries. Lower right: Jaako Vuormaa and his band, from Finland, on VE Day, 1945.

latter was initially leading virtually the same personnel. In later years Tuxen became well known as the leader of the Danish State Radio Symphony Orchestra, a post he held until his death in Copenhagen on 28 August 1957.

Anker Skjoldborg and Aage Juhl Thomsen both led bands on records during 1936 that produced excellent performances, but whether they were permanent groups I do not know. Niels Foss, born in Copenhagen on 28 January 1916, and Bruno Henriksen, born in Copenhagen on 6 January 1910, both came to the fore during the '40s, making records that show their orchestras to be highly proficient if not particularly individual. After Kai Ewans the best-known Danish musician and band-leader is undoubtedly pianist Leo Mathiesen, who, after directing small groups during the '30s, led a full dance band in the following decade. Mathiesen, born in Copenhagen on 10 October 1906, was strongly influenced as a pianist and singer by Fats Waller, in the latter capacity not always to good effect. Many of his band recordings are marred by what one might describe as an excess of bonhomie, but such titles as *Harlem*, *Hot Spot Blues*, *Leo's Idea*, *It's The Talk Of The Town* and *Opus Hansen* combine a high standard of ensemble work with generally first-rate solos from a core of talented musicians. When the band era passed Mathiesen worked as a soloist, and is today recognised by European collectors as a very good pianist and important pioneer in Danish jazz and dance music. He died in his home town at the age of 63 on 16 December 1969.

Neither Norway nor Finland produced dance bands whose records or personal appearances gained them other than local reputations, but a few individual jazz musicians from these countries are known to a wider European audience. The most modern Finnish band of the '30s was Klaus Salmi's Ramblers, which in 1932 recorded the first Finnish jazz record, while a swing craze during the '40s led to the formation of highly efficient big bands led by Erkki Aho and Jaako Vuormaa. To date, though, the story of dance music and dance bands in Norway and Finland is obscure.

British dance music was popular in Poland during the '30s, but poor economic conditions in that country made local bands of more than nine pieces a rarity. The most popular Polish bands were those of Frank Witkowski, Zdzislaw Gorzynski, Henry Wars, Henry Gold and George Peterburski (composer of *Oh, Donna Clara*, which became a big European hit in 1931). At least some of these combined American-styled dance music with national folk airs. The one Polish musician who did gain a European reputation during the '30s was trumpeter Ady Rosner, who toured France for three months in 1938. Rosner frequently led a band with the unusual line-up of three trumpets, tenor saxophone and three rhythm; visitors to Poland were astonished by the strength and imaginativeness of his playing. In the summer of 1938 Rosner played in Holland and Denmark, returning to Poland at the end of the year with the intention of taking a short holiday. However, he was persuaded to re-form his local band and commenced working at the Esplanade at Warsaw, his salary of £32 a week being the highest ever paid up to that time to a Polish musician. Rosner, unfortunately, became a war victim in the early '40s. Another bandleader, Lofka Ilgowski, was reported by visitors to Poland in 1939 to be leading a modernish dance band, with Ilgowski himself playing clarinet in the Benny Goodman manner. Unfortunately no recorded evidence exists of these bands, and owing to Poland's wartime sufferings most of the documentary material has been destroyed too.

The story of dance music history in other eastern European countries is also obscure, though records by Jan Sima's Orchestrem Gramoklubu (1936) and Ladislava Hobarta's Orchestra (1945) are good enough to suggest that Czechoslovakia certainly had bands which were by European standards of a very high calibre. After the period with which this book is concerned,

such Czech bands as those led by Karla Vlacha and Gustav Brom deservedly gained wide European reputations.

Italy is another country which failed to produce any dance band that acquired other than a local reputation, and the dance band centre of Europe from the early '20s until the rise of the Nazis was undoubtedly Germany. The '20s in particular saw Germany as a haven for dance music and jazz musicians, and apart from local talent there were musicians and bands working regularly there from countries such as Britain, Denmark, Holland, Sweden and the United States, in addition to the less likely ones of Canada, Russia and Turkey.

Ragtime became popular in Germany in the early years of the century, but by the '20s dance music and jazz had taken over, and leaders such as Marek Weber and Dejas Bela were building a considerable local reputation. The latter recorded both under his own name and that of Clive Williams, and such early titles as *Deep Henderson* and *Say Mister! Have You Met Rosie's Sister* show a strong Fletcher Henderson influence. Marek Weber's *Crazy Words*, like so many European hot performances of the time, is interesting for both its good and its bad points, the latter including the jerkiness and stiffness of the rhythm. That progress was being made in this sphere is revealed by Ben Berlin's *Button Up Your Overcoat* – Berlin's real name was Hermann Bick – recorded two years later in 1929, for here the rhythm is much more flowing and there is also a considerable improvement in the technical standard of both

solos and ensemble playing. The outlawing of Jewish and negro music by the Nazis brought the halcyon years to a close, but some leaders at least appear to have ignored directives during the '30s. Die Goldene Sieben's *Quartier Latin* (1937) and Heinz Wehner's *Bugle Call Rag* (1936) are creditable hot performances, the former in particular having a number of excellent solos.

Despite the fact that many of the German bands were of an excellent standard, virtually none seems to have become known to British or American dance band followers, though one record, *Tiger Rag/Jungle Jazz* by James Kok and his band, was issued on English Decca. Kok, a Romanian by birth, went to Germany in the late '20s and organised a small dance band, which he subsequently enlarged to fifteen pieces; he worked in both Germany and Switzerland. Kok was a great admirer of the Casa Loma Orchestra and his own group played and recorded in the style of that band with great proficiency; the technical assurance shown on such titles as *Tiger Rag*, *White Jazz* and Eddie Carroll's *Harlem* is equal to that of most European bands of the day. Kok's band became immensely popular in Germany, but, no doubt for political reasons, Kok left the country in 1935, passing over the leadership to clarinettist Erhard Bauschke, who continued to record, though with generally less impressive results, until 1942.

As well as the Belgian and Dutch bands which were recording, and presumably performing in public, in a swing style during the early '40s in Germany, there was also a number of German swing bands recording and working during the same period. Among the most adept were the groups led by Willy Berking, Benny de Weille, Freddie Brocksieper, Lutz Templin, Kurt Widman, Horst Winter and, perhaps best of all, Kurt Hohenberger. It is ironic that, at a time when the Nazi authorities officially banned swing music, German bands reached a peak of proficiency in the idiom, but such performances as de Weille's *Heute Macht Die Ganze Welt Musik Fur Mich*, Winter's *Studie In F* and Hohenberger's *Amorcito Mio* not only are excellently played, have good solos and are well scored, but do actually swing. Quite how these bands were able to defy the authorities to such an extent, even obviously copying from such frowned-on American musicians as Benny Goodman and Bunny Berigan, is a mystery. The fact that Nazi Germany, at the height of the campaign against 'decadent Western music', should become the swing band centre of Europe is the supreme irony of dance band history. The course of the war brought a rapid end to this period, and when German bands again became established the dance band era was past.

It is clear that in many European countries there were outstanding dance bands to be heard. The near future will, I hope, see the appearance of many reissues which will help to illuminate what is, in some instances, a subject little known except to the nationals of the countries concerned.

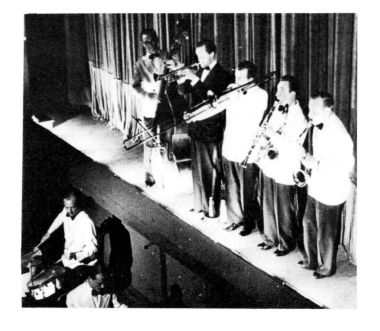

Left: James Kok and his band, c. 1935. Above: Heinz Wehner and his Telefunken Swing-Orchester, 1936. Below: Kurt Hohenberger with some of his soloists during a stage show in 1941.

THE
WAR YEARS
AND THE
AFTERMATH

In its second wartime issue the *Melody Maker* carried a headline that dance music was booming; London's West End, in particular, reported record business at night-clubs and theatres. Though some restaurant and club owners initially panicked – a number closing down altogether and firing their bands peremptorily – the more far-sighted amongst them were quick to realise that the demand for entertainment would be considerable, and that opportunities of making money were there for the taking. The government of the day, particularly in the 'phony war' phase, had no very clear policy on the question of whether theatres and clubs should remain open, though in July 1940 the Home Office brought in an ordinance closing down bottle parties. Amongst the first clubs to be affected were the Paradise and the Stork. The official police explanation included the comment that drunkenness took place on the premises, an accusation that drew from a representative of the Paradise the plaintive statement 'We have the finest people in the land among our guests and have always conducted a perfectly run establishment'. When the blitz began, the government did seriously think at one time of imposing a 4 pm curfew on all theatres, dance-halls and clubs, but ultimately decided that its effect on morale would outweigh its advantages. Throughout the height of the blitz, hotels, clubs and theatres remained open. The Mayfair Hotel reported early in 1941 that it not only presented Jack Jackson and his band but had resumed a cabaret policy, with a success that can be measured by the fact that it had to enlarge its facilities to cope with the crowds. A rundown of West End restaurants and hotels, in a 1941 *Melody Maker*, gave details of nightly dancing to resident dance bands at such venues as the Berkeley, Dorchester, Mayfair and Savoy Hotels. It suggested that their socialite clientele was determined not to let the war interfere too deeply with its pleasures. There were, of course, blitz casualties at some entertainment centres, and by late 1940 the Holborn Empire, London Coliseum, Finsbury Park Empire and Stratford Empire had been badly damaged, though with one notable exception clubs and hotels seemed to bear a charmed life.

The boom in entertainment was not confined to London, and amongst typical reports of the early war years were those of Joe Loss and his band attracting over 10,000 patrons during a week's residency at Glasgow's Playhouse Ballroom, and an opening night audience of 2,183 at the same dance-hall to greet Lew Stone's three-week engagement there. Not only live entertainment flourished, for 1940 was also a peak year for the sale of sheet music. The big hits at the end of December included *Sierra Sue*, *I'm Nobody's Baby*, *I'll Never Smile Again*, *Sleepy Lagoon*, *All Over The Place* and *There'll Come Another Day*, with only the humorous *Bless 'Em All* directly reflecting the war. At the start of the war there had been a spate of patriotic numbers of the *We're Gonna Hang Out The Washing On The Siegfried Line* variety, but, as the reality of the situation became apparent, bellicosity was little evident in songs that became popular hits.

Most of the leading bandleaders were past the age of being called up for military service. (One exception was Sydney Lipton, who joined the Royal Corps of Signals in March 1941 and served throughout the war.) The government used dance music as a propaganda weapon, and in 1941 commenced a special series of daily, hour-long, radio programmes beamed at German forces personnel. Wednesday was reserved for the Luftwaffe, who were not infrequently regaled with bands composed of RAF players! A neutral journalist who arrived in this country in May 1941 reported that the programmes were well received in the officer's mess at many a German aerodrome.

The service bands were by now superior in the main to the civilian units, which struggled to maintain standards in the face of the call-up of key personnel. The daily newspapers from time to time printed highly colourful stories about musicians attempting to evade military service. The *Evening Standard* in January 1940 reported 'Swingsters Want Exemption From Military Service', while the *Daily Express* of 26 June 1941 announced that 'Many Dance Band Boys Dodge The Army'. The trade press of the time reacted indignantly to such accusations, the *Melody Maker* fulminating at what it described as 'a slur on the profession', and there is no evidence whatsoever to suggest that dance band musicians made more strenuous efforts to avoid military service than any other section of the community. Dance and jazz band musicians have always been a good target for hack journalists when hard news is in short supply, and in the hysteria engendered by a wartime atmosphere they suffered their share of bizarre accusations. For example, a rumour circulated in some quarters during the autumn of 1940 that Charlie Kunz had been arrested for sending messages to the enemy through the medium of his piano-playing during broadcasts, and was serving a sentence – variously estimated at between seven and twenty years – in the Tower of London. Another victim was the famous French bandleader Ray Ventura, who suffered from a story, concocted by the Italian propaganda machine, that he had been killed on the Eastern front while fighting for the Finns against the Russians. This tale was taken up by some sections of the British press under such headings as 'A Dance Band Quisling'. The sheer unlikelihood of Ventura becoming a member of the Finnish army might be thought enough to have deterred any rational press writer, but reason and bellicosity – particularly when the latter is conducted from a safe position in a newspaper office – are not characteristics that go well together.

The dance band profession did suffer its casualties during the war, from both active service and bombing attacks. Al Bowlly was killed on 17 April 1941 when a land mine fell outside the block of flats in which he lived, and a month previously the West Indian bandleader Ken Johnson and his tenor saxophonist Dave Williams died when a bomb fell on the Café de Paris, where they were in residence. Grotesque and horrifying scenes followed the hit on the Café de Paris: one woman had her broken leg washed in champagne, and looters plundered rings from the fingers of the wounded and dying. The leading hotels and clubs were remarkably lucky in escaping bomb damage. Although sixty cinemas were destroyed in London during the war, and of the theatres only the Windmill could boast 'we never closed', the Café de Paris was the sole major casualty of the hotels and clubs. Hotel patrons also enjoyed privileges denied to the less affluent citizens who made do in crowded shelters, for ballrooms were frequently shifted to the safest possible locations, and well constructed shelters were provided. The Dorchester, for example, converted its Turkish-baths into shelters; according to Ralph Ingersoll there was

. . . a neat row of cots, spaced about two feet apart, each one covered with a lovely fluffy eiderdown. Its silks billowed and shone in the dim light in pale pinks and blues. Behind each cot hung the negligee, the dressing-gown . . . the pillows on which the heads lay were large and full and white . . . There was a little sign pinned to one of the Turkish-bath curtains. It said, 'Reserved for Lord Halifax'.

It seems that, as in the '30s, it paid to be a member of the socially privileged class during the war, if one wished to hear the leading dance bands under the best possible conditions.

Within a few months of the outbreak of war many of the leading dance band musicians found themselves together as members of service bands. The most famous of these was the RAF No. 1 Dance Band, better known as the Squadronaires. The idea of the band originated with Squadron-Leader O'Donnell, leader of the RAF Central Band at Uxbridge, who approached Les Brannelly and suggested that, as many leading dance band musicians were to be called up, they should enrol together in the RAF and form an orchestra to play to service personnel. Brannelly fell in with the suggestion and, together with other members of the Ambrose band, became a founder

The Squadronaires. Above: at a wartime dance, the line-up is (left to right): unknown, George Chisholm, Eric Breeze, Tommy McQuater, Archie Craig, Kenny Baker, Monty Levy, Tommy Bradbury, Andy McDevitt, Jimmy Durant (saxophones), Jock Cummings (drums).

member. The initial personnel included Tommy McQuater, George Chisholm, Andy McDevitt, Harry Lewis, Ronnie Aldrich, Jock Cummings, Sid Colin and Jimmy Miller. Brannelly (whose real name was Leslie Holmes) was the first director of the band, but in July 1940 he was promoted to Orderly Sergeant and as a result found himself unable to tour. He decided to continue working for the Squadronaires in an organising

capacity, but to hand over the leadership to Jimmy Miller, late of the Ambrose Octette. The band soon began broadcasts, and a report of one that took place in January 1941 moved 'Detector' of the *Melody Maker* to enthuse:

Any of you who were lucky enough to hear this airing will, I am sure, agree that I am not exaggerating when I say that it was the greatest dance band performance that has ever been broadcast this side of the Atlantic.

The programme performed on this date was representative of the Squadronaires, including a high proportion of jazz standards such as *South Rampart Street Parade*, *Farewell Blues* and *I Got*

Rhythm, with other numbers including several arranged by George Chisholm. Nine months later 'Detector' was still enthusing about the band, claiming that it was 'the greatest thing in jazz this country has produced'. The line-up of the band remained fairly unaltered throughout the war years; Clifton Ffrench brought the brass section up to five when he joined early in 1942, and Harry Lewis was invalided out of the RAF in September 1943 and not, for a time, replaced. A 1945 personnel included twelve of the original members – Lewis is the only absentee – with Ffrench and the newly joined saxophonists Cliff Townshend and Monty Levy. Until the final dissolution of the band in the '60s it retained some of its founder members. Throughout the war years the Squadronaires broadcast frequently; made many public appearances, such as a featured spot in the 'Dance Music Festival of 1942' at the London Coliseum and a variety booking in March 1943, when they doubled at the Chiswick Empire and the Hammersmith Palais; and provided the music for, and were seen in a dance sequence in, the 1943 film *The Life And Death Of Colonel Blimp*.

In the immediate post-war period the band played for service personnel in various European countries, deciding to remain together on a co-operative basis after demobilisation in 1946. It was booked for a summer season at a holiday camp, made some variety appearances and filmed a short for Pathé. A fairly steady broadcasting schedule was undertaken during the remaining years of the '40s, but a review of a 1947 radio transmission claimed that the 'band sounded tired, *Air Mail Special* showed ragged section work, there were uninspired solos, the whole programme judged by any standards was grim'. A month later the same reviewer judged another broadcast and was happy to report that the Squadronaires were back in form. That the band retained a wide popularity is made clear by the fact that in the 1947 *Melody Maker* readers' poll it came third in the dance band section and ninth in the 'sweet' section, but by the mid-'50s popular entertainment was taking a new direction and in 1964 the Squadronaires disbanded.

Initially all the band's Decca records were issued as by the Royal Air Force Dance Orchestra, though naturally in peace-

Above: a section of the Squadronaires when it became a civilian band. Below: Ronnie Aldrich, pianist leader of the band. Right: top: the Skyrockets Dance Orchestra, with vocalists Doreen Lundy and Cyril Shane sitting in front. Bottom: an RAF dance band directed by the Kahn brothers in the early '40s. Alfie Kahn is on the far left, Dave on the far right. The saxophonist is Charlie Barlow.

WELCOME

time they were listed as by the Squadronaires. One of the highspots of their output is a Ronnie Aldrich arrangement of Spike Hughes's delightful *Donegal Cradle Song* scored for five saxophones and featuring Monty Levy on soprano, while versions of *Jeepers Creepers*, *No Name Jive* and *C Jam Blues* (a George Chisholm arrangement) adequately reflect the high competence of the soloists and the precision of the ensemble. Though it made many entirely commercial recordings of a nondescript nature, and veered in its instrumentals between the stylistic extremes of big band Dixieland on the one hand and Stan Kenton on the other, the Squadronaires at their best were a very musicianly and versatile combination – without doubt the finest of the service bands.

The Squadronaires' chief rivals during the war years were the No. 1 Balloon Centre Dance Orchestra, better known as the Skyrockets, and the Royal Army Ordnance Corps Blue Rockets. The former originated during 1940 at Blackpool, where a number of musicians were undergoing training to become balloon rigger fabric workers, prior to transfer to the No. 1 Balloon Centre at Kidbrooke, just outside London. After completing their training the musicians formed a band to play in off-duty periods, and its reputation grew sufficiently to attract the attention of the Air Ministry, who booked it to undertake a two-year series of propaganda broadcasts to the German Luftwaffe. By 1942 the band .had been heard in numerous broadcasts, and in October of that year it appeared in the annual 'Jazz Jamboree' and played its first public concert at the Colston Hall, Bristol. The Skyrockets were led for the greater part of their existence by Paul Fenhoulet, a trombonist/arranger who worked with Carroll Gibbons at the Savoy Hotel in the pre-war period, but their initial leader was George Beaumont, until he received a posting to another station. The wartime history of the Skyrockets closely approximated that of the Squadronaires, though it was not until Balloon Command ceased to exist and the band was posted to Fighter Command that it received official recognition as a service dance orchestra. Frequent broadcasts, recordings for the Rex and later Parlophone labels, and occasional public appearances made the band popular with audiences throughout Britain, and like the Squadronaires its members decided to continue as a group after demobilisation.

In the post-war period the band was owned by thirteen of its members who employed the remaining musicians. Some of its best known stars were Les Lambert, Don Macaffer, Pat Dodd, Chick Smith and Pat Smuts, and a *Melody Maker* poll of 1946 placed the band fourth in the swing section and third in the 'sweet' section. It was in this year that the Skyrockets became the pit band for the show 'High Time' at the London Palladium, a show which incidentally included a feature act by what the *Melody Maker* described as an 'infant drum prodigy' called Victor Feldman. Paul Fenhoulet was interested in building the band to André Kostelanetz-like proportions, but the fact that other members of the personnel were not happy with the direction of its music became a talking point in the musical press, and in November 1947 the news broke that by general agreement Fenhoulhet would be leaving, and that his successor would be Woolf Phillips. Curiously enough, it was reported in the *Melody Maker* that Fenhoulet had been feeling for some time that the band was getting too commercial, and that he was keen on modern progressive music. A week later, Phillips reported his plans to 'modernise' the band. There was no detectable change in musical policy in the event, and the band continued to work regularly at the London Palladium during a great deal of 1948, including an engagement in support of Danny Kaye. It finally disbanded during the '50s.

The Army's answer to the two RAF bands was the RAOC Blue Rockets, formed by Eric Robinson. (In later years a well-known TV personality and leader of a large orchestra specialising in light classics.) After a while Robinson was transferred to the Army Radio Unit and the direction of the Blue Rockets

fell to trombonist Eric Tann – who had worked with Stone, Hall and Fox – until he was invalided out of the army in April 1943. The band initially specialised in swing arrangements of light classics, but before long took on the characteristics of one of the pre-war show orchestras, and signed a year's recording contract with HMV early in 1942. Early in that year there was a sustained press campaign against musicians in the services, described in one newspaper as 'toy soldiers', and though they received only normal army pay plus an allowance of ten shillings a week towards the hire, wear and tear of instruments, the outcry resulted in the disbandment of the Blue Rockets in February. A month later they re-formed and in the following years undertook their share of broadcasting, recording and occasional public appearances when army engagements permitted. In February 1943 it was reported that the Blue Rockets were to be featured in a film for the Ministry of Information, *Swinging Into The Attack*, with Miff Ferrie re-orchestrating several Spike Hughes compositions for use in the film. Whether the film was ever completed I have been unable to ascertain, and the activities of the band during the latter part of 1943 and much of 1944 are poorly documented. In 1945 it was reported that most of the original personnel had split up, but a peace-time band under the name of the Blue Rockets Dance Band was formed with many of the war-time musicians present, led once more by Eric Robinson. By early 1947 Robinson had left and the leadership passed to saxophonist Benny Daniels. Some important additions for a nation-wide tour at that time were the outstanding West Indian saxophone stylist Bertie King and vocalist Judy Johnson. The band survived into the early '50s but, though a highly competent unit, never really succeeded in matching its RAF rivals in popularity or musical interest.

Other service bands attained some degree of popularity, among them the naval Blue Mariners – led by pianist George

Crow and including the brilliant reedman Freddy Gardner, whose playing was always singled out for praise by broadcast reviewers – and the band of the RAF Fighter Command, which had such fine musicians as trumpeter Kenny Baker and saxophonists Joe Crossman and Aubrey Franks. Tiny Winters was a member of a station dance band led by Billy Amstell, there was an Ack Ack Dance Band stationed in Scotland, a Bomber Command Orchestra which recorded in 1947 for Regal Zonophone (as Leslie Douglas and his Orchestra), and even a London Fire Force Band of whom *Melody Maker* wrote, in October 1942, that it was 'now easily our second best National Services band and that's equivalent to saying second best in the whole country'. Only the Blue Mariners survived into the post-war years, but considering the conditions under which they played many of the service bands achieved a remarkable degree of proficiency, and the Squadronaires' accomplishments entitle them to be considered the finest dance band of the war years.

With most of the leading dance band musicians in the services, civilian groups struggled on as best they could. Sidemen ineligible for military service found themselves in a position to earn better money than ever before. Some leaders bemoaned the situation, and George Scott-Wood complained to the *Melody Maker* in September 1942 about having to pay superior salaries to inferior musicians, who, he claimed, did not give their employers the loyalty and consideration they had the right to expect. Despite this some bands achieved popularity greater than they had enjoyed in the pre-war years, one such being that led by the perennial Joe Loss, still active as a leader in 1971. He was born in Liverpool on 22 June 1910 and in the early '20s completed musical studies at the Trinity College Of Music and the London School Of Music. He led a youthful orchestra called the Magnetic Dance Band in 1926, shortly afterwards took a professional job as a violinist, and followed it in the next year or two with a variety of jobs with dance bands in Blackpool and London. In September 1930 he led a seven-piece band at London's Astoria Ballroom, playing opposite Oscar Rabin and his Romany Band, and a year later he moved

to the Kit-Cat Club, where he remained as resident bandleader for three years, in the course of which he made his broadcasting debut on 9 December 1933. Loss had broken into variety while at the Kit-Cat, topping the bill at the Holborn Empire early in 1934, but in the latter year he once more changed his location and returned to the Astoria Ballroom, now leading a twelve-piece group. In the next few years he combined this resident job with frequent broadcasts, recordings and annual touring. His band became immensely popular, partly on the strength of

Joe Loss gains pride of place on an October 1940 supplement.

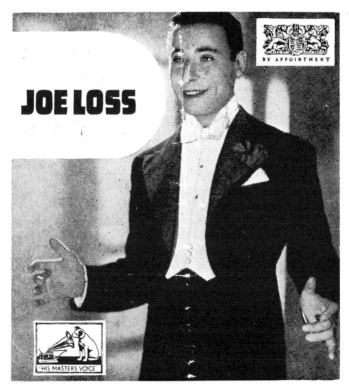

JOE LOSS

such heavily featured vocalists as Chick Henderson – lost at sea during the war – Monte Rey, Marjorie Kingsley and, for a period, Adelaide Hall.

At the outbreak of war the Loss band was in the middle of a summer tour, at the completion of which he returned to the Astoria Ballroom, but early in 1940 he went over to France to play for the British Expeditionary Force and soon after his return to England announced that he would finally be leaving the Astoria to undertake extensive touring schedules. His increasing popularity was underlined by a new recording contract, which meant that in future his records would appear on HMV rather than the cheaper Regal-Zonophone label. The war years were triumphant ones for Loss, for everywhere he went he attracted huge crowds and at many venues broke existing box-office records. One of his most curious broadcasts occurred on 15 November 1941, when his band was conducted by a notorious nonagenarian anti-jazz knight called Sir Henry Coward, who unbent sufficiently to remark that 'dance musicians are far superior to the type of music they play'. Sir Henry led the band in a version of the *Poet And Peasant Overture*, donating his fee to a wartime charity.

Loss has an unbroken record of leading a band for over four decades, always preferring to play in dance halls rather than hotels. He once said that 'the better the restaurant or hotel the lower the standard of dancing', adding 'fortunately there are still thousands of young workers who take a pride in their dancing, and my band is their band – the band for dancers'. Today he has modified his musical policy to incorporate contemporary developments in popular entertainment, but still occasionally makes records in an older style, retaining his popularity as a recording and TV artist.

Loss's best band was undoubtedly that of the late '30s and early '40s, which produced such popular recordings as *In The Mood*, *Woodchoppers Ball*, *Blues Upstairs And Downstairs*, *Honky Tonk Train Blues* and various more commercial titles with vocals from Chick Henderson and his other singers. Though few of Loss's recordings can compare in individuality with the output of the leading '30s bands, they are invariably technically impeccable. Some of the early '40s performances show the band off to its best advantage.

Oscar Rabin was another leader who achieved great popularity during the war years. Rabin was born in Riga in Russia

in 1899 but came to this country as a child. He met Harry Davis in 1924 and formed a friendship that spilled over into professional fields. The Rabin–Davis Band had its first engagement at the Palace Hotel, Southend, in 1925, subsequently being billed as 'Oscar Rabin and his Romany Band with Harry Davis'. In the years after it achieved some success as a Palais band at various London venues, breaking into recording and broadcasting in 1935. For part of its life at least the band was a co-operative unit, and during the war regular touring and ballroom appearances gained it a considerable following. During the early '40s I heard the band on a number of occasions in London; at this time it was following a more adventurous musical policy than it had done in the past – not in fact a difficult achievement – and included in its ranks some good musicians. It continued to be popular for a while after the war,

sometimes recording swing numbers, but, though a proficient band, it lacked any real individuality or creativity.

In many ways the band that dominated the '40s in Britain was Geraldo's; its output underwent considerable changes over the years. Geraldo (real name Gerald Bright) was born in London in 1904 and was a youthful piano prodigy who studied at the Royal Academy of Music. His first professional job was as a relief-pianist at a cinema in London's famous Old Kent Road, following which he became an organist at a restaurant. Then, during the '20s, he formed various dance combinations both in England and on the Continent, gaining popularity with frequent broadcasts from the Hotel Majestic at St Annes-on-Sea, where he led the resident band for nearly five years.

If certain press releases were correct – and this I take leave to doubt – Geraldo became enamoured of South American music while engaged in a study tour of several countries on that continent. It is undeniable that in August 1930 Geraldo's Gaucho Tango Band opened at the Savoy Hotel in London. The musicians were colourfully attired in what were accepted as the accoutrements of genuine gauchos, as supplied by the best theatrical costumiers, and the music had about as much

RECORDS FOR JUNE 1940

GERALDO and HIS SWEET MUSIC

Left: Geraldo and his band. Top: outside the Berlin Chancellory, 1945; left to right – Archie Lewis, Eddie Calvert, Joe Ferrie, Dereck Abbott, Dorothy Carless, Sid Bright, Jack Collier, Jimmy Watson, Freddy Clayton, two unknowns, Alfie Noakes, Dougie Robinson. Bottom: in the '50s with Lonnie Donegan and Patti Lewis. Below: Leslie 'Jiver' Hutchinson and his band, 1946.

authenticity as the uniforms. Gaining himself a reputation as the 'Tango King', Geraldo was awarded an appearance at the 1933 Royal Command Performance, but in September of that year he decided to form a straight dance orchestra too, and by 1937 the Gaucho Tango Band was no more.

Geraldo was always a popular broadcaster and appeared in a variety of formats, even leading large concert groups, but it was not really until the late '30s that the music he performed could be rated anything but competent. Early in January 1939 he made changes in a personnel that had been remarkably stable for some years, bringing in an excellent trio of saxophonists in Harry Hayes, Andy McDevitt and George Evans, all of whom were good jazz soloists. Around the same time Geraldo launched his relatively short-lived 'Sunday Night Swing Club' sessions at the St Martin's Theatre, all of which featured prominent jazz groups and individual soloists. On the outbreak of war Geraldo led a good band at the Savoy, but during the following August he severed his contract with the Savoy and decided to concentrate on touring. Soon afterwards he was appointed supervisor of the ENSA Band Division, in 1944 touring the Middle East, North Africa and Italy. Throughout the war years he strengthened his band, running against the current in this respect. Some of his most prominent additions were the late West Indian trumpeter Leslie 'Jiver' Hutchinson and singer Beryl Davis, daughter of Harry Davis, who left the Oscar Rabin band in June 1942. In April of the latter year Geraldo presented a swing concert at London's Stoll Theatre which attracted an audience of three thousand and ecstatic reviews in the musical press. His personnel at the time included such prominent musicians as Harry Hayes, Ivor Mairants, Norman Stenfalt, 'Lad' Busby and Nat Temple. For the rest of the '40s and part of the '50s Geraldo was the dominant dance band leader in Britain, his roster of musicians including a contingent of jazz stars who were often heavily featured both on record and in concert.

In the post-war years Geraldo, in addition to leading his own orchestras, became heavily involved in band management, supplying the groups who played on the major Cunard liners.

HARRY LEADER
& HIS BAND.

Far left: a series of shots of the Harry Leader Band taken from a publicity folder. Left: Jack Payne acting as guest conductor for the Ted Heath Band. Below: Eric Winstone and his band on stage, c. 1950. Below, centre: Harry Hayes (standing) with his septet during the late 'forties: left to right, other musicians are Alan Clare, Brian Gray, Danny Craig, Pete Peterson, Coleridge Goode and Jan Smits, with vocalist Primrose Hayes. Bottom left: The Basil and Ivor Kirchin Band. Bottom, centre: Vic Lewis directs his band at the Beaulieu Festival. Bottom, right: Harry Roy with his band, c. 1948.

He also controlled the pit orchestras of a well-known theatre circuit, was for a while musical director of Scottish Television, and was the first bandleader to appear on British TV when it reopened after the war. By the mid-'50s he had retired from leading an orchestra, but he still presents occasional concerts for his former audiences.

Geraldo's earliest records – over the years he was a prolific recorder – are uninteresting, but from the early '40s numerous titles combine a high standard of ensemble work and excellent solos, with altoist Harry Hayes being heard to advantage on such numbers as *Soft Shoe Shuffle* and *Idaho*. In the mid-'40s the Geraldo band was recording swing numbers from the books of such American leaders as Charlie Barnet and Stan Kenton, and not long afterwards a less derivative approach was apparent in a number of versions of jazz themes, some written by members of the band. It is a far cry from the Gaucho Tango Band to the bop-influenced group sometimes featured in the early '50s, and Geraldo's bandleading history is one of increasing adventurousness in both performance and use of material. Although Geraldo still retains a large public following, he himself is dissatisfied with all his recorded work, and will not give permission for any of it to be reissued. There is no doubt that to a generation who missed the halcyon dance band era of the '30s and grew up during the early war years, Geraldo occupies much the same niche in Britain as does Glenn Miller in the United States.

There were of course other attempts at leading bands during the war and post-war years. Carl Barriteau attempted to carry on the traditions of the late Ken Johnson from 1942, while another ex-Johnson musician, trumpeter Leslie 'Jiver' Hutchinson, led a band from 1943 that recorded in Prague late in 1947. Trumpeter Teddy Foster, once of the Ambrose and Billy Cotton bands, made several unsuccessful bandleading attempts, but became popular for a while in the '40s. George Evans led a rather unusual band for a short period; it had five alto saxophones and five tenors. After being associated with a Dixieland-type small group, Vic Lewis branched out in the late '40s to lead a big band heavily influenced by Stan Kenton, while John Dankworth made considerable impact with a band that featured modern jazz arrangements. The real success story of the late '40s was that of the late Ted Heath, who, after decades as a sideman with innumerable major dance bands, formed his own jazz-influenced big band and became immensely

Top: Joe Daniels, formerly Harry Roy's drummer, led his own 'Hot Shots' for some years. Here he heads his sextet at a recording session. Bottom: the late Ted Heath, who led Britain's most successful postwar big band.

popular on both sides of the Atlantic. However, whatever their merits, these groups were not dance bands as the term is used in this book, and their story is outside its scope.

With perhaps the single exception of Geraldo, none of the pre-war dance band leaders made musical progress during the '40s. It would, on the whole, be unrealistic to expect them to have done so, for the war took away many of the best musicians to the forces, and the social structure which gave them pre-war stability was fractured. By the end of the '40s British dance music was not in a healthy state. One of the more regrettable aspects of the period was the increasing sentimentality and banality of popular songs. Those leaders who resisted this trend seemed to fall back on a variety of derivative styles that echoed some of the popular American bands, but in any case the public was turning to other areas of popular entertainment. The series of events taking place in the United States, which caused the end of the big band era in that country, took a little longer to achieve their full effect in Britain, but inevitably their force was felt here within a short while. An unbiased observer of the British dance band scene during the late '40s would not have needed great prophetic powers to know that he was witnessing the end of an era of popular entertainment. When Bill Haley came to Britain a few years later an older generation of listeners and musicians fulminated – some are still fulminating seventeen years afterwards – but his triumph ushered in a new age in entertainment, one with developments that must be surprising Haley himself. Dance bands have continued to exist, but have become a small section of the whole popular entertainment field, and, barring some extraordinary turn of events, are likely to remain so in its future history.

The United States enjoyed peace for a little longer than Europe, and the Japanese attack on Pearl Harbor came at a time when the American entertainment industry was enjoying something akin to boom conditions. As a result of Roosevelt's public work projects and a great upsurge in the output of the armaments industry, prosperity was slowly returning, though until the outbreak of World War II unemployment figures never fell below eight million. In the months just before Pearl Harbor, re-employment, national defence spending, tension over possible involvement in the war, and a search for amusement were reflected in soaring record sales, which were confidently expected to reach one hundred million by the end of the year, almost double the 1940 total. The war put an end to such spectacular expansion, for in May 1942 the United States Government issued an order that ensured a cut in record production of some 70 per cent. Shellac had to be imported from India and, what with shipping difficulties and the increasing need for shellac in war production (wires on bomber planes were dipped in shellac for protective coating, and it was also used as a base for various plastics), the record industry's requirements became of secondary importance. The companies decided to concentrate on the best-selling commercial bands and the maintenance of their classical catalogues, though one significant decision that they made was that the 'race' and 'hillbilly' lists would be kept up, a move that in retrospect can be seen as highly important.

The popularity of the leading dance and swing bands seemed unassailable during the early '40s, but certain events took place which at the time seemed unrelated to their future but were in fact to alter profoundly the course of American popular entertainment. One was a disagreement in 1941 between ASCAP (American Society of Composers, Authors and Publishers) and the radio networks, over the terms for a renewal of a contract giving the latter the right to public performance of ASCAP-controlled music. ASCAP had been formed in 1914 to protect composers' interests and owned the rights to virtually all music written and published in the United States after 1884, but when they demanded an annual S9 million from the radio networks – almost twice what they had received previously – the latter were enraged and in October 1939 set up a rival organisation, Broadcast Music, Inc. There is no doubt that ASCAP had grown conservative and somewhat autocratic over the years, and its members showed almost open contempt for hillbilly and blues composers – who saw in BMI a heaven-sent opportunity to fight back. For the first ten months of 1941 the radio networks banned all ASCAP material from the air, and in this time BMI, after a hesitant start, attracted more and

more composers, until by October it had built up a catalogue of 36,000 copyrights from 52 publishers. By the time ASCAP and the networks settled their differences, hillbilly and, to a lesser extent, race music had secured a foothold in broadcasting that was to be decisive in the years ahead.

Less than eight months after the outbreak of war the record companies were faced with a strike called by the American Federation of Musicians. Its president, James C. Petrillo, argued that juke boxes (which now numbered almost half a million) and radio stations which played records for most of the day were increasing unemployment amongst musicians. He demanded that the recording companies establish a fund for these musicians, payable from their profits. All recording ceased on 1 August 1942 and, though the companies had tried to alleviate the situation by round-the-clock sessions in the previous week, by 1943 they were beginning to feel the pinch. The first company to give in was Decca, which, faced with bankruptcy, signed a contract with the AFM in September 1943. Columbia and RCA Victor held out until November 1944 before meeting the AFM's demands, but in the interim numerous small companies were established which signed agreements with the AFM and filled the vacuum left by the majors. The latter did attempt to provide new recordings by the use of· vocalists supported by choirs, but in retrospect the action of the AFM can be seen to have damaged the interests of its members very severely. Again, what was striking about the recordings made by most of the newer companies was their emphasis on hillbilly and race releases, which offered an ever greater challenge to the supremacy of the bands.

One of the most unfortunate effects of the AFM recording ban is that it denied us the opportunity of studying various interesting changes in the band scene. Some writers have claimed that by the early '40s the big bands were entering an era of degeneration, but this seems totally exaggerated when one considers that in this period Duke Ellington reached perhaps the highest creative peak of his career, Benny Goodman led what is arguably his most outstanding band, the Earl Hines band was by all accounts the most adventurous he ever led, and even some of the most commercial bandleaders were unexpectedly attempting to improve the quality of their music. In the last category we can use as an illustration the surprising metamorphosis in the musical output of Horace Heidt.

In the world of the theatre the clown who yearns to play Hamlet is a familiar figure; Heidt's activities in the early '40s proved that he had his counterpart in the dance band world. For years Heidt had led one of the most commercially successful but musically dismal bands in the United States, reaching a peak of popularity in the mid-'30s when his music was compounded of every gimmick in the book, from the electric guitar effects of Alvino Rey and the flashy showmanship of pianist Frankie Carle to a saxophone section that out-Lombardoed Lombardo. In 1939 the musical world was astonished when Bobby Hackett accepted an invitation to join Heidt's band, and even more surprised when several of the leader's sidemen provided adequate backing to Hackett on a number of small-group jazz recordings. Around 1942–3 Heidt totally revamped his band and style, bringing in jazz stars like Jess Stacy, Shorty Sherock and Joe Rushton, but unfortunately this group was active during the recording ban and so there is no recorded evidence of Heidt in a role other than that of a purveyor of musical dross. In recent years Heidt has become a successful business executive, though his continuing interest in music was shown when, in 1965, he presented an hour-long television programme over a Los Angeles station that included the last TV appearance of trumpeter Red Nichols. Heidt and Nichols had first met forty-five years before, when Nichols was organising a jazz group while attending Culver Military Academy in Indiana. On that occasion Nichols declined to give the piano chair to Heidt on the ground that his playing was too square. Heidt's perennial fate was to be dismissed as a square;

but for a brief period he was actually the musical equivalent of the clown who did finally get to play Hamlet!

In terms of popular success, though leaders as diverse as Benny Goodman and Guy Lombardo retained their considerable followings, the early '40s were dominated by the Dorsey brothers – leading separate bands – and, above all, Glenn Miller. To generalise, the leading dance bands in those years (not the jazz ones, of course) slowly veered away from swing instrumentals and increasingly featured sentimental ballads, a process further developed during the height of the war years. One corollary of this shift was the emergence of the dance band vocalist to a position of increasing prominence. Though many such singers had achieved considerable popularity before the war, it was in the '40s that they began to acquire box-office appeal equal to that of the bands with whom they were featured.

After the break with brother Tommy, Jimmy Dorsey retained most of the original Dorsey brothers personnel and for some years fronted it with a reasonable degree of success. The band's style varied between what were basically two-beat instrumentals and commercial ballads with vocals by Bob Eberly and Helen O'Connell, but the breakthrough to the big time came in 1941, as a result of a recording of *Green Eyes* with a vocal duet by Eberly and O'Connell. The pattern of this performance, with an opening chorus by Eberly, a double-tempo section with Dorsey soloing, and a return to the original

Left, top: Jimmy Dorsey (centre) with his vocalists Helen O'Connell and Bob Eberle. Bottom: Paul Whiteman (on dais) with the Dorseys in a scene from the film The Fabulous Dorseys. *Below: Jimmy Dorsey (lower right) with members of his band.*

tempo for O'Connell's closing vocal, reportedly arose from the requirements of a sponsor of Dorsey's commercial radio programme who requested a finale featuring its stars. Tutti Camarata devised the routine to meet the demand and after *Green Eyes* it caught on with the public, though at least one of the Decca executives thought the record would be a disastrous failure. Another big hit in the same vein was *Tangerine*, written by Johnny Mercer. In addition to the duets, both Eberly and O'Connell were also featured on many records singly; perhaps the best performance by the latter is heard on *Embraceable You*. When Helen O'Connell left the band she was replaced by Kitty Kallen, a more technically accomplished singer, and the duet tradition was continued until Eberly was called up for army service.

Probably the best band Dorsey led was that of 1943, which included such soloists as Babe Russin and Ray Linn, but because of the recording ban only a few records were made, of which *King Porter Stomp* and *Sackhouse Stomp* are the most impressive. At this time the popularity of the band in the United States, though not in Europe, equalled that of Tommy's, but though Jimmy led bands for a further decade, several with some degree of popular acclaim, he inevitably felt the growing weight of the recession that was taking place in the dance band world. In February 1953 he joined forces once more with Tommy, recording with the combined group until 1956. In November of that year he recorded a version of *So Rare* that became his last popular hit. By now gravely ill, Jimmy Dorsey died of cancer on 12 June 1957, outliving Tommy, who had died on the previous 26 November, by a mere seven months.

In view of Jimmy Dorsey's awesome reputation amongst

other musicians as a virtuoso alto saxophonist there is some irony in the fact that he is chiefly remembered by the public for the recordings which featured Bob Eberly and Helen O'Connell. The best of Dorsey's purely instrumental records, particularly those made in the '40s with a modern-styled band, deserve better than the neglect they have received from most critics, and their reissue would help place Dorsey's not inconsiderable musical achievements in perspective. Well over a decade after his death, Jimmy Dorsey is remembered today with affection by his public and with respect by other musicians.

Once Tommy Dorsey formed his own band he straightaway adopted a musical policy that was much more swing-oriented than his brother's, achieving a hit on his third Victor recording session with his famous version of I'm Getting Sentimental Over You. Although he always included a strong jazz contingent within his ranks Dorsey did not consider himself to be a jazz musician, and built his reputation partly on the versatility of his approach. He recorded much of the popular hit material of the day, featuring vocals by Edythe Wright and Jack Leonard, but hit the big time in 1937 with Marie, which featured a group vocal behind Leonard (copied from the version he had heard played by a little-known black band called the Sunset Royals), and a series of swing versions of light classics such as Song Of India and Liebestraum. Well established as a popular favourite by 1940, he reached a peak of acclaim in that year when Frank Sinatra joined the band and he commenced to feature him heavily on recordings, with the vocal group The Pied Pipers. This culminated in the enormous success of such titles as Hear My Song, Violetta, I'll Never Smile Again, Yours Is My Heart Alone and Oh! Look At Me Now. Sinatra

remained with the band until summer 1942, subsequently becoming the most widely acclaimed of all popular vocalists until his retirement in 1971 and, incidentally, the singer who received the greatest praise from musicians for his musical sensitivity.

The shift in Dorsey's musical policy during the '40s did not preclude occasional instrumental recordings, particularly as he had added to his staff the brilliant ex-Lunceford arranger Sy Oliver, responsible for hit versions of Yes, Indeed, Well Git It!, Opus No. 1 and On The Sunny Side Of The Street, but in general the increasing tendency of vocalists to emerge as dominant figures in their own right was echoed in his output. Another tendency amongst bandleaders was underlined by Dorsey's decision in the '40s to add a string section to his normal personnel, a move that contributed little to enhancing musical standards. Dorsey remained active as a leader, except in 1946–8, but though his later bands had many star sidemen he was never again able to recapture the spirit and individuality of the best of his earlier groups.

George T. Simon described Tommy Dorsey's as 'the greatest all-round dance band of them all', and though I at first thought this a fanciful judgment, on reflection I feel it is not too wide of the mark. In everything that he attempted, Tommy Dorsey applied perfectionist criteria, and if, during the '40s, much of the material he recorded was banal in the extreme, there is no denying the high musical standards that he maintained throughout his career. More flamboyant and explosive as a personality

Tommy Dorsey and his band, at a Victor recording session in the late '30s (below) and in a film of the early '40s (right).

than his brother Jimmy, Tommy Dorsey shared with him the admiration of other musicians for the sheer technical perfection of his own playing. On the strength of this alone he was undeniably one of the major figures in the history of dance music.

No leader in the world of dance music has created a style that has retained its appeal for as long as Glenn Miller's. To this day there are bands in both the United States and Britain whose repertoire consists mainly of note-for-note copies of Miller recordings, and they invariably draw large crowds wherever they perform. Miller's real break came when he led his band at the Glenn Island Casino during 1939, for although the engagement was not lucrative in itself it carried with it ten weekly broadcasts, which led to the band's widest exposure. It is ironic that not long before securing this booking Miller had become so discouraged by his failure to make any impact on the dance band scene that he seriously considered returning to studio work. After the Glenn Island Casino date, however, the Miller band became the biggest attraction in American music, breaking attendance records wherever it played. Miller's fans were dismayed when in 1942 he announced that he intended to volunteer for the armed forces, and the final engagement of the civilian band at the Central Theater, Passaic, New Jersey, on 27 September of that year was an emotional occasion. In 1943 Miller organised his famous AAF Orchestra which, after a heavy schedule in the United States, went to Britain in spring of 1944. This wartime band became a legend on the strength of its many BBC broadcasts and hundreds of appearances before service personnel, and at the end of the year it was decided to send it to Paris to commence a lengthy series of engagements in Europe. Miller himself set off for the flight to Paris with three others on a foggy day in December, intending to finalise the arrangements for tours of service camps. No trace of the plane or its occupants was ever subsequently discovered.

Over a quarter of a century after Miller's death the mystique that surrounds his name and his music remains as potent as ever. Part of the explanation may lie in the fact that his music provided much-needed relief from wartime cares, but, more than that, he possessed, as Benny Goodman wrote, 'a great sense of the commercial, of what would attract the average listener, and this he managed to do without sacrificing his musical integrity'. Certainly almost no other leader was able to produce, in a period of only just over three years, such a string of hit records: *Moonlight Serenade, Little Brown Jug, In The Mood, Tuxedo Junction, Pennsylvania 6–5000, Anvil Chorus, Perfidia, Chattanooga Choo Choo, A String Of Pearls, American Patrol, I've Got A Gal In Kalamazoo, Serenade In Blue* . . .

Listening to Miller's music today I must confess that, nostalgia apart, I find much of it somewhat tedious; the famous reed voicing, with clarinet over four saxes, and the repeated riff that fades away and then reappears, sound mechanical. Miller himself greatly admired the Jimmie Lunceford band, though he never claimed he was leading a jazz group, and there is no doubt of the polished musicianship present on all his recordings. There were certainly several more interesting bands about than Miller's, but he, more than anyone, personifies an era when sentimentality gained ground as a reaction to the brashness of the swing bands, and few other leaders have enjoyed such a rapport with their audiences. His vocalists, particularly Marion Hutton and Ray Eberle, typified the popular girl/boy next door image, and his music, however carefully planned, was outgoing

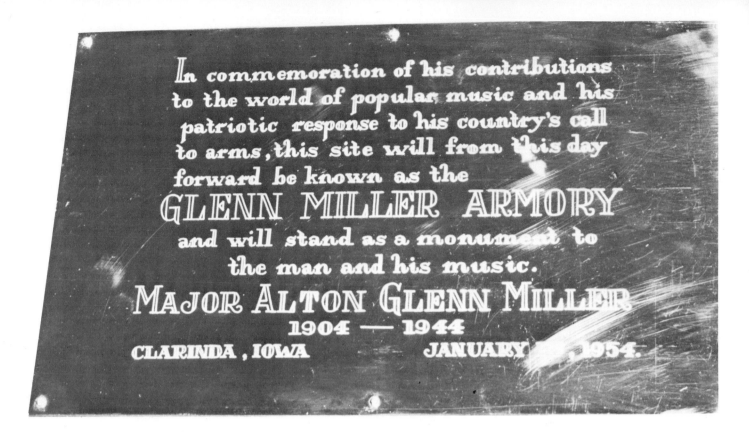

and relatively unsophisticated in character. Like Whiteman in the '20s, Miller seemed to summarise in his music the hopes and aspirations of a generation, and, also like Whiteman, he was rewarded with a degree of loyalty and affection from his listeners that few other leaders in the history of dance music have been able to achieve.

If the Dorseys and Miller dominated the opening years of the '40s from a commercial viewpoint, there were many other interesting bands to be heard, apart from the long-established ones. One of the finest and in many ways least appreciated orchestras was that led by pianist Claude Thornhill, who, like Miller, first received some public acclaim after an engagement at the Glenn Island Casino. The strength of the band lay in its brilliant and unusual voicings, with passages often played by six or seven clarinets, and french horns used to impart an unusual ensemble timbre. After creating a stir amongst critics and discerning listeners, Thornhill enrolled in the navy in October 1942 and was inactive in music until 1946, when, upon his discharge, he reorganised his band with many members of the earlier personnel present. Thornhill owed much to his brilliant arrangers Bill Borden and Gil Evans for the musical success of his band, its repertoire varying between beautifully played melodic ballads and bop-influenced jazz instrumentals. Despite the high esteem in which the band was held by musicians, however, it never really gained sufficient public support to survive, and broke up in 1948. On the surface, the Thornhill band possessed all the qualities needed for commercial success, particularly as its ballad interpretations were so ravishingly presented and it had several excellent singers, but in all probability its music was a little too subtle, its appeal too dependent on musically sophisticated listeners. Thornhill continued to work in music, though now well away from the limelight, until his death in July 1965. He is still remembered with great respect and affection by hundreds of musicians as one of the truly individual and creative figures in dance music history.

After leading several bands with only moderate success, Les Brown finally made it commercially in the early '40s, and for some years survived at the top while other leaders were disbanding or fronting small groups. Brown led, if not a particularly creative band, certainly a versatile one, which maintained high standards of technical proficiency. Its first breakthrough

was achieved by a combination of well-scored and played ballads and a series of novelty swing versions of classics. Its biggest selling records were an ingeniously scored *I've Got My Love To Keep Me Warm* and a bright version of *Sentimental Journey* with a vocal by Doris Day. Musically, the band is heard at its best in two LPs recorded at the Hollywood Palladium in September 1953, the arrangements of numbers such as *Street Of Dreams, I Let A Song Go Out Of My Heart, Speak Low* and *Laura* by Frank Comstock being outstanding, and the standard of ensemble playing impressive. Subsequently Brown was forced to compromise his music and his final batch of LPs is unimpressive.

Though American bandleaders and musicians were never forced to endure the dangers of bombing attacks on their home

Left, top: memorial plaque to Glenn Miller. Bottom: Tex Benecke – one of the stars of Miller's original orchestra – fronting his own band. Above, left: Claude Thornhill (piano) rehearses his band. Right: Les Brown holds the microphone for tenor-player Bill Usselton. Below: the famous Benny Goodman Quartet re-assembles for a record: Lionel Hampton, Gene Krupa, Teddy Wilson, Goodman.

territory, their problems as the war years unrolled were no different from those of their British counterparts. Key musicians were called up, travelling became difficult, and musical standards had to be compromised. Despite this, as in Britain, the war years were boom ones for the bands, and in the immediate post-war period it seemed that the process would be continued. By 1946, however, there were many warning signs that all was not well, not least the falling attendances at dances and concerts. Some leaders, aware that their fees had sky-rocketed outrageously during the war years, attempted to survive by accepting more modest economic returns, but the public still showed increasing reluctance to spend money on entertainment on the wartime scale. In late 1946 the full scope of the recession was revealed when Benny Goodman, Woody Herman, Tommy Dorsey, Benny Carter, Harry James and Les Brown all disbanded in a single month, though some of these leaders later re-formed with varying degrees of success. The great success story of the post-war years, however, was to be Stan Kenton's, and his music was a far cry from that of the major dance bands. In the circumstances, the second recording

Top: the full Woody Herman band, with an unknown lady trumpeter sitting in, in the film Winter Time. *Bottom: Charlie Barnet and his band in the film* Ideal Girl.

ban called by Petrillo and the AFM in 1948 seemed even more suicidal to the interests of its members than the first.

Though trade papers hopefully and with monotonous regularity reported signs of a revival of interest in the big bands, the halcyon days were over, and by the early '50s vocalists and vocal groups began to dominate the charts. The wartime tax on clubs providing entertainment was not rescinded, and in the circumstances few club owners were able to afford large bands. Television proved considerably less of a boon to bands than had the now old-fashioned radio. The despised hillbilly and race music, the latter now called Rhythm & Blues or Rock 'n' Roll, was taking over and would fashion popular entertainment in the years ahead. Record companies increasingly geared their output to a teenage market dominated by charts, the Top Twenty, and even A and B ratings on commercial issues. This last device has a much longer history than is generally assumed; Victor inaugurated it as early as 1909 to indicate which side of a record they considered had more popular appeal. Some companies disguised their rating; Brunswick for years placed a line under the catalogue number to indicate the B side, while Edison used the letters R and L, R marking the A (right) side and L the B (left) side. Some other companies, however, never used a grading system, either through indifference or to avoid annoying customers who might disagree with their rating. It is unlikely that more than a handful of early record buyers was even aware of the significance of the letters. Today pop record buyers are very conscious of the differentiation implied by the A/B rating, though now, as in the past, it carries no implication of musical judgement.

For the bandleaders who had dominated popular musical tastes for two decades such intricacies as A/B ratings on singles were of no interest, for singles by bands soon became a rarity in record issues. If things had been different, if the AFM had not instituted recording bans at vital moments, if ASCAP's demands had not led to the creation of BMI, if the entertainment tax had been abolished at the end of the war, could the bands have survived? It is an intriguing question, but the answer is probably that they might have survived a little longer but inevitably the factors which led to their eclipse would have ultimately prevailed, for new trends in popular entertainment are rooted in social and economic forces which cannot be turned aside. Rather than bemoan what has happened to popular entertainment since the dance band era, admirers of the bands should be grateful that they reigned for so long and in the process gave so much pleasure to millions of listeners. That so many combined popular appeal with high musical standards is a measure of their triumph.

THE
BUSINESS
OF
DANCE MUSIC

A number of top British leaders and musicians of the '30s certainly made good money, but probably a great deal less than is generally assumed. It must be remembered that the proportion of British dance band musicians who played in major bands or regularly worked on studio sessions was minute in comparison to the whole, and that the provincial rates were generally lower than those operative in London. How much a leader or sideman was able to earn during the '30s is essentially a private matter, but now and then the trade press of the day carried reports that enable one to make reasonably accurate surmises about basic rates. It is clear from these that the stories of leaders and musicians making vast sums of money are grossly exaggerated.

The problem is complicated by the fact that leaders would generally be unwilling to deny reports of huge earnings, for these could be advantageous in any bargaining with club or hotel managements. Then, even when what seems a spectacular fee for a date turns out to be, for once, correct, there may have been special circumstances governing its payment. One such example is a reported fee of £1,250 for the Ambrose band to play a week at the Glasgow Empire Exhibition in May 1938 – which would be atypical. One can best get some idea of musicians' wages during the '30s from contemporary reports of disputes between leaders and the Musicians Union. A 1938 *Melody Maker* described one involving Geraldo, then in residence at the Savoy Hotel.

After a holiday recess Geraldo had called his musicians together to commence rehearsals for a forthcoming cabaret at the Savoy, when he was faced by a sudden ultimatum from the Musicians Union: unless he increased their salaries to conform to the minimum of ten guineas a week, they would order the musicians not to resume work. Geraldo had already been approached by the union on the matter and had said that the situation was made difficult for him by the terms of his contract with the Savoy and by the need to pay above minimum rates for certain key personnel. What is significant is that some members of a well-known band, working at one of the major London hotels, were apparently earning less than ten guineas a week. Although by 1938 standards this was a high wage, musicians had expenses to meet – evening dress, band uniforms, upkeep of instruments – that were also above average.

Then in July 1939 Harry Leader fell foul of the union over his payments to fifteen musicians for a dance date at Folkestone, involving 3½ hours' playing time. His original offer of £2 10s. a man (with expenses) failed to meet the union minimum of four guineas. On this occasion Leader resolved his problem by dropping five members of the personnel and paying the four-guinea fee to the ten he retained.

According to Wemyess Craigie, a former associate of the Roy Fox organisation, the 1936 wage bill for Fox's band amounted to £30,000, or an average of £577 a week. In 1935 Fox would not accept an engagement for less than £600 a week, but he often fared better than this by taking a percentage of receipts. Record grosses of £4,000 were achieved at two theatre dates in Glasgow only seven weeks apart. Craigie's figures, however, seem optimistic in the light of those produced by the Fox office in July 1938, after 14 members of the band wrote to the MU claiming that they had been asked to accept stringent salary cuts, and, rather than agree, were leaving the band. Fox's certified salary figures are very interesting, revealing that in 1936–7 the lowest-paid musician received a weekly salary of £13 6s. while the others received sums between £14 10s. and £24. In 1937–8 nine of these eleven musicians remained, of whom seven had accepted weekly salary cuts ranging from ten shillings to thirty shillings; the other two had received rises of £2 10s. and £5 10s. In October 1938 six of these musicians had accepted further salary reductions ranging from ten shillings to £1 a week; two musicians who were present in 1936–7 re-joined at weekly salaries of £4 10s. and £3 less than they had previously made; and one

singer had reached a peak weekly salary of £25. Of the fourteen members who had signed the letter to the MU, in October 1938 one was receiving £25 weekly, one £22 10s., two £20, one £17, one £16 10s., one £16, one £14 10s., two £14, one £13 and three £12 – an average of about £14 17s. 6d. At this time Roy Fox employed a total of twenty-one musicians (including vocalists and orchestrator) and the certified weekly salary list was £295 10s. It is worth stressing that Fox, unlike some leaders, paid full salaries to musicians if they were absent through illness, made extra payments of £2 a week when the whole week was taken up with one-night stands, and added 7s. 6d. accommodation allowance when a Sunday concert entailed an overnight stay. (These bonuses are not included in the figures listed above.) Fox's was, of course, one of the leading British bands of its day, and his salaries would be well above normal, but here again one sees that, while key figures were making good money for the period, the rewards for some of the musicians, though reasonable, were anything but lavish.

Various factors make the press releases about salaries received by the leading bands of the '30s highly suspect. Mrs Joyce Stone, widow of Lew Stone, discussed this subject with me, drawing on the painstakingly detailed books kept by her husband. Though sums like £600 and £800 were bandied around as weekly payments for the services of a leading '30s band, Mrs Stone revealed that the mere size of the clubs and hotel rooms in which the bands performed would make them unlikely. A hotel might conceivably subsidise its restaurant from other takings, but it was certainly not common practice. The figure of £280 a week offered to Stone for a twelve-piece band at the Trianon in 1938 was somewhere near the norm, and the average salary of a musician in the Monseigneur band would have been between £10 and £12 10s. a week. Although Lew Stone was not by nature a man given to driving hard bargains, he was in the very top bracket of British bandleaders and would receive a salary which took recognition of this, so it seems most unlikely that other leaders would receive amounts two or even three times larger. All the really popular bands were able to add substantially to their earnings by recording and radio work, though the latter sometimes actually cost the leaders money; but here again it was only a few top instrumentalists who secured most of the session work.

From the musicians' viewpoint the immediate effect of the outbreak of war was disastrous, for West End employers ignored contractual obligations and often dismissed their orchestras without notice, some reopening soon afterwards with reduced personnels paid at less than union rates. In the October 1939 *Melody Maker* a report on the situation concluded with the words, 'it ill behoves any restaurant manager, maître d'hôtel or head waiter, many of whom are aliens enjoying a unique hospitality in our country, to attack standards of living of a section of our community, to the members of which so few months are left for putting their domestic houses in order.

As the war years unfolded and many musicians were called up, the position of those remaining was strengthened, but in 1941 the MU demanded increased recording fees, drawing a reply from E. R. (now Sir Edward) Lewis of Decca that the demands were not economically feasible for the companies to meet. The union wanted a new scale for all recording musicians, dance or 'straight': £2 per man for not more than two sides performed in two hours, or part; £3 for not more than four sides performed in three hours, or part; and an overtime rate of 5s. per fifteen minutes up to half an hour, after which payment should be made as if a new session had commenced. Up to this time a sixteen-piece orchestra accompanying a soloist on a three-hour session cost the company £30, a forty-four-piece 'straight' orchestra £74 6s. for a similar period, and a seventy-strong symphony orchestra £129. Dance musicians hitherto received more than their 'straight' colleagues, but even so, about £1 18s. for a three-hour session was hardly over-generous, and a musician lucky enough to do studio work five days a week would still add less than £10 to his income. In a ten-year period there must have been some increases in recording fees, so the rates in the early '30s must have been lower than those quoted. A really famous leader would undoubtedly have been able to negotiate his own contract and to have gained scales of payment well in excess of minimum rates, but it is doubtful if they were quite as spectacular as some sources have suggested.

Of course, the top bandleaders and musicians of the '30s did not live in penury. In an exceptional week a performer with a wide reputation could earn, from work in a regular band, recording and broadcasting fees, with perhaps a little doubling, about £40 or £50 – a considerable sum for the time. But it *would* be an exceptional week; average earnings were a great deal less. Also, then as now the regular recording musicians were a select band, accounting for only a fraction of even the men who played in the leading orchestras. The leaders clearly had more opportunities for making extra money – apart from the fact that they received the largest individual share of all monies earned in any case – and one of the sources was publishers' fees for broadcasting their numbers. As late as April 1939 the BBC was still desperately engaged in a hopeless battle with the songpluggers, calling on all leaders to sign an agreement refusing to accept money for playing certain numbers. No doubt their efforts were as unsuccessful as all their previous ones in that direction. One leader estimated that he might lose £200 on a broadcast, what with engaging extra musicians, paying his regular personnel additional fees, commissioning new orchestrations and meeting travelling expenses. Broadcasts were for many leaders an important source of publicity, hence they were willing to spend quite heavily on ensuring their success, but there must have been very few who resisted all the blandishments of the songpluggers, and under the circumstances one can hardly blame them. Though a leader might have a considerable sum in hand after paying his musicians, there remained other calls on the money: agency fees, the salaries of non-playing members of his organisation, entertaining, and considerable mailing costs.

On scanty information it is difficult to summarise the economic rewards of the British dance band musicians of the '30s. Undeniably a number of musicians in the leading bands earned excellent salaries for the period, and those who could augment their incomes by studio and recording work had a great advantage. The most prominent bandleaders achieved incomes that were sometimes considerable, particularly the more perspicacious ones who started their own agencies and became successful impresarios. Even so, the tales of vast sums of money earned and lost, and showbiz stories of high living, need to be treated with caution. It is salutary to remember that at least some of the most famous leaders died in circumstances hardly suggesting affluence. For the less fortunate musician, unable to make the major bands or find any foothold in the recording or broadcasting studios, the glamour associated with his profession must have seemed a little tawdry at times, for his rewards were only fractionally better than those enjoyed by citizens in more humdrum occupations. The '30s were indeed the 'golden years' for the dance bands, but for the actual musicians the gold must at times have seemed a mirage.

By comparison with Britain the United States did offer considerable financial rewards to its most successful leaders and musicians, and several of the former acquired great wealth over the years. The country probably afforded wider opportunities for high earnings to musicians and entertainers in general than any other in the world, so even the performers who failed to reach the top rank could be assured of some economic stability. On the other hand the pressures were much greater than in Europe, and the fight for survival at the top produced its fair share of casualties.

Paul Whiteman's payroll for a week in January 1928 reveals that the lowest-paid member of the personnel received $150 a week, while four received $350. Thirty-three musicians (including vocalists and arrangers) received a total of $6,420, an average close to $200 per man. (Interestingly enough, Henry Busse received $150 a week more than Bix Beiderbecke.) For the time such wages are staggeringly high, but while Whiteman was both a generous payer and an immensely successful leader, there is evidence that in later years other bandleaders were able to pay wages on a similar scale. We can contrast Whiteman's 1928 payments with those of the Bob Crosby band for early 1940 – bearing in mind that although Crosby led a popular band, run on a partly co-operative basis, it is unlikely that scales of pay would have equalled those of a Tommy Dorsey, Benny Goodman or Glenn Miller. Crosby himself received $400 a week, one musician who doubled as band manager $320 weekly, and the other salaries ranged from $125 to $320 weekly. The one person receiving what was by American standards a miserly wage, $50, was the band's vocalist, the then little-known Doris Day. Considering that quite a few of the Crosby personnel would make extra money from arranging and freelance recording sessions, it can be seen that, even allowing for higher living standards, they were generally better off than their British counterparts. No doubt the reimbursement of musicians in more obscure bands, based away from the major centres, were very different indeed. Tales are legion of performers who found themselves stranded and broke in small towns, after the sudden disintegration of the bands in which they were playing.

The boom years for the American bands were during World War II. It has been estimated that any leader could claim a guarantee of $1,000 for a one-nighter with a clause enabling him to take 60% of the takings if that proved greater, and that the major leaders such as Goodman, James and Shaw were asking $4,000 nightly at this time. There had been a few leaders in the past who claimed such amounts – Paul Whiteman, Rudy Vallee, Fred Waring – but their earnings were greatly in excess of the majority of their fellow bandleaders, whereas in World War II several leaders could command top rates. Even before this Kay Kyser received $10,000 or more for a week's engagement in Cleveland during March 1939, a remarkable figure when one considers that Kyser's was not one of the leading bands of its day. Even allowing for some exaggeration, there is no doubt that any really popular leader in the United States during the peak years of the band era would have had to be singularly reckless or inefficient as a businessman not to have made enough money to keep himself in comfort for the rest of his life.

Affluent or penurious, famous or obscure, purveyors of advanced jazz or of sickly sentiment, bandleaders of the 'golden era' generally agree on one subject – the perfidy of their booking agencies. Few went quite as far as Tommy Dorsey, who, when his MCA contract expired in 1950, booked a full-page advertisement in *Billboard*: 'PHEW! After 15 Years I am finally out of the clutches of . . . YOU KNOW WHO ! ! ! I am being Booked exclusively by . . . TOMDOR ENTERPRISES, Inc.'

If this is an extreme example of the reactions of one leader, there were others who felt little less enraged at what they regarded as poor treatment from their agencies, though most preferred to fight the matter out in private. Yet, given the growth of the dance bands during the '20s, agencies were inevitable, and initially at least they performed their functions ably enough.

Meyer Davis was running an agency for dance bands as early as 1920, but while he may have been the pioneer in this field the establishment of the booking agent within popular entertainment must have a lengthy history. The origin of nation-wide booking agencies for dance bands can be traced fairly accurately to the setting up by Jules Stein of the Music Corporation of America (MCA) in Chicago during 1924. For the first three years activity was confined to the Chicago area, but in 1927 a New York office was opened, to be followed in due course by other offices in Atlanta, Beverly Hills, Cleveland, Dallas, San Francisco and London. In the early years of the agency in Chicago – when, rather surprisingly, it booked King Oliver's Creole Jazz Band and Jelly Roll Morton for a series of one-night stands – affairs were conducted on a somewhat hit-or-miss basis. It was the discovery of Guy Lombardo and his Royal Canadians in a small Cleveland roadhouse, and the finding of Wayne King locally, that led to the success of MCA in 1927, and though the agency fared poorly in the first two depression years it gradually outstripped all its rivals with an impressive roster of over a hundred well-known bands.

Other important agencies were active during the '30s, chief of which were the Rockwell–O'Keefe Agency (later General Artists Corporation), the William Morris office, and Joe Glaser's Associated Booking Corporation, which in 1949 bought the band section of the Morris office to add to its own impressive list of artists.

For geographical reasons individual booking by the bandleaders themselves was hardly practical, and for tours the major agencies built up a list of locations which, in association with various promoters, became virtually exclusive to them. As these venues were often key ballrooms or theatres they provided an incentive to bandleaders to sign with the agencies, whose job it was to promote the interests of the bands under contract to them by any reasonable means. The percentage the agency received from all the engagements it booked was variable; a general scale was 10% for location work and 20% for one-night stands, but in many cases the agency's share was much higher. Once it had achieved a position of strength an agency could lend financial support to a band which it believed to have a good chance of attaining popular success. The organisation of a new band is, after all, an expensive business, embracing outlay on band uniforms, a library of music (including special orchestrations), musicians' wages for rehearsal prior to accepting engagements. Possibly a band might carry a considerable wages bill for some months before it achieved sufficient recognition to make it a viable proposition.

An individual in an agency could play an important part in the launching of a band. Willard Alexander of MCA, despite a lack of enthusiasm amongst his senior executives, helped Benny Goodman in the early days of his bandleading career by his encouragement and practical help in securing enough engagements to keep the band in existence. A few leaders ignored the big agencies and placed their business affairs in the hands of an individual, who was in effect a booking agent with only a single client, but until the closing years of the dance band boom even the more disenchanted seldom thought of organising all their own engagements.

Although there were a number of prominent agencies in Britain none achieved the pre-eminence of MCA, though there was a rapid growth of the MPM Entertainments Corporation, formed by Leslie Macdonnell early in 1937. Macdonnell had worked as an agent for Roy Fox for some years before this and at the start of his MPM enterprise Fox was his only client, but by the end of 1937 Billy Cotton and Mantovani had joined his list of bands, as had numerous solo artists, including visiting American stars contracted to the Rockwell–O'Keefe Agency, whom Macdonnell now represented in Europe. By 1939 MPM handled the bookings for Carroll Gibbons, Ken Johnson, Joe Loss, Lou Preager, Van Phillips, Jack Jackson, Maurice Winnick and other well-known leaders. A 1940 advertisement in the *Melody Maker* optimistically included Louis Armstrong, Jimmy Dorsey, Woody Herman, Glenn Miller and Artie Shaw in its list of clients, but none of these artists ever undertook a European tour under its aegis.

The large agencies were probably never quite the villains that some bandleaders have claimed, but the latters' complaints were very far from being always without foundation. The

agencies undoubtedly became too big and wielded a disproportionate amount of power, and with so many clients on their books there was inevitably a temptation to concentrate on the successful bands and neglect those with less drawing power. The organisation of one-night touring schedules was often undertaken without thought for the comfort of the artists, and distances of 400 or 500 miles between engagements were not as uncommon as they should have been. When the shift in popular entertainment away from the dance bands took place several of the agencies were swift to drop their former clients, many moving into the lucrative field of films and TV. An ex-bandleader once commented acidly that he knew numerous musicians who were penniless, but had yet to hear of an impoverished agency executive.

The relationship between agencies and musicians would have been a great deal grimmer, were it not that virtually all the highly successful dance bands in the United States were white. The position of the leaders of the large black bands was very different, for not only were the choice location jobs denied to them – so that they were forced to undertake more one-night tours – but they were much more likely to be exploited by unscrupulous managers and promoters. Managerial cuts in the region of 40% were commonplace when a black leader was involved, and travelling arrangements were often difficult in the South. Because the large black bands were jazz units rather than dance bands, their exploitation at the hands of agents, managers and promoters must await another volume; but those writers who wish us to believe that jazz was solely a 'happy music', and its practitioners permanently happy people, should talk to the musicians who played in the big bands during the '30s. If they did, one myth at least could be decently laid to rest.

This chapter has necessarily been somewhat inconclusive, for hard facts and figures on the business side of dance music have always been difficult to come by. That a few people won great rewards by their efforts as musicians is certain, and many others were able to make a comfortable living. The well-known bands, however, were only the tip of the iceberg, and for the leaders and individuals who never made the big time the glamour of the profession must soon have worn off, and the profits must have been at best unimpressive. Musicians who complain that they were exploited may sometimes be exaggerating, but the dance band business did have its fair share of rogues – a fact which was brought home to me some years ago when, searching through some old record-company files, I found details of a recording session. On the sheet of paper was pencilled the words: 'Fee for the session £40. Mr. X requests that payment should not be made in the presence of the musicians.' Mr. X was the nominal, non-playing leader!

An interesting point which Mrs. Stone explained to the author was that bandleaders who topped the bill in variety theatres were responsible for the payment of the other acts. This was satisfactory when attendances were good, but when they were not the bandleader could find himself out of pocket at the end of the week. Every leader who worked under this arrangement feared bad weather, and it was the appalling winter of 1946/7 that chiefly motivated Roy Fox's decision to cease his bandleading activities.

POSTSCRIPT

The zenith of the dance band era is now three decades behind us and in the meantime most of the the leaders and sidemen who came to fame during the '30s have either died or retired from music. Roy Fox and Henry Hall have, as we have seen, retained a foothold in music by running entertainment agencies, a field in which a number of other, once prominent, dance musicians have tried their luck with varying degrees of success. In the United States rather more survivors of the pre-war years continue to direct successful bands. Apart from the large jazz orchestras of Count Basie, Duke Ellington and Harry James, veteran leaders who have remained in business to the present day include Guy Lombardo, Freddy Martin, Lester Lanin, Dick Stabile, Benny Strong, Charlie Spivak and Lawrence Welk. The latter's 'Champagne Music' has for some years been featured in an immensely popular hour-long weekly TV show. Other survivors are probably still active in less publicised areas than New York, Chicago and Los Angeles. Then there are those like Charlie Barnet and Woody Herman, who form orchestras for specific engagements or tours.

Every New Year's Eve, between midnight and 4 am, American radio stations revert to the pattern of former years and relay broadcasts of bands from hotels and ballrooms throughout the country, generally featuring up to a dozen well-known names, ranging from Ellington and Basie to Lombardo and Martin. This annual programme must provide nostalgic moments for dance band followers, and nostalgia must indeed be a potent factor in the popularity of such bands as the Glenn Miller Orchestra in the United States and Syd Lawrence's in Britain.

Ever since Miller's death 'Glenn Miller Orchestras' have proliferated, sometimes in competition with each other. The Miller estate finally resolved the problem by giving its official blessing to a chosen orchestra, and currently the 'authentic' Glenn Miller band is directed by the talented jazz clarinettist Buddy De Franco, at one time a regular winner of the jazz clarinet division in *Down Beat*'s annual polls. A spring 1971 tour of Europe by this group had sell-outs wherever it played. There is little to be said for such bands as creative units, particularly since their repertoire consists mainly of re-creations of 30-year-old hits, and anyone aware of De Franco's past achievements in jazz must feel slightly saddened at his almost apologetic manner when he announces that he is about to feature himself on clarinet. Glenn Miller's music possesses a unique ability to evoke nostalgic memories, perhaps because of its association in the minds of many listeners with the World War II years and – for Britons – with memories of the broadcasts of his AAF band. A British leader who has successfully capitalised on this nostalgia is Syd Lawrence. He came to prominence in the late '60s leading a band that specialised in performing flawless copies of the original Miller hit recordings. (In my listening experience, the Lawrence band makes a better job of this than the official Glenn Miller Orchestra!) Recently Lawrence has broadened his repertoire to include numbers associated with such prominent bands of the swing era as Charlie Barnet's, Benny Goodman's, Tommy Dorsey's and Artie Shaw's, and he has claimed that in due course he will present original material in the swing band manner. Interestingly enough, Lawrence has succeeded in building a nation-wide following with his records and personal appearances, and he increasingly draws listeners too young to have heard the originals at the time of their initial release.

In the economic conditions prevailing in the '70s few hotels still have resident bands and those that do exist are virtually unknown to anyone but their clientele. Such hotel bands as remain are normally limited to six or seven musicians, the ubiquitous Hammond organ frequently being the lead instrument, and though their style is conservative and repertoires include many show tunes and standards of earlier decades, they are a far cry from their counterparts of the '20s and '30s.

Above: Syd Lawrence. Right: Billy Ternent. Far right: Bert Ambrose.

In Britain the remaining large ballrooms, such as the Mecca chain, do retain links with the balmier years of the dance band era, for the featured bands appear to make only token gestures to the contemporary pop scene. Their music, however, is notable more for its high level of technical execution than for its individuality or novelty.

Most survivors of the big band era who are still leading permanent bands are lone figures, able to follow their own course because they have acquired almost legendary reputations that attract audiences in several continents. Others, lacking such advantages, are forced to bow to a combination of circumstances that make the maintenance of a full-time big band an impossibly hazardous venture. Hotels and variety theatres were the stand-bys of the bandleaders of the '30s, but today the former can seldom afford to retain resident bands and the latter hardly exist at all. Big band directors are forced to concentrate on concert presentations, with the summer festivals providing additional work for jazz units. Frequent overseas tours may be practical for Count Basie or Duke Ellington, who have international reputations, but are clearly impossible for leaders of lesser stature. In the years ahead musicians who have a yen to lead a big band will probably follow the example of the Thad Jones–Mel Lewis Band in the United States or the Kenny Clarke Francy Boland Band in Europe, organising a core of sympathetic musicians who will come together to play for specific tours or the rarer resident location jobs. Such bands do work quite a few months in the year, but the rehearsal bands, of which there are several in the United States and Europe, only occasionally secure engagements, usually of short duration. Now and then a former leader may follow the example of Geraldo who, in 1970, assembled an orchestra for a concert at London's Royal Festival Hall, relying on the loyalty of his old fans to produce a capacity audience.

In some European countries the problems of a few big band

leaders are eased by the willingness of radio networks to provide sponsorship, even to the extent of having resident orchestras. In recent years official attitudes to jazz and dance music in Czechoslovakia, Hungary and Poland have become surprisingly liberal, and several big bands are thus assured of regular radio, TV, concert and recording outlets. Some of the bands involved seem to be partly jazz, partly dance and partly show units, but one welcome result of this official sponsorship is that the more experimental bands are much freer to pursue an independent line at recording sessions than they would be if economic considerations alone governed the selection of material. In Britain, in contrast to past decades when the BBC's attitude to any form of popular music was at best condescending, the growth of the teenage audience, allied to that of the now banned pirate stations, has finally led to the creation of a channel devoted almost entirely to contemporary pop. A few programmes on another channel are slanted towards the older generation whose tastes in popular music were formed in earlier decades. That there remains an audience of some size for the dance music of the '30s was shown by the success of a weekly radio series which featured a band led by Billy Ternent, at one time chief arranger for the late Jack Hylton. The music that Ternent presented was essentially that of the '30s, and as he was working in a tradition of which he has always been a part, the results were far more satisfactory than those of other bands whose stock-in-trade is the re-creation of thirty-year-old hits.

A recurring theme of music journalism is that the big bands are on the way back. Earlier I sketched the events that led to the emergence of Rhythm & Blues, Country & Western, and Rock 'n' Roll as the cornerstones of contemporary popular music, and the years since have seen no fundamental changes in the idiom – except perhaps the emergence of the blues as a major influence. A growing eclecticism has caused a number of groups to employ elements of rock, jazz, blues and even diluted Indian music simultaneously. In the '70s only the wildest of optimists could imagine that in some magic way the big band era could return, for, leaving aside questions of public taste, it

is clear that the dance bands were to a large extent a product of economic and social conditions which, happily, are not with us today. This fact in no way invalidates their music, but, unless we recognise the social forces that influence developments in popular music, much of its history appears arbitrary and even mystifying.

The one thing that partisans of any style or era of popular music are unable to accept is that change is inevitable. Followers of '30s dance music are no exception to the rule, and magazines devoted to the subject, though they include much interesting historical and factual material, read at times as though the contributors have become frozen in time. One is reminded of the title of Caitlin Thomas's autobiography, *Leftover Life To Live*. It is everyone's right to like or dislike any kind of music, but it is ironical that the people who fought against misrepresentation and dismissal when it was applied to their style of music are so ready to employ similar tactics against later developments – particularly when their criticism descends to banalities about the clothes and hair-styles affected by current pop groups. One writer I read recently commented smugly that The Beatles would have been booed off the stage thirty years ago, presumably implying that this would have showed the audiences' perspicacity; yet he would have been – and rightly so – the first to deplore the hostile reception given to Fred Elizalde by certain theatre audiences during the late '20s. Alas, tolerance is not a characteristic of partisans of any cause, and too many dance band enthusiasts view attempts to apply even partially objective standards to their music as akin to treason.

It is my belief that the percentage of what is valuable in any form of popular music, artistically and as entertainment, does not significantly vary from one decade to the next. The profusion of dance bands in the '20s and '30s was such that, inevitably, much of the music produced was entirely mediocre, and even among the recordings of the major bands there is still a good deal of dross. With popular music, distance in time does indeed lend it enchantment, and reissues, which are selected to present artists at their best, sometimes lead one to assume that the highspots are representative of the whole. One myth about the '30s is the belief that all the decade's popular songs were notable for their melodic and technical excellence. The truth is that, although the '30s did indeed see a peak of popular songwriting, the good songs represented only a fraction of the whole. It is salutary to examine the monthly release sheets of the leading record-companies of the '30s, for the standards are far outweighed by the hundreds of tunes that show hack songwriting at its worst. The output of a popular band, Henry Hall's BBC Dance Orchestra, for example, includes well-written standards like *Moon Song, I Cover The Waterfront, The Song Is You* and *Don't Blame Me*, but for each of these there are a dozen songs of such excruciating banality as *The Old Kitchen Kettle, Let's All Sing Like The Birdies Sing, Horses Carry Tails, My Old Irish Mother* and *Does Santa Claus Sleep With His Whiskers On?* – and among the tunes recorded by other artists at the same time are such gems as *When I Passed The Old Church Door, Put Your Worries Through The Mangle, Songs I Heard At Mother's Knee* and *Are You Russian (Or Just In A Hurry)*. Though songs like these are no worse than many of the following decades, including some that have topped the Hit Parade, they serve as useful reminders that not every songwriter of the '30s was a Gershwin or Cole Porter.

If dance band enthusiasts sometimes show a lack of balance in their writings, so too do the more strident propagandists for contemporary pop. Today pop is big business on a scale unknown in the '30s, and every new manifestation is attended by a barrage of high-powered publicity, some of which, employing a style that is positively biblical in tone, makes claims that can only be described as messianic. Only the blinkered would deny that some modern pop is exciting and original; one of its most welcome ingredients is the element of reality and toughness which it has incorporated from the blues. At its best – a best which it does not often attain – the music has great vitality and freshness, but such manifestations as 'protest' songs and 'underground' music, performed by middle-class practitioners whose adherence to revolutionary philosophies must be highly suspect, give cause for justified cynicism.

What is perhaps most fascinating about pop music today is its eclecticism, for both its audience and its performers contain many people who seem to be genuinely interested in exploring the roots of the various forms which have gone into it; among them are many who show a degree of tolerance towards past popular music that puts their elders to shame. There is even an interest in the better dance bands of the '30s amongst this youthful audience, which, while it may be in part expressive of a bogus nostalgia, is often surprisingly discerning. After all, the basic factor governing individual taste is generally commitment to the music with which one came in contact during one's youth. Recently, for instance, in a TV interview, an ex-rocker of the Bill Haley period bemoaned the degenerate taste of his daughter, who preferred underground music.

When one considers that the great days of the dance bands were already past a quarter of a century ago – a span of time which in popular music terms is enormous – what is remarkable is not that there are so few survivors but that there are any at all. There remains a considerable interest in dance bands, which is a tribute to the manner in which their music touched so many people's lives. Presumably, as long as ballroom dancing survives in its present form, dance bands will be with us, just as dance band records will continue to appear as long as a public exists to purchase them. It could even be that the nostalgia both of those who remember the bands in their heyday, and of others who wish they could, will lead to the formation of new bands, though such a development would necessarily be outside the mainstream of contemporary popular entertainment.

Revivalism in popular music is an interesting subject; I have an unprovable and decidedly unscientific theory that it runs in approximately twenty-five-year cycles and is conditioned by economic factors. The basis of the theory is that people who are deeply involved with popular entertainment in their youth have to forego spending money on records and concert and club attendances when they are married and have children, but, when their children grow up and are economically independent, they again have spare money to devote to hobbies or pleasures, and sometimes resume former interests. It may be significant that, whereas jazz reissues have been available since LPs first appeared, dance band reissues were few and far between until quite recently. The companies who own the rights to original recordings by the major dance bands could, if they wished, obtain a modest but steady return on reissues of this nature, but, now that the record industry is increasingly structured to think only of sales figures in the tens of thousands, it is possible that the practice will grow of leasing masters to small independent companies, who will best cater to specialist tastes.

Although few could have recognised it at the time, the outbreak of World War II sounded the death knell of the dance band era, primarily because the social structure in which the dance bands operated was shattered. The era represented a high point in popular entertainment, and at least some of the leading bands brought a degree of creativity and technical expertise to their work that resulted in performances which it is not too extravagant to hail as masterpieces of popular art. The leaders and musicians who formed the bands probably viewed their role in a functional light, and the best strove to strike a balance between the claims of dancers and those of the listening public, which, they realised, included a discriminating minority able to appreciate the finer points of scoring and technical finesse. Primarily, no doubt, they regarded themselves as entertainers, but entertainers whose tradition embraced a concern with craftsmanship and inventiveness that could be expressed in ingenious scoring and distinctive ensemble textures, as well as in the more obvious form of solo passages. Their days of glory are long past, but the best of the music that they created has, over the years, acquired the timeless character of all that is best in popular art. That is their triumph and our good fortune.

DISCOGRAPHY

The Formative Years

Almost no records by the earliest American dance bands have been reissued in microgroove form. The following provide examples of the development of syncopated music referred to in this chapter, the French 'La Préhistoire' item being particularly interesting as it includes both French and American groups.

'Golden Age of Ragtime', BYG(F) 529.060
'Ragtime, Cakewalks and Stomps, Volume 2', Saydisc(E) SDL-210
'Pianola Ragtime – The Golden Age of Mechanical Music, Volume 1', Saydisc(E) SDL-132
'New York Jazz Scene 1917–1920', Riverside(E) RLP-8801
'La Préhistoire du Jazz en France 1918–1930', Pathé(F) C 054-10656

The following item is a modern recording, but a fascinating recreation of a type of small-orchestra ragtime which was played for dancing in the early years of the century.

New Orleans Ragtime Orchestra, Pearl(A) PLP-7

The United States – The Twenties

CALIFORNIA RAMBLERS
'California Ramblers 1925–27 – Miss Annabelle Lee', Biograph(A) BLP-12020
'Hallelujah! Here Comes the California Ramblers 1925–1929', Biograph(A) BLP-12021
'California Ramblers – Vol. 1, 1925–1927', The Old Masters(A) TOM-20
COON-SANDERS NIGHTHAWKS
'Radio's Aces', RCA Victor(A) LPV-511, (E) RD-7697
JEAN GOLDKETTE ORCHESTRA
Several titles included in 'The Victorious Bix' [2-LP set], Divergent(Sw) 301/2
Three titles included in 'The Bix Beiderbecke Legend', RCA Victor(A) LPM-2323, (E) RD-27225
BERT LOWN ORCHESTRA
'Bert Lown and his Orchestra 1929–1932', The Old Masters(A) TOM-18
GEORGE OLSEN ORCHESTRA
'George Olsen and his Music', RCA Victor(A) LPV-549, (E) RD-7925
BEN POLLACK ORCHESTRA
'Ben Pollack and his Orchestra', Only For Collectors(Arg) OFC-40
'Ben Pollack Orchestra 1928–1929', The Old Masters(A) TOM-22
Two titles included in 'Jack Teagarden', RCA Victor(A) LPV-528, (E) RD-7826
FRED RICH ORCHESTRA
'Fred Rich Orchestra 1929–1930', The Old Masters(A) TOM-27
FRED WARING'S PENNSYLVANIANS
'Waring's Pennsylvanians', RCA Victor(A) LPV-554
PAUL WHITEMAN ORCHESTRA
'Paul Whiteman, Volume 1', RCA Victor(A) LPV-555, (E) RD-7954
'Paul Whiteman, Volume 2', RCA Victor(A) LPV-570, (E) RD-8090
'Paul Whiteman and his Orchestra', Columbia(A) CL-2830
'Paul Whiteman's 50th Anniversary Record', Grand Award(A) GA33-901, Music For Pleasure(E) MFP-1183
'Pops Remembers', Coral(A) COPS-3871, (E) CPS-60
Several titles included in 'The Victorious Bix' [2-LP set], Divergent(Sw) 301/2
Seven titles included in 'The Bix Beiderbecke Legend', RCA Victor(A) LPM-2323, (E) RD-27225

ANTHOLOGIES
'Collectors Items', IAJRC(A) 1 [contains one track by the Phil Baxter Orchestra]
'Hot Jazz 1927–1929', The Old Masters(A) TOM-19 [contains tracks by Hale Byers, Tom Gerunovich, Harris Brothers' Texans, Benny Meroff, Jesse Stafford and Herb Wiedoeft]

Britain – The Twenties

AMBROSE AND HIS ORCHESTRA
'The Best of Ambrose and his Orchestra at the Mayfair Hotel, London, 1928–1932', Music For Pleasure(E) MFP-1258
FRED ELIZALDE ORCHESTRA
'Jazz at the Savoy – the 20's', Ace Of Clubs(E) ACL-1102 [includes piano solos]
'Fred Elizalde Orchestra 1927–1929', The Old Masters(A) TOM-30
SAVOY ORPHEANS and SAVOY HAVANA BAND
'The Savoy Bands' [2-LP set], World Record Club(E) SH-165/6
ANTHOLOGY
'Jazz in Britain – the 20's', Parlophone(E) PMC-7075 [includes tracks by Jack Hylton's Kit-Cat Band and Rhythmagicians, Fred Elizalde, and the Piccadilly Revels Band]

The United States – The Thirties

GUS ARNHEIM ORCHESTRA
Nine titles included in 'The Young Bing Crosby', Vik(A) LX-995, RCA Victor(E) RD-27075
CASA LOMA ORCHESTRA
'Great Recordings', Harmony(A) HL-7045
'Smoke Rings', Decca(A) DL-8570
'Casa Loma Orchestra 1934/38', Brunswick(G) 87.534
Five tracks included in 'Great Jazz of 1930', The Old Masters(A) TOM-4
DORSEY BROTHERS ORCHESTRA
'The Fabulous Dorseys Play Dixieland Jazz 1934/35', Decca(A) DL-8631, Coral(E) CP-27
ISHAM JONES ORCHESTRA
'The Great Isham Jones and his Orchestra', RCA Victor(A) LPV-504, (E) RD-7643
'Swingin' Down the Lane', Ace of Hearts(E) AH-110
HAL KEMP ORCHESTRA
'Great Dance Bands', RCA Victor(A) LPM-2041
'Hal Kemp Orchestra 1927–1931', The Old Masters(A) TOM-24
GUY LOMBARDO ORCHESTRA
'The Sweetest Music This Side of Heaven' [4-LP set], Decca(A) DXM-154
'The Sweetest Music This Side of Heaven', Ace Of Hearts(E) AH-86
'Lombardoland', Decca(A) DL-8249
    Other LPs by Lombardo on Capitol(A) and Decca(A).
FREDDY MARTIN ORCHESTRA
'Shall We Dance ?', RCA Victor(A) LPM-1160
'Greatest Hits', Decca(A) 7-4908
    Other LPs by Martin issued on various American labels.
RAY NOBLE ORCHESTRA
'Ray Noble', RCA Victor(A) LPV-536, (E) RD-7881
'We Danced All Night', Camden(A) CAL-380, (E) CDN-5131
LEO REISMAN ORCHESTRA
'Leo Reisman', RCA Victor(A) LPV-565
TED WEEMS ORCHESTRA
'Ted Weems Orchestra 1928–1930', The Old Masters(A) TOM-23

Britain – The Thirties

AMBROSE AND HIS ORCHESTRA
'The Best of Ambrose and his Orchestra at the Mayfair Hotel, London, 1928–1932', Music For Pleasure(E) MFP-1258
'London Jazz Scene, the 30's' [with Lew Stone], Ace Of Clubs(E) ACL-1103

'Tribute to Cole Porter', Ace Of Clubs(E) ACL-1186
'Champagne Cocktail', Ace Of Clubs(E) ACL-1246
'The Bands That Matter', Eclipse(E) ECM-2044
BILLY COTTON AND HIS BAND
'Billy Cotton and his Band', World Record Club(E) SH-141
ROY FOX AND HIS BAND
'At the Monseigneur Restaurant, Piccadilly', Ace Of Clubs(E)
    ACL-1172
'Fox Favourites', Ace Of Clubs(E) ACL-1240
'The Bands That Matter', Eclipse(E) ECM-2045
'Let's Reminisce', Music For Pleasure(E) MFP-1179
CARROLL GIBBONS AND HIS SAVOY HOTEL ORPHEANS
'The Magic Touch of Carroll Gibbons', Music For Pleasure(E)
    MFP-1230
HENRY HALL AND HIS ORCHESTRA
'Henry Hall and the BBC Dance Orchestra', World Record
    Club(E) SH-140
JACK HYLTON AND HIS ORCHESTRA
'Jack's Back', Encore(E) ENC-162
'Jack Hylton and his Orchestra', Ace Of Clubs(E) ACL-1205
'The Bands That Matter', Eclipse(E) ECM-2046
'Jack Hylton and his Orchestra', World Record Club(E) SH-127
RAY NOBLE AND HIS ORCHESTRA
'The Ray Noble Story, Volume 1', Encore(E) ENC-140
'The Ray Noble Story, Volume 2', Encore(E) ENC-160
'Ray Noble – Al Bowlly, Volume 1', Monmouth-Evergreen(A)
    MES-6816
'Ray Noble – Al Bowlly, Volume 2', Monmouth-Evergreen(A)
    MES-7021
'Al Bowlly' [includes two titles with Carroll Gibbons], World
    Record Club(E) SH-146
JACK PAYNE AND HIS BBC DANCE ORCHESTRA
'Jack Payne with his BBC Dance Orchestra', World Record
    Club(E) SH-143
HARRY ROY AND HIS BAND
'Hotcha-Ma-Cha-Cha!', Music For Pleasure(E) MFP-1135
'The King of Hot-Cha', Regal-Starline(E) MRS-5068
'The World of Harry Roy', Decca(E) SPA-141
LEW STONE AND HIS BAND
'London Jazz Scene, the 30's' [with Ambrose], Ace Of Clubs(E)
    ACL-1103
'10.30 Tuesday Night', Ace Of Clubs(E) ACL-1147
'Al Bowlly with Lew Stone and his Band', Ace Of Clubs(E)
    ACL-1178
'My Kind of Music', Ace Of Clubs(E) ACL-1231
'The Bands That Matter', Eclipse(E) ECM-2047
AL BOWLLY
'Al Bowlly Sings Again', Ace Of Clubs(E) ACL-1162
'The Ambassador of Song – Al Bowlly', Ace Of Clubs(E)
    ACL-1204
'By the Fireside', Halcyon(E) HAL-2
'The Big Swoon of the Thirties', Music For Pleasure(E)
    MFP-1178
     [On the above LPs Bowlly is accompanied by a variety of
     groups, ranging from studio units to regular bands.]
ANTHOLOGIES
'My Baby Loves to Charleston', Music For Pleasure(E) MFP-1158
    [contains tracks by Bert Firman and his Orchestra and The
    Rhythmic Eight]
'The Golden Age of British Dance Bands' [2-LP set], World
    Record Club(E) SH-118/9 [includes Roy Fox, Ray Noble,
    Harry Roy and Lew Stone]

The Swing Era

The bands of the '30s and '40s are represented on many LPs. This
selection is chosen to relate to references in the text of this chapter.
CHARLIE BARNET ORCHESTRA
'Charlie Barnet, Vol. 1', RCA Victor(A) LPV-551, (E) RD-7965
'Charlie Barnet, Vol. 2', RCA Victor(A) LPV-567, (E) RD-8088
COUNT BASIE ORCHESTRA
'Count Basie and his Orchestra', Decca(A) DL-8049, Bruns-
    wick(E) LAT-8028
'Jumpin' at the Woodside', Ace Of Hearts(E) AH-111
WILL BRADLEY ORCHESTRA
'Boogie Woogie', Epic(A) LN-3115
TOMMY DORSEY ORCHESTRA
'Yes, Indeed!', RCA Victor(A) LPM-1229

'Hawaiian War Chant', RCA Victor(A) LPM-1234
DUKE ELLINGTON ORCHESTRA
'In a Mellotone', RCA Victor(A) LPM-1364, (E) RD-27134
'At His Very Best', RCA Victor(A) LPM-1715, (E) RD-27133
BENNY GOODMAN ORCHESTRA
'The Golden Age of Benny Goodman', RCA Victor(A) LPM-1099
'The Best of Benny Goodman', RCA Victor(E) RD-8001
'Clarinet a la King', Epic(A) EE-22025
WOODY HERMAN ORCHESTRA
'The Band That Plays the Blues', Ace Of Hearts(E) AH-156
'The Turning Point 1943–1944', Decca(A) DL-9229, Coral(E)
    CP-2
EARL HINES ORCHESTRA
'The Grand Terrace Band', RCA Victor(A) LPV-512, (E)
    RD-7720
GENE KRUPA ORCHESTRA
'Drummin' Man' [2-LP set], Columbia(A) C2L-29
JIMMIE LUNCEFORD ORCHESTRA
'Lunceford Special', Columbia(A) CL-2715, CBS-Realm(E) 52567
RED NORVO ORCHESTRA
'Mildred Bailey' [3-LP set], Columbia(A) C3L-22
JAN SAVITT ORCHESTRA
'Jan Savitt Orchestra', Decca(A) DL-9243
ARTIE SHAW ORCHESTRA
'Free For All', Epic(A) EE-22023, CBS-Realm(E) 52636
'Any Old Time', RCA Victor(A) LPM-1570, (E) RD-27065
CHICK WEBB ORCHESTRA
'Spinning the Webb', Coral(E) CP-3

European Dance Music

COLEMAN HAWKINS
'Coleman Hawkins with the Ramblers', Ace Of Clubs(E) ACL-1247
LEO MATHIESEN
'Take It Easy', Odeon(D) MOCK-1003
'How How', Odeon(D) MOCK-1005
ANTHOLOGIES
'Czech Jazz 1920–1960' [2-LP set], Supraphon(Cz) DV 10177/8
    [includes titles by Ladislava Habarta, Jaroslav Jazek, Jan Sima,
    Karla Vlacha and others]
'Dansk Guldalder Jazz', Vols. 1–4, Odeon(D) MOCK-1006-9
    [Vol. 1 includes the bands of Kai Ewans with Benny Carter,
    Anker Skjoldborg and Aage Jule Thomsen; Vol. 2, Kai Ewans
    and Leo Mathiesen; Vol. 3, Neils Foss and Leo Mathiesen;
    Vol. 4, Bruno Henrikson and Leo Mathiesen.]
'Jazz in Deutschland', Vols. 1–6, Historia(G) H-630-5 [Produced
    as three 2-LP sets. The first has tracks by Clive Williams (Da-
    jos Bela)'s Original Jazzband and the orchestras of Bela and
    Marek Weber; the second, Ben Berlin, Oscar Joost, James Kok,
    Die Goldene Sieben, Heinz Wehner, Teddy Stauffer and his
    Original Teddies and Kurt Hohenberger; the third, Ernst van
    t'Hoff, Hohenberger, Willy Berking, Horst Winter, Benny de
    Weille, Jean Omer, Kurt Widmann, Lutz Templin and
    Freddie Brocksieper.]
'La Préhistoire du Jazz en France', Pathé(F) C 054-10656 [in-
    cludes one track by Gregor and his Gregorians]
'Swing From Belgium, Vol. 1, 1940–1942', Swingfan(G) 1002
    [includes titles by Fud Candrix, Jean Omer and Eddie Tower]
'Swing! Vol. 3 – Svenska Swingepoken 1935–1939', Sonora(Sd)
    SOLP-108 [includes tracks by Håkan von Eichwald and Arne
    Hülphers]
'Swing in Europe 1935–1947', Brunswick(G) 87.520 [includes
    titles by Stan Brenders, Freddie Brocksieper, Jack Hylton,
    James Kok, Lutz Templin and Ernst van t'Hoff]
     Although most of the records listed above are devoted to
    jazz or swing, many titles are actually dance music.

The War Years and The Aftermath

LES BROWN AND HIS BAND OF RENOWN
'Sentimental Journey', Columbia(A) CL-649
'Concert at the Palladium', Vols. 1 and 2, Coral(A) CRL-57000/1,
    (E) LVA-9001/2
JIMMY DORSEY ORCHESTRA
'The Great Jimmy Dorsey', Decca(A) DL-8609, Ace Of Hearts(E)
    AH-114
'Latin American Favourites', Decca(A) DL-8153

TOMMY DORSEY ORCHESTRA
'Tribute to Dorsey', Vols. 1 and 2, RCA Victor(A) LPM-1432/3
'Frankie and Tommy', RCA Victor(A) LPM-1569
'That Sentimental Gentleman' [2-LP set], RCA Victor(A) LPM-6003
GLENN MILLER ORCHESTRA
'Glenn Miller Memorial 1944–1969', RCA Victor(A & E) GM-1
SQUADRONAIRES
'Contrasts in Jazz', Decca(E) LF-1141
CLAUDE THORNHILL ORCHESTRA
'The Thornhill Sound', Harmony(A) HL-7088
'Snowfall – A Memory of Claude', Monmouth-Evergreen(A) MES-6066
ANTHOLOGY
'Jazz in Britain – the 40s', Parlophone(E) PMC-7121 [contains one track by the No. 1 Balloon Centre Dance Orchestra]

Unfortunately, several of the above LPs have been deleted for some years. As we go to press, however, we hear that a Claude Thornhill LP is to be issued in Japan, incorporating Harmony(A) HL-7088 with additional titles, and that an LP by The Squadronaires may be issued in 1972 on Eclipse(E).

Postscript

SYD LAWRENCE ORCHESTRA
'Syd Lawrence with the Glenn Miller Sound', Fontana(E) SFL-13178
'More Miller and Other Big Band Music', Philips(E) 6499 100/1
GLENN MILLER ORCHESTRA (directed by Buddy de Franco)
'Do You Wanna Dance', Command(E) SCMD-507
BILLY TERNENT ORCHESTRA
'That Unmistakable Sound', Ace Of Clubs(E) ACL/SCL-1267

BIBLIOGRAPHY

Books

CHARTERS, Samuel B., and KUNSTADT, Len. *Jazz: A History of the New York Scene*. Doubleday, New York, 1962.
FITZGIBBON, Constantine. *The Blitz*. Wingate, London, 1957.
GOODMAN, Benny, and KOLODIN, Irving. *The Kingdom of Swing*. Frederic Ungar Publishing Co., New York, 1939. [Reprinted 1961.]
INGERSOLL, Ralph. *Report on England*. The Bodley Head, London, 1941.
JORGENSEN, John, and WIDEMANN, Erik [eds.]. *Jazzens Hvem-Hvad-Hvor*. Politikens Forlag, Copenhagen, 1962.
LANGE, Horst. *Die Geschichte des Jazz in Deutschland*. Verlag Uhle und Kleimann, Lubbecke, 1960.
LANGE, Horst. *Jazz in Deutschland 1900–1960*. Colloquium Verlag, Berlin, 1966.
MALONE, Bill C. *Country Music, U.S.A.: A Fifty-Year History*. University of Texas Press, Austin and London, 1968.
PERNET, Robert. *Jazz in Little Belgium*. Robert Pernet & Ets 'Sigma', Brussels, 1967.
SCHLEMAN, Hilton. *Rhythm on Record*. Melody Maker, London, 1936.
SCHWANINGER, A., and GURWITSCH, A. *Swing Discographie*. Ch. Grasset, Geneva, 1946.
SIMON, George T. *The Big Bands*. The Macmillan Co., New York, 1967.
TRODD, Kenith. *Lew Stone – A Career in Music*. Joyce Stone, London, 1971.
WALKER, Edward S., and WALKER, Steven. *English Ragtime: A Discography*. The authors, Mastin Moor, Derbyshire, 1971.
WALKER, Leo. *The Wonderful Era of the Great Dance Bands*. Howell-North Books, Berkeley, Ca., 1964.

Articles

AMBROSE, [Bert]. 'Come, Come Mr Elizalde'. *The Gramophone* March 1929. [This article was ghosted by Roger Wimbush.]
BADROCK, Arthur. 'Spreadin' Rhythm Around'. *Collecta* May–June 1969.
COLTON, Bob, and KUNSTADT, Len. 'The Story of Coon-Sanders'. *Record Research* June–July 1957.
COLTON, Bob, KUNSTADT, Len, and NELSON, John R. 'The extraordinary Bert Lown'. *Record Research* January–February 1958.
CRAIGIE, Wemyess. 'From The Fox's Lair'. *The Street Singer* May–June 1969.
CROSSMAN, Joe. 'Reminiscences'. *The Street Singer* November–December 1968.

ELIZALDE, Fred. 'Jazz – What Of The Future?' *The Gramophone* February 1929. [This article was ghosted by Roger Wimbush.]
ELLIS, Chris. 'Some West Coast Bands of The 1920s'. *Storyville* February–March 1969.
GRONOW, Pekka. 'The Finnish Jazz Scene'. *Jazz Monthly* November 1965.
GRONOW, Pekka. 'Discography As A Science'. *Jazz Monthly* August 1968.
KALSBEEK, Wim H. 'The Ramblers Dance Orchestra'. *Memory Lane* May 1969.
KEEPNEWS, Orrin. 'Louis On The Spot'. *Record Changer* July–August 1950.
KIEFER, Peter T. Notes on 'Waring's Pennsylvanians', RCA Victor(A) LPV-554. 1968.
KRAMER, Karl. 'Jelly Roll in Chicago; The Missing Chapter'. *Ragtimer* April 1967.
KUNSTADT, Len. 'Filling In Discographically'. *Record Research* July 1964.
LANGAN, Dan. Notes on 'Leo Reisman, Vol. 1', RCA Victor LPV-565. 1969.
MCANDREW, John. 'Ted Weems'. *Record Research* August 1965.
MAHER, James T. Notes on 'The Great Isham Jones and his Orchestra', RCA Victor(A) LPV-504, (E) RD-7643. 1964.
'NEEDLEPOINT' [Edgar Jackson]. 'Ambrose v. Elizalde – Which Is Right?' *The Gramophone* April 1929.
PERNET, Robert. 'Charles Remue'. *Jazz Monthly* March 1967.
[RAMBLERS THE.] 'The Ramblers 1926/1946'. *RSVP* 46 March 1969.
RETTBERG, Harvey. 'Those Nostalgic Nighthawks'. *Record Research* August 1962.
RUST, Brian. 'Diggin' The Dust No. 4'. *Vintage Jazz Mart* July 1956.
RUST, Brian. 'The Benson Orchestra of Chicago'. *Vintage Jazz Mart* October 1967, December 1967, April 1968.
TANNER, Peter. 'Dynamic Prelude To The Thirties – Fred Elizalde'. *The Golden Years* January 1969.
TANNER, Peter. 'The Incomparable Ambrose 1923–1934'. *The Golden Years* October 1969.
TANNER, Peter. 'The Incomparable Ambrose 1933–1970'. *The Golden Years* October 1970.
TANNER, Peter. 'A Tribute To The Coconut Grove – From Gus Arnheim To Freddy Martin'. *The Golden Years* July 1970.
TANNER, Peter. 'Stompin' At The Savoy With Fred Elizalde'. *Jazz Monthly* January 1971.
VAUCHANT, Leo. 'Le Legendaire Leo Vauchant' [talking to Louis Victor Mialy]. *Jazz Hot* December 1969, January 1970.
WALKER, Edward S. 'Early English Jazz'. *Jazz Journal* September 1969.
WALKER, Edward S. 'Stomping At The Savoy'. *Storyville* August–September 1970.

Compiled by Penny Martin

Page numbers in *italic* refer to illustrations.

Munn, Billy 111
Murray, Don 24
Murray, Ken 122
Musicians' Union (Britain) 132, 164
Musolina, Nick 28

N

Nanton, Joe 127
Neagle, Anna 81
Nelson, Stanley 49
New Mayfair Novelty Orchestra see Ray Noble
New Mayfair Orchestra see Ray Noble
New Orleans Rhythm Kings 25
New Savoy Orpheans 41
Newton, Cyril 38, 41
Newton, Ramon 41
New York Havana Band 38, 38
Nichols, Loring 'Red' 29, 30, 33, 33, 48, 50, 52, 54, 111, 155
Night Club Kings 79
Noakes, Alfie 77, 78, 79, 81, 83, 85, 87, 93, 111, 151
Noble, Ray 38, 50, 52, 61, 62-4, 77, 78, 79, 80, 81, 82, 106, 129
Noble, Mrs Ray 77
No. 1 Balloon Centre Dance Orchestra see Skyrockets
Nooner, Roy 36
Norman, Cecil 78, 79
Norman, Jose 118
Norvo, Red 123, 125, 127
Novatones 85

O

O'Connell, Helen 157, 157, 158
O'Donnell, Johnny 34
O'Donnell, Squadron Leader 142
O'Farrill, Chico 127
O'Hara, John 24
Oliver, Joe 'King' 71, 123, 166
Oliver, Sy 125, 127, 157
Olsen, George 19, 29, 53-4
O'Malley, Pat 79, 96, 98
Omer, Jean 134
Oppenheimer, Mrs Louis 49
Orchestre Jazz de l'INR 134
Original Crichton Lyricals 104
Original Dixieland Jazz Band 13, 14, 38, 102, 104, 106
Original Havana Band 41
Original Lyrical Five 104
Original Ramblers see Ramblers
Original Savoy Orpheans 41
Original Teddies 135
Osborne, Will 34
Overdon, Jack 120
Owen, Reg 105

P

Packay, Peter 101, 134
Paquinet, Guy 132, 133
Parker, Charlie 61
Parkes, Ennis see Ennis Hylton
Parry, Harry 104
Payne, Jack 48, 50, 52, 76, 78, 101, 111, 153
Payne, Laurie 106
Payne, Norman 48, 79
Penn, Jack 112
Peterburski, George 138
Peterson, Pete 153
Petrillo, James C. 155, 162
Pettis, Jack 34
Philburn, Al 29, 33
Phillips, Sid 77, 92, 94, 95, 96
Phillips, Van 166
Phillips, Woolf 146
Piccadilly Revels Band 47
Pied Pipers 157
Pilney, Jack 120
Pitt, Freddy 47
Plant, Jack 79, 92
Pletcher, Stew 127
Pogson, Edward O. 'Poggy' 100, 101
Pollack, Ben 19, 24, 25-7, 27, 33
Polo, Danny 54, 92, 94, 95
Pope, Bob 28
Porter, Cole 30, 95, 170

Powell, Mel 127
Preager, Lou 166
Princeton Triangle Band 44
Pursglove, Reg 43
Purvis, Jack 70

 Q

Quealey, Chelsea 33, 44, 48, 50, 72
Quicksell, Howdy 24
Quinquaginta Club Ramblers 47
Quintet of the Hot Club of France 132

R

Rabin-Davis Band 149
Rabin, Oscar 147, 148-9, 149, 151
Radcliffe, Dennis 52, 54
Radio Rhythm Boys 78
Ragas, Henry 13
Raiderman, Max 52
Raine, Jack 53, 101
Ralfini, Jan 110
Ralton, Bert 38, 38, 41, 80, 111
Ramblers 132, 133
Rank, Bill 23, 24-5, 24
Rasmussen, Peter 137
Read, Bert 54
Redman, Don 22, 72, 123, 127
Reid, Neil 125
Reinhardt, Django 134
Reisman, Leo 68, 69
Reith, Sir John 54, 77
Remue, Charles 38, 134, 135
Reser, Harry 34
Rey, Alvino 155
Rey, Monte 118, 148
Rhythm Boys 67
Rich, Freddie 34
Richardson, Andy 47
Richolson, Joe 28
Rinker, Al 21
Riskin, Andy 24
Ritte, Ernest 81, 83, 85
Robey, George 38
Robinson, Dougie 151
Robinson, Eric 146, 146
Robinson, J. Russell 38
Rodin, Gil 25, 27
Rollini, Adrian 29, 30, 33, 44, 48, 49, 50
Rollini, Arthur 48
Rosebery, Arthur 111, 112
Rosing, Val 79
Rosner, Ady 138, 138
Roy, Harry 52, 76, 104-5, 105, 110, 153
Roy, Sidney 104, 105-6, 105
Royal Air Force Dance Orchestra see Squadronaires
Royal Army Ordnance Corps Blue Rockets see Blue Rockets
Rushton, Joe 155
Russell, Luis 19, 87, 123
Russell, Pee Wee 33
Russin, Babe 157
Ryker, Doc 24

S

Salmi, Klaus 138
Sanders, Joe 27, 28, 29
Sargent, Kenny 57, 58
Sartell, Frenchie 106
Sauter, Eddie 127
Sauter-Finegan Orchestra 127
Savitt, Jan 124
Savoy Havana Band 38, 41, 44, 50
Savoy Orpheans 38, 38, 41, 41, 43, 44, 48, 50, 106, 106
Savoy Quartette 38, 41
Sawyer, Joan 9
Sbarbaro, Tony 13
Schutt, Arthur 34, 72
Scott, James 9
Scott-Coomber, Billy 101
Scott-Wood, George 147
Selma Four 44
Seven Spades see Ciro's Club Coon Orchestra
Shakespeare, Bill 110
Shand, Dave 115, 118
Shane, Cyril 144

Shaw, Artie 123, 124, 125, 127, 129, 165, 166, 168
Shearing, George 118
Shelton, Anne 94
Sherock, Shorty 25, 155
Shields, Larry 13, 14, 106
Shilkret, Nat 53-4
Shirley, Eva 30
Siday, Eric 101
Sima, Jan 138
Simon, George T. 56, 158
Sinatra, Frank 157
Sinclair, Teddy 38-41, 38
Singleton, Zutty 64
Skidmore, Jimmy 105
Skjoldborg, Anker 138
Skyrockets 144, 146
Slack, Freddy 25
Slavin, Archie 85
Smith, Chick 146
Smith, (Whispering) Jack 100
Smith, Tom 52
Smits, Jan 153
Smuts, Pat 146
Somers, Debroy 41
Spanier, Muggsy 35, 67
Spargo, Tony 14
Specht, Paul 10-1, 34, 34, 44, 69
Spivak, Charlie 68, 168
Squadronaires 93, 119, 142-6, 143, 144, 147
Stabile, Dick 168
Stacy, Jess 125, 130, 155
Stafford, Jesse 34
Starita, Al 43, 44, 45, 47, 52, 101
Starita, Ray 44, 45-6, 47, 48
Starita, Rudy 44, 45-6, 47, 47
Stark, John 9
Stauffer, Teddy 135
Stedeford, Dorothy 106
Stein, Jules 166
Stenfalt, Norman 151
Stewart, Ian 106
Stillwell, Ray 34
Stone, Christopher (James Caskett) 44
Stone, Eddie 72
Stone, Fred 118
Stone, Joyce 164
Stone, Lew 38, 43, 52, 54, 57, 76, 80-7, 82, 85, 87, 89, 89, 93, 94, 95, 96, 104, 113, 118, 123, 132, 142, 146, 164
Stonecrackers see Lew Stone
Stout, Russ 28
Straight, Charlie 10-1, 33
Straus, S. W. 20
Strauss, Richard 44
Stravinsky, Igor 20, 96
Strong, Bennie 168
Sunset Royals 157
Sweatman, Wilbur 10, 11
Sylvians 44
Syncopated Five 67

T

Tann, Eric 146
Tanner, Elmo 69
Teagarden, Charlie 22
Teagarden, Jack 21, 22, 27, 27
Temple, Nat 105, 151
Templeton, Alec 96
Templin, Lutz 140
Ternent, Billy 96, 98, 100, 101, 118, 168, 169
Thiell, Harold 28
Thiell, John 28
Thomas, Bert, Snr. 43
Thomas, Caitlin 169
Thompson, Leslie 102
Thomsen, Aage Juhl 138
Thorburn, Billy 41
Thornhill, Claude 62, 72, 160, 161
Thorpe, Tony 38, 38
Thow, George 61
Three Rhythm Sisters 95
Tipping, Bernard 53
Tizol, Juan 127
Todd, Tommy 127
Törner, Gösta 136
Tower, Eddie see Emile Deltour
Towne, Jack 33
Townshend, Cliff 144
Trotter, John Scott 69-70

Trumbauer, Frank 21, 22, 22, 23, 24, 24, 33, 35, 54
Tucker, Sophie 67
Turpin, Tom 9
Tuxen, Eric 137-8
Tyers, William 10

 U

Ure, Alec 43
Usselton, Bill 161

 V

Valentino, Rudolph 9
Vallee, Rudy 36, 38, 41, 44, 165
Van t'Hoff, Ernst 133, 134
Vauchant, Leo 98, 133
Ventura, Ray 132-3, 133, 142
Venuti, Joe 21, 22, 23, 24
Vickers, Norman 120
Vlacha, Karla 139
Vodery, Will 44
Vola, Louis 132
Voorhees, Don 33
Vries, Louis de 133
Vuormaa, Jaako 138, 138

W

Wadmore, Teddy 87
Walker, Edward S. 14
Waller, Fats 30, 113, 138
Waring, Fred 10-1, 30, 30, 53-4, 165
Wars, Henry 138
Watson, Jimmy 151
Weber, Kay 62
Weber, Marek 139
Weeks, Anson 74
Weems, Art 69
Weems, Ted 69
Weersma, Melle 96
Wehner, Heinz 140, 140
Weille, Bonny de 140
Welk, Lawrence 64, 66, 168
Whetsol, Arthur 127
Whidden, Jay 90
White, George 20
White, Norman 105
Whiteman, Paul 19-23, 19, 21, 22, 30, 33, 43-4, 45, 52, 53, 67, 69, 71, 98, 123, 132, 157, 160, 165
Widman, Kurt 140
Wiedoeft, Herb 34
Wilbur, Jay 77
Wilcox, Herbert 81
Wilcox, Spiegan 24
Wile, Ray 18-9
Wiley, Lee 69
Wilkins, Dave 94
Willard, Clarence 72
Williams, Art 87
Williams, Clive see Dajos Bela
Williams, Cootie 127
Williams, Dave 118, 142
Williams, Ken 142
Wilson, Garland 101
Wilson, Teddy 161
Wiltshire, Basil 53
Winestone, Benny 113, 115, 118
Winnick, Maurice 108-10, 108, 111, 166
Winstone, Eric 153
Winter, Horst 140
Winter, Marius B. 38
Winters, Tiny 77, 78, 79, 81, 85, 93, 115, 118, 147
Wise, Bob 77, 78, 79
Witkowski, Frank 138, 138
Wornell, Jimmy 44
Wright, Edythe 157
Wright, Herbert 10
Wright, Lawrence 78

Y

Yorke, Peter 96
Young, Victor 71-2, 71

 Z

Ziegfeld, Florenz 12, 29